Public Lands and Political Meaning

Public Lands and Political Meaning

*Ranchers, the Government, and
the Property between Them*

Karen R. Merrill

UNIVERSITY OF CALIFORNIA PRESS
Berkeley · Los Angeles · London

Chapter 2 is reprinted in revised form with the permission of the *Western Historical Quarterly*. The original
article appeared as "Whose Home on the Range?"
Western Historical Quarterly 27 (Winter 1996):
433–51.

University of California Press
Berkeley and Los Angeles, California

University of California Press, Ltd.
London, England

Library of Congress Cataloging-in-Publication Data

Merrill, Karen R.
    Public lands and political meaning : ranchers, the
government, and the property between them / Karen R.
Merrill.
        p.   cm.
    Includes bibliographical references and index.
    ISBN 0-520-22862-6 (cloth : alk. paper)
    1. Public lands—United States—History.   2. Gov-
ernment ownership—United States—History.
3. Ranchers—Legal status, laws, etc.—United States—
History.   4. Pasture, Right of—United States—History.   I. Title.
    KF5605 .M47   2002
    333.74'0973—dc21

                            2001003100

Manufactured in the United States of America
10   09   08   07   06   05   04   03   02
10   9   8   7   6   5   4   3   2   1

The paper used in this publication meets the minimum
requirements of ANSI/NISO Z39.48-1992 (R 1997) (*Permanence of Paper*). ⊗

For my parents—
for letting me find my own West
and for Martha—
from the woods to the sea and back again

Contents

Illustrations

Preface

During the final months of revising the manuscript of this book, I took a short vacation in Provincetown, Massachusetts, as far away as one can imagine in the continental United States from the geography, climate, human culture, and animal populations of the western public grazing lands. While walking down the main street one foggy morning, I was stunned to see a faded sticker on the back of a stop sign reading: FREE OUR PUBLIC LANDS and END DESTRUCTIVE WESTERN LIVESTOCK GRAZING. I could quickly hazard a guess about when someone must have affixed that sticker—most likely in the early to mid 1990s, when the Clinton administration launched a battle to raise grazing fees, touching off yet another sagebrush rebellion over the public lands. I marveled that someone standing at the very tip of Cape Cod on the eastern coast of the United States had felt so passionately about America's public grazing land. And after living in the East and the Midwest for years, during which time I had often had to perform great verbal calisthenics to convince people that the public grazing lands were important, I was elated to find traces of someone who had stood on that exact spot and believed those lands were relevant enough to easterners to deface a sign.

But I wondered how other people would read the sticker. Would they know what and where the public lands were? Would they care about public grazing? Whereas in the nineteenth century the existence of an enormous public domain excited great political debate, it now attracts only peripheral national attention.[1] Like others who care about these

lands—including, presumably, the activist bearing the sticker—I want
to "free our public lands" from that obscurity. Although national media
such as the *New York Times, Newsweek,* and *Time* occasionally focus
on the political struggles over the public grazing lands, the players are
so stereotypically portrayed that little new understanding emerges. The
public-minded bureaucrat versus the land-grabbing rancher; the hard-
working cowboy versus the rule-bound district supervisor; the altruistic
environmental lawyer versus the mean-spirited sagebrush rebel; the sil-
ver spoon–fed mountain biker versus the real working man of the West
—such portrayals, while generally capturing a nugget of truth about the
battles, rarely help a reading audience understand what's at stake when
different groups make claims on the public lands. Most important, time
and again the conflicts over western grazing are cast as simply a western
issue, unrelated either to those who live east of the Missouri or to any
national governmental problem.

Not surprisingly, perhaps, the field of American history has repro-
duced such a pattern, and my aim is also to bring the public lands to the
attention of mainstream American historiography, particularly as practiced by professional historians. Patricia Nelson Limerick has spoken
eloquently on this subject. In a 1994 article on how college textbooks
integrate western history (very poorly), Limerick noted that "only a
student miraculously capable of reading between the lines could learn
much of anything about the history of the public lands" from the textbooks she reviewed. She singled out the treatment of the Taylor Grazing
Act of 1934 as a particularly egregious example of the way American
historians have ignored the history of the West in the twentieth century,
preferring instead to follow the tried-and-true practice of closing the
frontier in 1890 with nary a second glance. In Limerick's view, American history textbooks would not have room for the Taylor Act, even
if their authors knew anything about it. Although it ended decades
of homesteading, authorizing the government to manage the public
domain and signaling a critical shift in the government's stance toward
the West's natural resources, the Taylor Grazing Act "simply missed the
deadline." With the frontier comfortably closed in 1890, and all ranchers
apparently quieted, American history textbooks have "no imaginable
reason for the Taylor Grazing Act of 1934 or for the continued, bitter,
sometimes violent conflicts over grazing on Western public lands in our
own time." [2]

In order to understand the modern West, historians will have to in-
corporate the Taylor Grazing Act into their understanding of the New

Deal in much the same way that they understand the significance of the Wagner Act of 1935, which gave industrial workers the right to join unions, authorized collective bargaining, and brought the federal government fully into mediating conflicts between workers and employers. The Wagner Act occupies a central place in the political history of the twentieth century and is an absolutely critical lens for both teaching and interpreting the New Deal, as it brought a certain resolution to the explosive labor problem and helped mark "the establishment of a new era," as Katherine Van Wezel Stone has argued. By setting up an administrative machinery in the federal government to help resolve labor-employer conflicts, the Wagner Act laid the groundwork for an ongoing battle in the twentieth century to define the rights of workers and employers.[3] Similarly, the Taylor Grazing Act sought to create the administrative machinery to launch a "new era" of public land use by resolving the decades-long struggle over the public domain lands in the West, which had been open for homesteading since the 1862 Homestead Act. Although it did solve some of the problems involving the western grazing lands, the act also gave rise, however, to a continuing battle over defining the rights of public land ranchers and the federal government. In both the Wagner Act and the Taylor Grazing Act, in other words, we see the federal government developing administrative structures that laid the groundwork for debates about the relationship between economic and political rights that continued for the rest of the century.

Needless to say, there are many differences between the two acts, but by remarking on their similarities, I want to emphasize that the Taylor Grazing Act should, like the Wagner Act, be accorded a central place in our understanding of the New Deal. What justifies doing so? First, the size of the area involved. Historians and policymakers typically use the word "vast" to describe the western public lands, and it is an apt choice. But how vast is vast? Currently, the federal government manages close to 300 million acres of public grazing lands, an area equivalent in size to all the eastern seaboard states from Maine to Florida, including Pennsylvania and New York. Most of this land had been acquired by 1950, the point at which this book ends. This analogy should make clear the uniqueness of public land holding in the West—that it is one of the things that sets the region apart from the rest of the country. In a nation devoted to ideals of private property, the existence of so much public land administered by the federal government creates a political pickle of monumental proportions. How politicians, bureaucrats, and westerners have tried to get out of that pickle is a story that should engage American political historians of every stripe.

Furthermore, although the Taylor Grazing Act and the politics of the public grazing lands have not found their way into the political history of the twentieth century, they have had a starring role in political science. In his 1966 book *Private Power and American Democracy,* undoubtedly one of the more influential works in American political science in the second half of the twentieth century, Grant McConnell argued that American government had largely been "captured" by private interests, and among the areas he singled out for examination was that of public grazing under the Taylor Grazing Act. Indeed, for McConnell, the ranchers' capture of public land administration presented "a picture bleaker and starker than any to be found anywhere" in postwar American politics.[4] Much more remains to be said about McConnell's argument in the following pages, but I mention his work here to emphasize that the politics of public grazing land can shed light on national politics in the twentieth century and should not simply be dismissed by American political historians as a quirky western problem or relegated only to the field of environmental history.

Simply put, the politics of public grazing are a particularly informative arena in which to investigate the debates over federal power in the first half of the twentieth century—the most extended period of government reform in the nation's history.[5] For one thing, the role of the federal government in land use was a significant feature of that reform, albeit often ignored in general accounts of early twentieth-century American politics. Moreover, the stakes were high in resolving the question of what to do with the public lands, because the property arrangements of the West so directly hinged on governmental action. Of course, that had been true throughout the nineteenth century, as Congress forged different land policies to promote the settlement of the public domain. At the center of those policies, of course, was a belief that the public lands should leave the government's hands to become private property in the hands of individuals. By the early twentieth century, however, the equations had changed, for now the question of appropriate governmental action involved a possibly permanent federal presence in western public lands.

If the history of the public lands should occupy a more central place in national history, it is also a history that is important in its own right, and given how much serious attention has been devoted to the subject, it is a mystery that so much twentieth-century U.S. history remains oblivious to it. Nonetheless, although I deeply admire a great deal of work that historians have produced on the public lands, and on public grazing lands specifically, this book seeks to "free" those lands from the history that historians have written about them.

As Richard White observes, historians of the public lands "created a body of scholarship so grand, so sweeping, so detailed that it finally came to a halt by its own accumulated weight." [6] Paul Gates remains the dominant presence in the field, and to his name I could add a dozen more, including that of E. Louise Peffer, whose 1951 *Closing of the Public Domain* has been my touchstone in writing this book. This historiography encompassed many different projects, and much of it focused on the policy shifts toward the public lands, investigating the legislative changes in Congress, administrative experiments in the executive branch, and attitudinal transformations among government elites that led the federal government toward greater management over the public lands. But the "accumulated weight" of this work and this paradigm indicates that it is clearly time to ask new questions about the place of the public lands in American history. Environmental historians, for instance, have been doing so for some time, exploring the ecological consequences of different government policies. Returning to the subject as *political* history, however, I have departed from public land historians of the past in seeing this geography, not as land that was either disposed of or kept in federal hands, but as property to be negotiated. And I argue that only by examining how organized ranchers and federal officials understood the public grazing lands as property can we grasp the true depths of their political conflicts.

Property—in the form of the actual land in question, but also as an organizing vision of society, as a set of legal tools, and as a structure of language—brought ranchers and the federal government together in a truly dynamic political relationship. It was dynamic because from the late nineteenth century onward, the two sides never lost sight of each other; at times, their understandings of property and the public lands would coincide, while at other times, those understandings parted ways so severely as to produce political explosions. By portraying ranchers and federal land managers either as irrevocably bitter enemies or as unholy allies in a conspiracy to defraud the public of these lands, the historiography on this issue has, I think, contributed to obscuring the real story. The only way out of that obscurity, and the only way to understand today's political discourse on the subject, is to listen carefully to what both ranchers and federal officials said in an era unchallenged by environmentalism. In doing so, I run the risk of being misunderstood. While I scrutinize both organized ranchers and federal officials, some readers may conclude that I've been politically "captured" by one side or the other. Of course, I do have hopes for the public grazing land of the West today: I would like to see policies developed that not only address environmental concerns but also put in place effective enforcement mechanisms; that genuinely negotiate the human uses of those lands with ecological needs; and that derive their legitimacy from *truly* democratic participation rather than from either interest-group power or executive authority. But my concern here has been with the past, with how the issue of America's public grazing lands became so soaked with competing visions of property and political power.

Land ignites passions. Who owns it? Who controls it? Who has access to it? How should it be used? These were all questions that lay at the heart of the debates over public grazing lands, and they remain front and center today. They are the issues that drove someone to affix a political sticker to that stop sign in Provincetown, just as much as they motivated me to write a book. Both of us, I imagine, were impelled by the same desire to bring these lands to more people's attention. The Provincetown sticker proposed a direct course of action: END DESTRUCTIVE WESTERN LIVESTOCK GRAZING. The pages that follow, however, like most histories, tell an intricate story that suggests no simple solution.

The path that this book has taken is itself a very intricate one: notes, drafts, and disks traversed a number of states, lay on shelves in different universities, apartments, and houses, and were packed and repacked too many times to remember. And throughout these travels, I was grateful to have the support and help of many people.

My interest in the subject of this book goes back to my first college course, as a high school senior, in environmental history with Clayton Koppes at Oberlin College. Several years later, Clayton served as my thesis adviser and mentor on a somewhat related subject in agricultural history: he was the very model of an adviser and encouraged me to pursue my love of American history. His friendship ever since has been an anchor to me through the ups and downs of graduate school and launching a career. The book itself had its origins as a dissertation in the history department at the University of Michigan, where I found tremendous intellectual company among my fellow graduate students and the faculty. Although this final version may not be fully recognizable to them all, Ken Church, Stephen Frank, Vicky Getis, Sarah Elkind, Erik

Seeman, Victoria Wolcott, and Caroline Winterer helped shape early drafts of this work. That Vicky Getis and I ended up living only five minutes away from each other in our post-Michigan lives meant that we could continue many of the conversations we began in graduate school (except we had to learn how to talk over the din of small children).

As members of my dissertation committee, Julia Adams helped lead me to my topic and Susan Johnson came in, at quite the last minute, as a very welcome western historian. David Scobey provided critical feedback as I wrote the dissertation; more significantly, his eleven pages of notes and questions on the dissertation as a whole presaged the direction I would eventually take, long before I knew it myself. As chair of the committee, Terry McDonald always made time for lengthy discussions of my research, which left me energized and inspired by his breadth of reading. His critiques were uniformly enlightening, if also occasionally skin-thickening, and I'm sure I was in need of both. I was also fortunate at Michigan to receive a Rackham Pre-Doctoral Fellowship and a Mellon Dissertation Fellowship, which helped to get the dissertation off the ground.

Other sources of funding also moved this project along. An alumni grant from Oberlin College, a summer grant from the Charles Redd Center, and funding from the University Committee on Research in the Humanities and Social Sciences at Princeton University all helped me to undertake archival research. I am grateful to Amherst College for a Copeland Fellowship in the spring of 1997, which allowed me the time to begin revising my manuscript. Grants from the Hoover Presidential Library Association and from the American Heritage Center at the University of Wyoming covered my expenses in what were especially important archival visits. I would like to thank their staffs, and particularly Rick Ewig and Lori Olson at the Heritage Center, for their help and guidance in my research. Gene Gressley also kindly shared his vast knowledge of the Heritage Center's holdings at an important early stage of my research.

This project would never have taken the shape it eventually did without the years I spent in the history department at Princeton University, and I'll always count myself fortunate to have landed in such an intellectually exciting and congenial place after graduate school. Simply being a part of the faculty opened my eyes to new worlds of doing history, but four colleagues in particular gave generously of their time (including reading my dissertation) to help me work through the direction this book has taken. Dan Rodgers brought to our conversations his rich knowledge of twentieth-century American culture and politics and provided especially sound guidance in thinking about the shapes the American state took. Jeremy Adelman was a constant model in his understanding of political economy, as well as a regular source of citations and information. Steve Aron and I overlapped at Princeton for only two and a half years, but his collegiality, scholarly advice, and friendship have been a great support to me over the years, as well as just a lot of fun. Finally, Dirk Hartog has given unstintingly of his time. From our first conversation about the dissertation over Chinese food on Nassau Street—when he asked, "This project isn't really about the state, is it?" (out of fear, I probably answered "no," but readers will see that it does say something about the American state)—Dirk helped me rethink the very conceptual framework of the book. He also bolstered my confidence when I grew fainthearted about tackling property law. On a more practical level at Princeton, Dan Rodgers and Phil Nord, as chairs, helped to arrange paid and unpaid leaves, as well as a teaching schedule that accommodated a difficult weekly commute, which gave me precious time to devote to revising.

After leaving Princeton, I was fortunate to find wonderful colleagues and institutional support elsewhere. At the University of California, Irvine, Steven Topik, Carolyn Boyd, and Robert Moeller inspired me to think in different ways about American political history, while Sharon Block and Alice Fahs provided moral support and much needed humor as I was completing the last revision of the manuscript. My affiliation with Williams College is still very recent, but I am thankful for the funding it has provided toward the publication of this book and for my colleagues' support of this project.

Just when I was beginning to present my work publicly, the field of western American history was transforming itself into what I think is one of the most vibrant areas of American historiography. I have benefited enormously from the works of many western historians, but I give special thanks to Clyde Milner, David Rich Lewis, and Anne Butler for their support of my work in the *Western Historical Quarterly;* to Marni Sandweiss, my lunch companion and professional comrade in *western* Massachusetts, for her friendship and visual perspective on the field; to Bob Righter and Sherry Smith, for their company and conversation in Jackson Hole, especially while floating down the Snake River; and to Jim Muhn, for his grasp of the details of public land law.

At the University of California Press, Monica McCormick not only waited patiently for this book but also supported its progress with enthusiasm; while the waiting was more prolonged than I would have wished, it did give me the opportunity to see her regularly at the Western History Association meetings (keeping her, of course, "up to date"), which I always enjoyed. Suzanne Knott provided enviable clarity about the details of readying the manuscript, while Peter Dreyer copyedited it with great care and an especially keen eye for prolixity.

My family has stood by me and by this project so unwaveringly and for so long that words can barely express my gratitude. I especially appreciate the fact that no one in the family ever asked, although surely they must have wondered, "So when is that book going to get done?" My parents, Marly and Dan Merrill, encouraged this project at every step, followed its metamorphosis, and always contributed important insights from their own scholarly worlds. Their immeasurable generosity is a wonder, and they have come to the rescue in more ways than I can either remember or would like to admit. My brother Steve Merrill and my sister-in-law Nancy Day Merrill have always provided great outlets from the pressures of completing this project. Now that it is finished, I can dote on their daughter, Annabelle Leigh, with extra energy. My aunt and uncle, Cynthia and Mike Tamny, moved to Golden, Colorado, at an opportune moment, when I could visit them as I finished my research; getting the chance to know them better at this point in my life has been a source of tremendous pleasure.

My deepest thanks go to my partner Martha Umphrey and our son Theo Jackson. Theo came along right at the moment when I was ready to reexamine my dissertation, and his arrival enriched my life in every way. His sweetness, his boundless love, his insights on the world, and his surreal humor have been a daily inspiration to me. So, too, have Martha's strength and stamina been a constant source of wonder. With her wide-ranging knowledge of the law and her remarkable ear for language, she has helped me over the years to clarify and give shape to the themes of this book. Her intelligence and compassion have sustained me, and with this book's completion I look forward to beginning a new page of our lives together.

Introduction

Movie producers have long kept a fascinated gaze on the American West, but few films capture the classic drama of the range as well as *Shane* does. Set in Wyoming in 1889, with the Grand Tetons looming over nearly every scene, the movie charts both the verbal and physical battles between a group of homesteaders and a pair of cattle ranchers named the Ryker brothers.[1] The Rykers and their disreputable hired hands try every trick in the book to run the homesteaders off the open range, from riding their horses through the settlers' gardens to violent intimidation. Clearly desperate to keep his range intact, one of the brothers approaches Joe Starrett, the leader of the homesteaders, to try to persuade him to give up his land claim. He begins by asking Starrett to work for him.

"I'll pay you top wages—more than you can make on this patch of ground," he says.

Starrett refuses.

"You can run your cattle with mine," Ryker adds. "What's more, I'll buy your homestead."

Starrett will have none of it. "You've made things pretty hard for us, Ryker," he answers. "And us in the right all the time."

Ryker explodes. "Right?! You in the right?!" As pioneers, he begins arguing, he and his fellow cattlemen had made the range safe for the very settlers who were now breaking it up, and he spells out how he had helped open up the West when Starrett was still a boy. "We made this

I

country, found it and made it," he declares. "And you say we have no
right to the range?! The men that did the work and ran the ranches have
no rights?!"

"You didn't find this country," Starrett answers calmly. "You talk
about rights. You think you've got the right to say that nobody else has
got any. Well, that ain't the way the government looks at it."

This book is about that conversation. It is about the remarkable set
of slippages in Starrett and Ryker's conversation about the public range,
where opposing visions of righteousness justify property rights and opposing assertions of property rights involve the government, which, on
the surface, seems so absent from the scene. It is about the political res-
onance of that conversation throughout the first half of the twentieth
century, when ranchers engaged in a national debate over the kinds of
claims they could make to western rangeland. It is certainly not the first
book to look at the debates over public grazing lands, nor will it likely
be the last. In fact, the political battles over the range have inspired a remarkable output of writings, some of which explore much the same historical landscape I take on here. Collectively, these studies show clearly
how Congress has legislated for the management of the public range;
how the politics of interest group power have functioned in that legislation; and how federal bureaucrats have managed public lands. In most
of the accounts, these officials are seen pitted against organized ranchers and western opponents of conservation in a struggle to protect the
public's interest in western rangeland. They fight to limit the number of
cattle and sheep on public grazing land, to cut down on erosion and
keep streams running clear, and to make ranchers pay what they consider to be a fair price for the use of these public lands. In some of these
battles, the federal officials are successful. In others, they find themselves
up against a wall of formidable western men, who seem strangely able
to dig in their heels for years at a time, refusing to allow anything more
than some frontier range code to govern their use of public lands.[2]

This account, which reigned in political histories of public grazing before the rise of the environmental movement in the 1960s, has often been
repeated and expanded in more recent works, covering the past few
decades. Books like Denzel and Nancy Ferguson's *Sacred Cows at the
Public Trough* and Lynn Jacobs's *Waste of the West* were part of a political movement among environmentalists that, by the early 1990s, embraced the idea that the West should be "Cattle Free by '93." Many environmentalists, the novelist Edward Abbey among them, saw public
land ranchers as "welfare cowboys," subsidized by the federal govern-

ment, whose cattle were trampling western rangeland into dust and consuming grass and forage that wild animals should be eating.[3] The bulk of scholarly works on this period likewise suggest that by and large ranchers are resistant to changing their old practices, so that the public lands may be restored to health, and that they are getting a free ride from the federal government.[4] More galling still, public land ranchers behave as if they own the lands on which they are allowed to graze their animals, despite the fact that every legal decision involved in public grazing has supported the government's claim that it, not the ranchers, may do with that land whatever it sees fit.[5] Such attacks on the range livestock industry have not gone unanswered, although the responses rarely reach a larger audience than the readership of western newspapers. What these rejoinders have emphasized is that the environmentalist critique of ranching has consistently refused to see how vital it is to local communities and how stultifying the management of the federal government is to ranchers' businesses.[6]

All these works—from those written before the environmental movement to those written afterward, from those that support the government's efforts to administer the lands in the name of the public to those that decry federal red tape—give us vast detail about the political manifestations of the conflict over the public range. But to my mind, they have not explained *why* that conflict has been so profoundly impossible to resolve and so cyclically volatile.[7]

There are two reasons for this failure. First, none of these works has attempted to make sense of the changing political positions of organized western ranchers over a lengthy period of time. Even the best histories, for instance, merely track how public land ranchers have reacted to particular policy initiatives by the federal government. Although ranchers were one of the most powerful political forces by midcentury in the West, perhaps scholars have not taken ranchers' views seriously, or perhaps the image of ranchers as hardy frontier individualists has worked against understanding what they stood for, and fought over, in their political organizations. This book is not an organizational history of the western livestock industry per se, but it looks at the industry's changing ideas about public rangelands from the time when ranchers began to organize to the time when they had clearly become a significant political lobby. Early on, I decided to examine the political positions of organized ranchers before they came under serious attack by wilderness preservationists, hoping to understand their relationship with the federal government prior to the current environmental battles. Historians who have

looked at this period have found the record blurred by rhetorical ex-
cesses when the industry ratcheted up its hostility to federal land management, and I have focused on ranchers' public utterances in an effort
to explain that rhetoric as expressing not simply economic self-interest
but also genuine political disagreement with federal policymakers.

What I found when I took this rhetoric seriously was that ideas about
property played a crucial role on both sides of the fence in the perpetu-
ation of the political conflicts. The overwhelming reason for the lack of
scholarly attention to the language of property is surely because the
Constitution makes clear that the public lands are the property of the
United States, and Congress has nearly limitless powers to make policy
for these lands. But that apparent clarity hides a striking opacity about
what public property ownership means politically and what relationship
public property has to those people who use its natural resources and
whose private property is intricately bound up with it. The chapters that
follow argue that relations of property stand at the center of the conflict
between the federal government and public land ranchers; they are what
drive the quotidian politics of embattlement over public grazing, as well
as the cyclical explosions we have come to label "sagebrush rebellions."

Scholars and journalists writing about the issue have long recognized
that for much of this century, both before and after the federal government took over the management of the range, ranchers have tried to lay
claim to public rangeland. No such claim has ever been legally recognized, these writers correctly note, returning us once again to the apparent clarity of the letter of the law: that public grazing lands are the
property of the United States and any property claims made on them by
ranchers are simply unfounded. But on both the government's side and
the ranchers' side, the documents tell a different story. If we look beyond
the technical fundamentals of public land law and expand our understanding of property to mean not simply what the courts define as legal
truths but also how interpretations of property weave their way into political discourse, we find property claims in almost every nook and
cranny of the debates.

I argue that in setting up permanent management of public grazing
lands, the federal government brought land managers and ranchers together in a political relationship fully defined by the structures and
meanings of private property. First, the two agencies that set up public
grazing management, the Forest Service in the Department of Agriculture and the Bureau of Land Management in the Department of the Interior, attached their adjudication and administration of the range to

ranchers' actual private property; ranchers could not attain grazing permits without owning private property and without meeting even more specific requirements about how their property had to function in their overall ranch operations. By making this connection, however, these agencies locked themselves into an unending circle of attempts to then detach grazing permits from the ways that ranchers both made use of them as property in practice *and* understood them as part of their private property. Second, the government and organized ranchers continually looked to private property relations to make sense of their own relationship. Both sides employed a language and a legal understanding of property, but as time went by, their ideas radically diverged.

So far, I have used the term "property" in a general sense, and indeed, throughout the debates over public grazing, participants in the conflicts often played fast and loose with it. It would therefore pay to reflect on what was involved when ranchers and government officials argued over the meanings of property. What do we mean by "property"? This deceivingly simple question has inspired casebooks of interpretations. Property theorists and pedagogues alike emphasize one critical point: property is not a thing but a right. It is an enforceable claim, recognized by the state, to use or benefit from something. Partly because Americans have tended in common usage to understand property as a thing, and partly because the property at issue was *landed* property, those involved in the debates about the range tended to focus on—and one might even say obsess over—the fact that the government legally owned the thing, the property, and the ranchers did not. They focused, in other words, on the government's claim to the property and, to the degree that they discussed rights, they focused on the government's immanent power as owner to deny ranchers the use of that property. With time, especially during the 1920s and after, ranchers began to pull apart this "thing-ness" in an attempt to differentiate what they saw as their right to use the public range from the government's rights as owner. The government's response was again to emphasize that it held the entire bundle of rights that came with owning this land, because most federal officials believed that giving away any "stick" in their bundle of rights was a step toward giving away the whole thing.

But what kind of property did these public lands represent? On the one hand, the public lands are property owned by the United States. But this answer begs the question of who actually *owns* the land. Because of the peculiar history of public land ownership, Americans have most commonly spoken of the federal government as the owner, because the

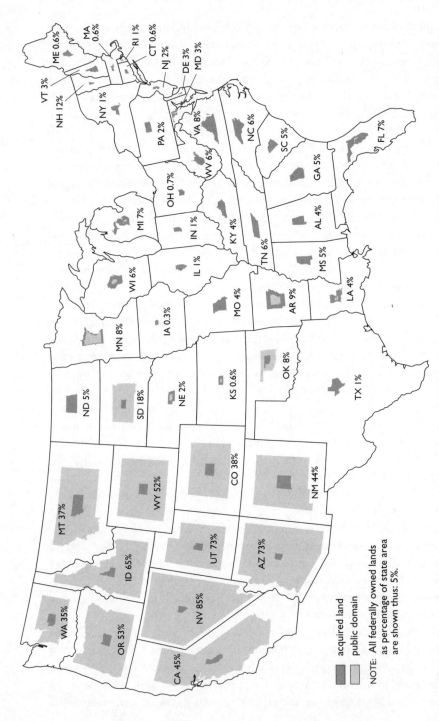

Figure 1. Proportion of federally owned lands as percentages of state areas, ca. 1955. Source: Marion Clawson and Burnell Held, *The Federal Lands: Their Use and Management* (Lincoln: University of Nebraska Press, 1957), 38.

acquired land

public domain

NOTE: All federally owned lands as percentage of state area are shown thus: 5%.

ME 0.6%
MA 0.6%
RI 1%
CT 0.6%
NJ 2%
DE 3%
MD 3%
VT 3%
NH 12%
NY 1%
PA 2%
VA 8%
NC 6%
SC 5%
FL 7%
GA 5%
WV 6%
OH 0.7%
IN 1%
KY 4%
AL 4%
MI 7%
IL 1%
TN 6%
MS 5%
WI 6%
MO 4%
AR 9%
LA 4%
MN 8%
IA 0.3%
ND 5%
SD 18%
NE 2%
KS 0.6%
OK 8%
TX 1%
WY 52%
CO 38%
NM 44%
MT 37%
UT 73%
AZ 73%
ID 65%
WA 35%
NV 85%
OR 53%
CA 45%

public lands came into existence in two ways: seven of the original thirteen states ceded their claims to western lands when the new federal government was launched in 1787, and the government subsequently acquired land through treaties and wars in the nineteenth century. Under
Article IV, section 3, of the Constitution, Congress was given the power
to legislate for the public lands however it chose, and that power has often specifically identified Congress as the owner of the lands. In contrast,
with the rise of the regulatory state in the early twentieth century, ownership of the public lands has also been seen to belong more fully to the
federal land agencies of the executive branch. The view that the public
lands are owned by what Carol Rose calls the "organized public," in the
shape of a government agency, competes with the view that the public
lands are owned by the American public. At least two versions of the latter opinion are evident in the history of public land policy. In the nineteenth century, it was common for officials in the eastern states to speak
of all the states owning and desiring to share the benefits of the public
lands; in the twentieth century, however, as the public lands have passed
into permanent federal management, we have seen conservationists and
environmentalists refer to these lands as the property of the American
people as a whole—the "unorganized public" of the United States—
with the government acting only as a kind of trustee (see figure 1).[8]

What is striking about the debates over public grazing is how deeply
muddied this question remained throughout the years. While it was one
thing to say that the American public owned the national parks, that
claim caused confusion when speaking of the public grazing lands,
which were used by only a handful of western ranchers. The result was
that it was profoundly unclear which "public" was being asserted to be
the owner of these lands: was it the organized public of government or
the unorganized public of the people? The ranchers, legislators, and bureaucrats who were involved in the political battles rarely addressed this
question directly, perhaps because the answer lay somewhere in between—that the government was responsible for keeping the lands public by denying any private property claims on them. In assuming that
mantle of responsibility, however, the government increased its powers
of regulation over the public lands in the early twentieth century, and
that authority to manage the lands, vested in the agencies in charge of
public grazing, had two significant effects. First, it increased the impression the agencies made that the federal government was the exclusive
owner of those lands, an impression that would lead ranchers to complain that the government was no better than a feudal landlord. Need-

less to say, such a connection provided plenty of rhetorical fuel in the political conflagrations over public grazing. But, second, it implicitly raised
a nettlesome question for federal land managers about the nature of federal sovereignty on the public lands. That is, did the government's legitimate authority derive from its ownership of the land or from a congressional mandate to administer public policy?

   Not surprisingly, land managers relied on both these explanations,
but it is their reliance on the government's ownership claims that war-
rants attention in light of the changes in American government during
the twentieth century. Throughout the Progressive period and the New
Deal, government at both the state and federal levels saw an expansion
of powers. While this was a piecemeal process that affected different areas of governmental activity at different rates and in an assortment of
ways, this growth in what scholars call "state capacity" is nonetheless
certainly one of the central stories of modern American political history.
And despite the fact that what emerged may have been an "uneasy
state"—one that decentralized power and was particularly permeable
by interest-group influence—the American state during the first half of
the twentieth century accrued a host of functions that it had not had before. Where officials in Washington were able successfully to carve out
arenas of federal activity—and public land management was one of
them, although it took many decades to build up the public land holdings that we know today—they did so through the creation of administrative structures that were legislated to regulate certain activities.
Whether the focus was railroad rate regulation or meat inspection, this
growth in federal oversight was understood to have congressional approval (thus representing the people) and to be justified by the government's need to protect the public interest in a time of rapid economic
and social change.

   Land managers also saw that the expansion in federal administration
of the public lands involved developing modern governmental institutions to protect the public interest. Indeed, conservation leaders did not
see land withdrawals as anything but a very modern governmental experiment in land policy. But there was another side to this liberal understanding of their work that was in distinct tension with it. The government held the authority to regulate the public lands withdrawn from
settlement, officials said, because it held sovereignty over all the lands
that it owned, just as any property owner held sovereignty over the land
that he or she owned. Thus, in the realm of the public lands, federal
officials saw the government's power as deriving not only from what

scholars of the state would call the new "administrative capacity" of the state but also from property ownership. This emphasis on property is striking, because it suggests that the American state was shaped by more than simply the constant struggle over the administrative organization of power and the access that private actors would have to public policy-making—a struggle that has largely defined how political historians have understood the development of the modern federal government. When land managers and Supreme Court justices asserted that the government was sovereign over the public lands because it owned them, and that this sovereignty then allowed the government a wide swath of public regulatory powers, that assertion rested on the claim to a private property right.

Of course, the American government was not supposed to rule through its property, the way that, say, a European monarch would once have done. And throughout the nineteenth century, the federal government sought ways to dispose of all its land (through sales, grants, or homesteading) in the belief that its sovereignty would only be deemed legitimate if it could both transfer clear property titles to individuals and organize the sparsely populated territories into states. The shift in that thinking to one of withdrawing land and conserving certain natural resources under federal management indicated, as has been pointed out time and again, a tremendous transformation in the way that the government and Americans understood the process of western settlement. The newness of the governmental structures should not, however, hide the fact that in focusing on *sovereignty,* land managers and numerous judges were implicitly drawing together two concerns that lay far outside the frames of liberal reform. One of those concerns had long-standing importance in the development of modern nation-states, involving how the state's sovereignty is expressed in actual territory. Is a state's legitimacy and authority unchallenged over the land under its jurisdiction? As we shall see, this question galvanized all sides in the conflict, from Supreme Court justices to federal bureaucrats, from conservationists to the many westerners who believed that the western states were sovereign over the public lands within their boundaries. But there was a second concern, which entailed another notion of sovereignty, that is, the sovereignty of the private property owner. In the final analysis, land managers argued, the federal government's proprietary rule could not be challenged because the government held all the rights that an individual owner would have.[9]

In other words, the source of power for the government's regulatory authority was not fully an invention of "modern" state structures. But, ironically, if that regulatory authority bolstered the claims of the government over the public lands, it also had the opposite effect; as the government established structures of property to manage public grazing, ranchers who were dependent on those structures for their businesses developed property interests in the public lands to which they could not lay claim before the lands were withdrawn. Of course, many public land ranchers before the forest withdrawals of the 1890s and the Taylor Grazing Act of 1934 had asserted that certain ranges were theirs simply by right of occupancy and labor. But the nature of that property discourse changed once the federal government began actively to manage these lands, because ranchers now had a set of structures that, to them, appeared to legitimate their property claims. Far from fighting the government because they felt overly dependent on the public lands, as western historians have argued, public land ranchers in fact engaged in fights with federal officials from a stance of political empowerment *because* of their access to this land. Thus, while the government was successful in keeping public land ranchers from gaining recognition of property rights from the courts, in no way did it succeed in keeping ranchers from claiming those rights in the language and arena of politics. Moreover, the nature of ranchers' discourse about property changed because, with the creation of agencies to manage public grazing, the government was asserting its ownership of these lands more profoundly than it had before. The very administration of the range, in other words, created by the government to protect the public's interest in the public lands, set the government and range users against each other in an intractable conflict over competing property claims to the same land.

All these assertions about property, then, lay at the heart of the expanding political polarization between organized ranchers and the federal government in the first half of the twentieth century. It was also a polarization whose shape, by 1950, will be recognizable to readers familiar with the contemporary battles between ranchers and environmentalists over the public lands. But approaching that familiar territory requires first stepping back to the end of the nineteenth century, when ranchers had very little political capital in the nation; in fact, it was widely hoped that they would fade from existence, as they were seen as land monopolists who were intent on keeping small homesteaders from settling the West. As discussed in chapter 1, Theodore Roosevelt and like-minded writers saw manly virtues in the ranchers' way of life, but

Roosevelt and others also believed that only the agricultural settlement of the West, with its emphases on private landownership and improvements, would bring the frontier region into the nation. The popular ambivalence toward ranchers was reflected in government policy as well; while ranchers had an "implied license" to use the public domain for their ranching enterprises, they only did so by "sufferance," in the Supreme Court's words. Although state governments in the West went ahead and developed laws that helped regulate the range livestock industry, those laws were interpreted as binding only so long as the federal government did not enact any policy with respect to its property.

By the early years of the twentieth century, however, much of this was already beginning to change, as explored in chapter 2. First, the government had begun making forest withdrawals under two expansive congressional acts in the 1890s, and those withdrawals would become the national forests under the management of the Forest Service in 1905, which would launch the first government grazing program. This departure from the long-standing government policy of disposing of the public domain has received much attention from historians. In this chapter, I examine the way that the Forest Service began articulating a different vision of settling the West, which involved settlers using public property rather than homesteading it. The national ranchers' organizations were then just testing the political waters, and the Forest Service became their political ally, accepting that ranchers played a legitimate role in settling the West. In opposition to this alliance stood eastern and western members of Congress who were wary both of big ranchers and government bureaucrats and supported expanding homesteading on the public domain. Although the homesteading policy triumphed in the Progressive period, it is also evident that ranchers and federal land managers ultimately succeeded in establishing new property relations in the West between ranchers and the federal government, linking ranchers' privately owned ranch operations and the public lands they used.

However, ranchers and Forest Service officials could not anticipate the explosive breakup of their alliance in the 1920s when the service attempted to raise grazing fees on the national forests. Little in the history of public grazing policy has provoked more misunderstanding than the issue of grazing fees. Ranchers' resistance to fee increases has been interpreted very simply as a desire to get something for (almost) nothing, and given how modest the increases have always appeared to be, it is difficult *not* to embrace this view. But as I argue in chapter 3, the issue of fees involved much more than money. It involved both the extent of federal power—because the Forest Service proposed to expand its administrative authority along with the increase in fees—and the ways in which the government understood itself to be the owner of the national forests. During this period, the Forest Service strongly articulated the analogy between itself and the individual property owner justifying its belief that it had a right to raise fees in order to capture more of the value of the public land.

Organized ranchers rejected that analogy, which in the end did not explain to ranchers why an increase in fees would serve the public interest. More important, the conflict over fees helped propel the political discussion of the public lands in new directions, which I examine in chapter 4. In challenging the government's authority in the grazing fee controversy, organized ranchers began to argue that the western states were the true sovereign powers over the public lands within their boundaries. Drawing on a language of property rights that they had developed in opposition to the Forest Service, ranchers argued that the western states had political rights to own the remaining lands in the public domain. In this they were aided by President Herbert Hoover, who proposed to give the surface rights of the public domain to the western states. But in the end his was a different vision than that of states' rights advocates, based more on his desire to streamline the administrative machinery of public land management than to bolster western states' sovereignty. Although the cession of the public domain to the states never occurred, it did have an important effect on the drafting of the Taylor Grazing Act, which in 1934 put all of the public domain under the Department of the Interior. In its resistance to federal land ownership and administrative expansion, the political discourse of states' rights helped lead organized ranchers and their allies in Congress to insist on provisions both to involve ranchers in administering the act and to give them secure access to the public range. I discuss these developments in chapter 5, where I pay particular attention to the ways in which the Interior Department's first director of grazing, Farrington Carpenter, interpreted the Taylor Grazing Act as establishing range rights for ranchers.

Carpenter's interpretation was at odds with Secretary of Interior Harold Ickes's understanding of the act, for while Ickes allowed for local autonomy in the administration of the new grazing districts, he drew the line, as the Forest Service had always done, at acknowledging that ranchers had gained any rights to the public domain. The gulf between Ickes's and Carpenter's understandings of the Taylor Grazing Act reflected the act's own profound ambiguities, which, as I argue in chapter 6, help explain the political explosions over the issue in the 1940s. This episode in the battles over public grazing has received a good deal of attention, in part because it has seemed so inexplicable: just as the management of the Taylor Grazing Act was getting off the ground, the major western livestock associations and key western legislators in Congress began attacking it. Given how much those associations had been involved in shaping the act and its subsequent administration, the attack, which ended up nearly destroying the grazing program in the Department of the Interior, looked like an assault on themselves. In fact, the episode makes little sense without an understanding of just how far ranchers' language of rights had come since the passing of the Taylor Grazing Act. By putting into place institutions and processes for adjudicating property claims, the act had restructured how ranchers saw the range: before the act, it had been a place of unregulated competition for grass; now it was divided into allotments, access to which was attached to ranchers' private property. These changes pushed some ranchers even beyond arguing for their rights to the range to the belief that they should be allowed to purchase the public rangeland itself. Such arguments did not go unopposed: by the mid 1940s, a counterattack by conservationists had begun to mobilize against the property claims that public land ranchers were making to the range. And in that mobilization, conservationists were articulating more boldly than ever that the public property of the West belonged to everyone in the nation, and that the public, as its owners, deserved to have it protected.

Of course, the political struggles over the public lands today still display many of the features of this earlier period in American history. The 1990s, for instance, saw the emergence of the wise use movement, which sought, among other things, to secure property rights for commercial users of public lands, including ranchers. But in between the conflicts of the 1940s and the last decade of the twentieth century, the modern environmental movement grew not only to achieve a prominent place in the politics of public grazing but also to challenge the discourse and structures of property that connected ranchers to the federal government. Environmentalists assailed both sides in the conflict, criticizing ranchers for overgrazing land that all Americans owned and the government for not protecting Americans' inherent interest in maintaining the ecological health of that land. The federal government responded in part to these criticisms, and Congress enacted several key pieces of legislation that sought to apply environmental values more fully to government grazing policy. Not surprisingly, since legislation is born of compromise, environmentalists have complained that such measures have not gone far enough, while ranchers have argued that they go too far. On the one hand, as I suggest in the epilogue, this intervention by environmentalists opened up a profoundly more expansive way to understand the property of the United States, one that brought a greater range of values into the policymaking of grazing managers. On the other hand, environmentalists have also at times been caught up in the terms of the prevailing property discourse that have ensnared ranchers and the federal government, thus locking them, too, into the scabrous political conflict over western rangelands in the twentieth century.

In examining the period preceding postwar environmentalism, this book explores how people's understandings of property wove their way into the political language and debates over public range policy. However, in that process—in the way that legal principles became translated into political rallying points—much clarity was often lost. For instance, as ranchers and their political allies increasingly emphasized their rights to the range, they were drawing on recognized legal relationships in property law, such as rules about easements and adverse possession. Sometimes they referenced those rules explicitly, and at other times implicitly; sometimes, too, they did so correctly, and at other times incorrectly. I have tried to make clear when participants in these debates were drawing on specific legal principles, more detailed discussions of which will be found in the notes.

Several central terms of the book also merit explanation. At stake in all the debates examined here was the rangeland owned by the United States, but that land was described in different ways. In 1890, it was open to homesteaders and was more often than not called the "public domain," although commentators also referred to it as "public land." After the forest acts of the 1890s, enabling the president to place public land in reserves—or national forests after 1905—the term "public domain" largely meant public land *other* than the reserves, the land that still lay open for settlement. The term "public land," then, typically meant all the lands under U.S. ownership, including those in the reserves. After the Taylor Grazing Act, which put what remained of the public domain under federal management, some people still referred to that land as the "public domain," although others referred to it as the "Taylor lands"—a name that helped to differentiate the area from those parts of the national forests devoted to grazing. Still other commentators have described all of the public lands of the United States as "federal lands"; while this is a term that immediately connotes the government's literal ownership of these lands, which itself requires examination, it is so common that I have sometimes used it interchangeably with the term "public lands." And when I have needed a very general term to describe the public lands on which ranchers grazed their animals, I have often simply used the terms "range," or "public range." In every instance where there might be confusion, and where there are clear indications, I have tried to specify what kind of rangeland commentators are discussing.

Finally, because this story is about a struggle on the national political stage, I have often had to generalize about the participants—and, in particular, about ranchers. Ranchers' political opinions were as varied as any group's, because they were people of different classes and racial origins, and one could even occasionally hear a woman's voice among them. But as is always the case with large, organized groups, only a limited number of ranchers participated in politics, and even fewer participated in national politics. Moreover, there were many ranchers in the West who did not ever graze their animals on public lands, either by choice or circumstance, and whose voices were rarely heard in the debates over public grazing. When I therefore refer to the views of ranchers or, more specifically, of organized ranchers, I am referring both to a very select group of men and to a set of positions that often excluded internal opposition by the time those positions filled the pages of the trade association journals and were heard in the halls of Congress. But that exclusion was never complete, particularly in the early years, when ranchers began involving themselves in policymaking. Most important, the public record that organized ranchers have left shows them in a lively and prolonged discussion among themselves over the very things that Rufus Ryker and Joe Starrett sparred over: what rights ranchers had to the "open" range and how exactly the government would view their attempt to control the vast public estate of the West.

CHAPTER I

Policing and Policymaking on the Range

> In its present form stock-raising on the plains is doomed, and
> can hardly outlast the century. The great free ranches, with
> their barbarous, picturesque, and curiously fascinating sur-
> roundings, mark a primitive stage of existence as surely as do
> the great tracts of primeval forests, and like the latter, must
> pass away before the onward march of our people; and we
> who have felt the charm of the life, and have exulted in its
> abounding vigor and its bold, restless, freedom, will not only
> regret its passing for our own sakes, but must also feel real
> sorrow that those who come after us are not to see, as we
> have seen, what is perhaps the pleasantest, healthiest, and
> most exciting phase of American existence.
>
> —Theodore Roosevelt,
> *Ranch Life and the Hunting-Trail*

Contemporary accounts of the western "cattle kingdom" of the late
nineteenth century were quick to herald its impending demise. Those
writers who were enchanted with it, such as Theodore Roosevelt, helped
to produce an almost instantaneous nostalgia that would characterize
accounts of the range cattle industry ever after. That nostalgia would
embrace a number of different things—the cowboys, the horses, the
wild animals, the life of adventure, the "open" range. All of these, it was
noted time and again, were merely the ephemera of a frontier industry.
Other observers were not so nostalgic and saw the "cattle kings" in a
colder light, but like Roosevelt, they understood their presence to be a
temporary one. For the western cattleman, wrote one newspaper editor,
"there was nothing of a permanent character about" the range cattle in-

dustry. "[I]t was simply a business opportunity of which he sought to make the most, and then quit as his pasture became crowded."[1]

The specific forms the cattle business took in the late nineteenth century did indeed pass quickly; it experienced an explosive rise in the 1870s and 1880s and dissolved rapidly thereafter, especially after the winter of 1886–87, when "cattle kings" on the range suffered huge losses and when many livestock owners quit the business.[2] However, the industry did not die. A new breed of ranchers, including sheep producers, would stake out the range and make a permanent place for themselves in the West. But while the transformation of the livestock industry would change the politics of the range substantially throughout the early twentieth century, as the federal government became more involved in it and as ranchers coalesced into national lobbying organizations, certain patterns were established in the late nineteenth century that would shape later conflicts. First, ranchers combined into local and state livestock associations both to secure their property (that is, their cattle) and to police the boundaries of their ranges against newcomers. Because the range was a vast grazing commons, however, conflicts inevitably erupted between ranchers competing for the same areas. And with no public land laws that would help ranchers secure enough grazing land to operate, they attempted to make this public property their own through a variety of methods, such as intimidation, illegal fencing, and controlling key water sources. The official response to such practices was mixed, as it would be for many decades. On the one hand, the federal government recognized and permitted grazing on the public domain and even allowed western states to regulate land use, although it occurred on federal property. On the other hand, the government began both to take stock of the public domain problem and to police it in the mid 1880s, in an attempt to take down illegal fences, thereby asserting its status as the landowner. Washington's authority over the public domain would then receive a tremendous boost with the congressional acts of the 1890s that created the forest reserves, which included a great deal of public grazing land. Thereafter, the regulated range of the reserves (later called the national forests) would serve as a pointed contrast to the unregulated range remaining in the public domain. Throughout all the battles over rangeland among ranchers and between ranchers and the federal government, the critical question remained whether ranching would *and should* survive into the twentieth century. This question bedeviled Washington policymakers, politicians, and ordinary citizens in the region, because it was so unclear where ranching fit within the frameworks in which people understood American society and the American economy. This confusion over what ranching was as an industry would influence the battles over the public lands for years to come, and until the question was settled, roughly after World War I, it stymied the best efforts of those engaged in trying to solve the public land problem.

"The cattle kingdom," wrote Walter Prescott Webb in a common portrayal, "was a world within itself, with a culture all its own, which, though of brief duration, was complete and self-satisfying. The cattle kingdom . . . formulated its own law, called the code of the West, and did it largely on extra-legal grounds." [3] If Webb romanticized the late nineteenth-century cattle industry, like many other writers, he nonetheless captured its uniqueness in American history. The qualities he highlighted were the result of an astonishing convergence of factors: the end of the Civil War, the exiling of Native Americans to reservations in the West, the expansion of urban populations, and therefore consumers, technology that made possible the transportation of dressed beef, and an expanse of land that served as an enormous grazing common. How the cattle frontier developed in what would become known as the public land states was, in Terry Jordan's words, "the result of chance juxtapositions of peoples and places." [4] Although Anglo-Texans shaped ranching in the West, ranchers also drew on other traditions (for instance, from California and the Midwest), and Anglo-Texan practices were themselves what Jordan calls a "syncretism" of herding traditions from the Carolinas and Mexico that dated back to the late eighteenth century. [5] In the end, western ranchers would substantially depart from this "Texas System," although this is our own starting point for understanding the history of public lands ranching, because it was predominately this "system" that observers saw in operation on the late nineteenth-century range.

Texas livestock owners had raised cattle on the open range before the Civil War, but with the end of the war the demand for beef increased rapidly and Chicago emerged as a leading market center, sparking the rapid rise of the western cattle industry. The war had cut off Texas cattle raisers from northern markets and created a bovine population explosion. With up to five million head grazing on the Texas plains, ranching entrepreneurs could buy cattle cheaply. As Edward Everett Dale notes dramatically: "Texas in 1865 was a vast reservoir fairly overflowing with cattle. To the north lay markets, to the north Texans must go with the only movable property left to them."[6] The initial cattle drives from Texas to the corn belt states, where farmers would fatten the animals before slaughter, were fiascoes; difficult river crossings and Indian skirmishes interrupted their movement, and farmers in other states feared the spread of Texas cattle fever, which had run rampant before the war.[7] In 1868, however, Joseph G. McCoy, an Illinois cattle trader, established Abilene, Kansas, as a shipping point from which to send cattle to other states. During the early 1870s, a number of western Kansas cattle towns also arose, including Newton, Dodge City, and Wichita, shipping on average a total of 200,000 to 300,000 head to market. These cattle went mostly to Chicago or Kansas City to be slaughtered, and to the corn belt states to be fattened or bred, but over the years, they were also increasingly sold to stock the northern ranges in Montana, the Dakotas, and Wyoming. From these Kansas cattle towns began the northern drives.[8]

The spread of the cattle industry over the northern plains only became possible with the destruction of the bison population and the suppression of Native Americans: ecologically speaking, cattle could not live off land occupied by bison, and cattle owners could not fully operate in Indian territory until they had broken Native Americans' subsistence on the bison. The slaughter began in full force by 1880, and in combination with drought and competition from domestic cattle, it devastated the bison population within a few short years, which in turn meant that Indians became increasingly dependent upon government beef rations, further encouraging the development of the range cattle business. In 1870, for instance, the government bought 12,669,790 pounds of beef on the hoof for the Indians. By the next year, that amount had increased to 27,441,750 pounds, and by 1880 the government was purchasing about eighty million pounds, which was equal to about fifty thousand head of cattle.[9]

Demand for beef increased for other reasons, as well. Most important of these was the building of the Union Pacific railroad, which in addition to helping populate the plains states also brought ranchers. The General Land Office estimated in 1871 that about fifty ranchers or ranch companies had established themselves in eastern Wyoming, and the overall number of cattle on the plains increased dramatically over the 1870s—from 11,130 in 1870 to 278,073 in 1880 in Wyoming, for instance, and from 70,736 to 346,839 in Colorado over the same period.[10]

Who were the men who became involved in the industry? Some were western entrepreneurs, such as John W. Iliff, who had come to Colorado territory in the late 1850s and bought Texan herds from Charles Goodnight after the Civil War. Taking advantage of the free grass and securing large beef contracts with the railroads, Iliff quickly built up a thriving business. Financial partnerships and incorporation agreements between eastern or foreign investors and western ranchmen brought hundreds more to the business.[11] As Gene Gressley has noted, in many cases the financiers invested in cattle companies after they had invested in other kinds of western enterprises.[12] What drew them, particularly in the boom era of the late 1870s and early 1880s, were spectacular profits, which could reach as high as 30 to 40 percent, helping to produce the gigantic ranches that so fascinated and repelled the American public. By the early 1880s, for instance, the Swan Land and Cattle Co., financed by Scottish and English investors, had control of a range in Wyoming and Colorado that was one hundred miles long by fifty to one hundred miles wide, was capitalized at over $3,000,000, and owned about 125,000 head of cattle.[13] The increased beef prices and general speculation fever induced a craze for cattle ranching among wealthy Scottish and English investors. "In Edinburgh, the ranch pot was boiling over," one agent for investors noted. "Drawing rooms buzzed with the stories of this last of bonanzas; staid old gentlemen, who scarcely knew the difference between a steer and a heifer, discussed it over their port and nuts." [14]

Foreign investments in the United States were nothing new, and in the West, they helped to build both the railroad and mining industries. But the influx of foreign capital into the cattle business, and thus into land ownership, set off typically American alarms. Some argued, for instance, that the industry was structurally a vestige of feudal Europe. As a *Nation* review observed: "Certain of these foreigners are titled noblemen of countries in Europe. Some of them have brought over from Europe, in considerable numbers, herdsmen and other employees who sustain to them the dependent relationship which characterizes the condition of the peasantry on the large landed estates of Europe." [15]

This argument had a potent appeal both in Washington and in American culture at large. Although more Americans than European and British noblemen were ranch owners, the epithets "cattle baron" and "cattle king" articulated many people's fears that a landed aristocracy would monopolize the West.[16] Although the cowboy was emerging as a kind of archetypal American man (despite the occupation's roots on Mexican ranchos), the industry itself was branded as outside the traditions of American agriculture.[17] Intensely masculine, without the "civilizing hand" of women, and occupying vast physical space, ranching clearly did not resemble eastern or midwestern family farming. Ranging large herds of cattle entailed entirely different notions of what constituted *productive* land use, which historically and legally meant making "improvements" on the land.[18] Ranchers in the nineteenth-century West did not grow crops, and ranches were noted for their crude buildings. Moreover, taking advantage of the expanse of public land, ranchers often owned only a small proportion of the land they used.

Indeed, for most interested observers in the late nineteenth century, ranching was distinctly undesirable, compared with farming. But rather than seeing the ranching industry as an outgrowth of eastern industrialization, commentators squeezed it into a proto-agricultural model and argued that ranching was simply a temporary stage in the evolution toward a more developed western society. One can clearly see this evolutionary view in Frederick Jackson Turner's thesis, of course. Or in the words of a Laramie, Wyoming, newspaper editorial in 1887, "[N]o country on the globe and at no period of the world's history has any nation or people who devoted themselves exclusively to stock-raising ever risen much above semi-barbarism." [19] For those who wanted cattlemen out of the West, ranchers were the enemies of the small landholder; they were semi-barbaric "land barons," or "cattle kings," with much more in common with the Jay Cookes of the world than with western settlers. But this complicated portrait of the cattle rancher—who was seemingly both primitive and feudal and a monopoly capitalist—also emerged from those observers who saw quintessentially American virtues in ranching. Such a portrayal is evident, for instance, in the work of one of the more prominent writers of the West, and one deeply associated with it: Theodore Roosevelt. The bundle of qualities that Roosevelt ascribed to ranching calls for a closer look, as these qualities would become common understandings of the industry and influence the paths policymakers and politicians would take in the twentieth century.

After going West to work on his Dakota ranch, Roosevelt published *Ranch Life and the Hunting-Trail* in 1888, already writing with both a vivid nostalgia for ranching and a belief that it was a critical part of the evolutionary development of western society. In the "far West," he wrote, "it is the men who guard and follow the horned herds that prepare the way for the settlers who come after." [20] Ranching was, Roosevelt believed, a "primitive" industry, "an iron age that the old civilized

world has passed by," which still pitted men against nature in a way
"unknown to the dwellers in cities." Distinguishing it further from the
rest of America, he wrote,

> The whole existence [of ranching] is patriarchal in character: it is the life of
> men who live in the open, who tend their herds on horseback, who go armed
> and ready to guard their lives by their own prowess, whose wants are very
> simple, and who call no man master. Ranching is an occupation like those of
> vigorous, primitive pastoral peoples, having little in common with the hum-
> drum workaday business world of the nineteenth century; and the free ranch-
> man in his manner of life shows more kinship to an Arab sheik than to a sleek
> city merchant or tradesman.[21]

On the one hand, Roosevelt liked to distinguish ranching from other
kinds of contemporary industries, including (and especially) farming.
While cowboys represented essential and noble qualities of American
manhood, ranching also did not fit into nineteenth-century, industrializing America. It was a "patriarchal" industry, an occupation structured
hierarchically by individual men (i.e., ranch owners) rather than by organizations, made up of self-contained economic units and lying outside
the rules of modern business.[22] But nearly in the same breath, Roosevelt
undermined his own myth-making by depicting ranch owners as proper,
if not superior, versions of eastern businessmen. This new and improved
variety of capitalist was a western phenomenon; range livestock owners,
in Roosevelt's words,

> certainly compare very favorably with similar classes of capitalists in the
> East. Anything more foolish than the demagogic outcry against "cattle
> kings" it would be difficult to imagine. Indeed, there are few businesses so ab-
> solutely legitimate as stock-raising and so beneficial to the nation at large;
> and a successful stock-grower must not only be shrewd, thrifty, patient, and
> enterprising, but he must also possess qualities of personal bravery, hardi-
> hood, and self-reliance to a degree not demanded in the least by any mer-
> cantile occupation in a community long settled.[23]

By making the ranch owner a hardy individualist or even an Arab sheik,
Roosevelt disconnected him from the capitalist market, while simultaneously depicting him as a good businessman. Thus ranching represented an industry that both ran on modern business principles and allowed men to return to a kind of primitive social unit.

The "primitive" nature of ranching was further embellished by Roosevelt's representation of it as a thoroughly masculine pursuit. Here,
women only flit like shadows, beyond the text. In his chapter on "The
Home Ranch," for instance, Roosevelt describes the difficulties and the

joys experienced by ranchers and cowboys living out on the plains: home was simply where a man could sleep and get his meals, and without a woman at the hearth, it had none of the moral or sentimental qualities that informed middle-class and agrarian paeans to domesticity. "There is an old and true border saying that 'the frontier is hard on women and cattle,'" he comments. "There are some striking exceptions; but, as a rule, the grinding toil and hardship of a life passed in the wilderness or on its outskirts, drive the beauty and bloom from a woman's face long before her youth has left her. By the time she is a mother she is sinewy and angular, with thin, compressed lips and furrowed, sallow brow." [24]

Although Roosevelt goes on to note frontier women's strength and courage, it is also clear that women do not gain health on the frontier, and unlike men who became more manly living and working on the plains, women lost both their femininity and all traces of maternal bearing. In contrast to farming, then, where the farm wife/mother occupied a significant symbolic space, ranching in Roosevelt's text, and elsewhere, was marked by the absence of women from a single-sex male world. [25]

The dichotomy in Roosevelt's description of the ranching industry of the late nineteenth century—that is, whether it embodied a primitive, temporary frontier economy or represented a modern industry—would continue into the public land debates in the early twentieth century. It simply could not be made to fit into agriculture or industry. For Roosevelt, its awkward place in society and in the economy engendered a deeper conflict: between his nostalgia for ranch life and his declarations as president that the real goal of western American development was agricultural settlement and widespread ownership of land. As early as *Ranch Life and the Hunting-Trail,* he had resigned himself to what he saw as the inevitable evolution of western society and to the passing of "what is perhaps the pleasantest, healthiest, and most exciting phase of American existence." [26]

While the free range was the reason for the western cattle industry's existence, because it was land that the federal government intended to dispose of rather than regulate, it also created a set of legal problems that the cattle owners often tried to address in extralegal ways. "The problem of controlling the grazing on the public domain in order to prevent overcrowding and to preserve the individual's share," Ernest Staples Osgood observes, "was the most difficult that the group had to face." [27] The problems of control centered around two separate issues: the animals and the land. In terms of the former, cattle were property that moved and could be moved, and thus early on in the industry, cattle owners combined to protect their herds from rustling, originally during the northern drives and later out on the range, particularly during roundups. Brand identification was central to the system. In Wyoming, for instance, each cattle owner had to register his brand with a local committee, and by 1879, illegal branding had become a felony.[28] And it was in Wyoming that livestock owners achieved their most legendary, even infamous, power. The Wyoming Stock Growers' Association (WSGA) was established in 1879, consisting largely of ranchers near and in Laramie County. By 1881, it began inviting other local associations within Wyoming and in surrounding territories to join it, and by 1883, its membership had grown to 363 and owned two million head of stock.[29]

Throughout the 1880s, the WSGA wielded extraordinary power in the territory, getting legislation passed that made the association nearly a separate political unit of the territory.[30] But as with other livestock associations in the West, the WSGA's primary purpose was to protect cattlemen's property and maintain control over the range, especially during roundups in the spring and fall, when different owners' cattle had to be sorted out. The WSGA divided the range into roundup districts, hired a foreman in each district to oversee the roundup, and established a legal date on which the roundup was to begin.[31] The association was also entirely in control of who could and could not enter the cattle industry. Livestock associations hired detectives to track down rustlers with illegally branded herds, and they often viewed smaller cattle operators with suspicion. Because the industry relied on a predominately transient labor force, associations kept close track of cowboys and other workers, routinely compiled blacklists of suspected rustlers, and forbade their members to hire these men.[32]

If cattle owners in these years consolidated their control over their animals as property to be protected, they had a remarkably laissez-faire attitude toward protecting their cattle as living creatures. During the boom years of the 1880s, cattle owners simply left their animals out on the range to forage for themselves during the winter. Under this system, largely derived from Texas methods and ill-adapted to the northern plains, there were "two kinds of cattle in the spring," as a Colorado officer of the Humane Society noted, "the dead ones and the living ones. There are others, tottering 'shades' of last year's prosperity. . . . They excite pity because *not* dead."[33] While the dead cattle were losses, they never made enough of a dent in cattlemen's profits to encourage less risky methods. This changed with the winter of 1886–87. After a hot and dry summer, on an overgrazed range, blizzards and bitter cold decimated western herds. Loss of cattle, by most estimates, averaged around 30 percent, and descriptions of the carnage provoked widespread disgust over the industry's inhumane treatment of its animals.[34] It was a disaster that reverberated in a number of ways for cattle operators. Thereafter, ranchers fought continually against a popular perception of them as cruel, a perception that had political consequences as the Humane Society grew in influence and lobbied Congress to improve safety standards in transporting livestock.[35] The blizzards also had a decisive effect on ranching methods in the West. In combination with already falling prices, the cattle losses forced many owners out of the business and the remaining ones cut down on their herd sizes and began growing hay to feed their cattle. Industry spokesmen argued that smaller ranches were more profitable and less risky, and smaller ranchers became interested in developing sound management and breeding higher-quality cattle.[36]

The blizzards highlighted the fragility of the cattle industry, and the ten years that followed saw tremendous upheaval in the range states and territories. As more ranchers vied for a diminishing piece of the range, they became involved in volatile disputes about controlling land use, particularly as sheep growers began very successfully to occupy the public domain. In fact, throughout the 1890s, the number of sheep grazing on western lands closed in on, and in some places, surpassed, the number of cattle, sheep often thriving in places most disturbed by the overgrazing of cattle.[37] Some of these disputes ended in violence, others in court. "Range wars" were the most notorious events, crystallizing the deepest conflicts over western range use and signaling the need for closer policing of the public lands. In the case of the Johnson County war in north-central Wyoming, for instance, a combination of factors created the setting for what would become a classic western conflict: livestock owners had overstocked an already overgrazed range, and after the winter of 1886–87, sheep owners and farmers moved into the area, competing for forage and space with cattle operations. Smaller cattle ranches, often owned by former cowboys, were also competing with larger outfits, whose owners accused them of rustling. In the spring of 1892, in an attempt to halt the rustling, the WSGA hired a group of armed men from Texas—the "regulators"—who eventually killed two suspected rustlers. An outraged mob of farmers and smaller livestock

owners later surrounded the "regulators" themselves, requiring the intervention of federal troops, which ended the conflict with only minor
skirmishes.[38]

In other parts of the West, cattlemen slaughtered sheep and drew
"dead lines" to keep sheepherders off the ranges they used; homesteaders cut barbed wire fences that ranchers had illegally built on the public
domain; and sheepmen "ate out" the ranges of both homesteaders and
cattle producers.[39] The rise of violence and conflict was a profound in-
dicator of the mixed signals ranchers received from Washington about
their use of the public domain. Because Congress intended to dispose of
the public domain in small parcels, it rarely exerted any governmental
authority at all over the use of the land. Indeed, Congress's *silence* on
range use was taken to be its most important policy statement, for that
silence was clearly translated into permission. As the Supreme Court argued in *Buford v. Houtz* (1890), "there is an implied license, growing
out of the custom of nearly a hundred years, that the public lands of
the United States . . . shall be free to the people who seek to use them
where they are left open and unenclosed, and no act of government for-
bids this use. . . . The government of the United States, in all its branches,
has known of this use, has never forbidden it, nor taken any steps to arrest it." [40]

As evidence not only of this "license" but also of the predominance
of public grazing in the West, the Court noted that all the western states
and territories had reversed the English common law rule that "a man
was bound to keep his cattle confined within his own grounds, or else
would be liable for their trespassing upon the unenclosed grounds of his
neighbors." On the contrary, said the Court, "[o]wing to . . . the great
value of the use of the public domain for pasturage," farmers were responsible for fencing their cultivated land from straying cattle.[41]

But if there was "an implied license" that all who wanted to could
graze their animals on the public range, this license did not translate into
a vested property right, and ranchers therefore tried in many ways to
control grazing lands for their exclusive use. One of the more widespread practices in the late nineteenth century was to fence off parts of
the public domain. As Osgood has written, by "the early eighties the
practice of enclosing portions of the public domain" with cheap barbed
wire fencing "spread so rapidly that the whole range industry was in
danger of being strangled to death in a web of its own making." The
Swan Land and Cattle Co. in southeastern Wyoming had one hundred
and thirty miles of fencing, for instance, and a company in Colorado

had fenced in almost a million acres of range. This fencing was "neither practical nor legal," as Osgood notes: it interfered with the purpose of the public domain, which was for homesteading, and it contributed to the large-scale losses during the winter of 1886–87 by not allowing cattle to continue moving in search of grass. In 1885, Congress attempted to halt the practice with the Unlawful Enclosures Act, the first use of federal police power on the range. But although the act forced many outfits to cut their fences, it was widely considered to be ineffective, and the problem of illegal fencing would reoccur throughout the period before the Taylor Grazing Act of 1934.[42]

The other common method ranchers used to gain control of their public ranges was to acquire them under the public land laws of the country. Although this outcome was clearly not intended by Congress when it established the laws, they were so "hopelessly inconsistent," Lawrence Friedman observes, that it is difficult to determine what overall goals Congress had in mind.[43] From the very beginning, American public land policy metamorphosed to serve a variety of interests and goals. The U.S. government granted lands to states for the benefit of public schools and colleges; it granted huge tracts of land to railroads to encourage western development along its routes; settlers could buy lands from railroad companies, states, and the federal government; or, they could file a homestead or other settlement claim. It was a system that created hundreds of thousands of homesteads, while also benefiting those with enough money to buy the better private lands. And the incongruities did not escape the many livestock owners who felt trapped in a nexus of land laws that worked against them.[44]

Land was, of course, fundamental to how Americans imagined the future of their country. Debates over land law, Richard White writes, were "about the very nature of American society and how it should replicate itself in new territories. . . . Land served as a sort of seal of approval for social consensus."[45] Over the course of the nineteenth century, the federal government did achieve some consensus over land policy; yet that consensus also froze certain ideas of what constituted proper land use, albeit conflicting, into place for decades. These notions then impeded the development of innovations in policy in the twentieth century.

The bases of American public land policy lay in the Land Ordinance of 1785 and in the Northwest Ordinance of 1787, which governed the organization of all the territory that the United States acquired in the nineteenth century.[46] In particular, the former stipulated that once Indians had given up their land, government surveyors would then survey and divide the public domain into townships of six square miles each. Every township would then be divided further into one-square-mile sections (640 acres) and each section would contain four quarter sections of 160 acres. The government would then sell these lands at auction.[47] It was a neat design and one that embodied republican ideals that a democratic government would be secured by widespread ownership of land. The problem, however, was that the government could not survey land as fast as people wanted to settle it, and the presence and political activism of squatters became a divisive political issue throughout the early nineteenth century. Certain politicians, especially eastern and southern Whigs, portrayed squatters as lawless ruffians who took advantage of the public lands at no cost to themselves. Westerners and most Democrats, on the other hand, saw them as the advance guard of civilization, willing to leave societal moorings to improve the land, ultimately for the greater good of the entire country.[48]

By the early 1800s, public land sales were so booming that Congress established the General Land Office, initially housed in the Treasury Department, but moved to the newly created Department of the Interior in 1849. By that point, the government's land office business was becoming increasingly complicated. In 1841, Congress had passed the Preemption Act, which allowed squatters first right to purchase 160 acres of land that they had settled on and improved. By acknowledging squatters' improvements, the Preemption Act opened the way for the Homestead Act of 1862, which became the centerpiece of American public land policy. While fraught with problems and abuses, the Homestead Act embodied the promises of a nation of small producers. Provided they paid a nominal filing fee to the General Land Office and testified that it was "for the purpose of actual settlement," homesteaders could enter a claim on 160 acres of surveyed public land. After five years, upon proof that they had improved the land—that is, cultivated it and constructed some kind of dwelling on the property—they would then receive a patent for it.[49]

Settlers also had the right to "commute" or buy their entries after six months, and the commutation principle received the bulk of criticism when the government first put the act into operation.[50] By the 1870s and 1880s, when the range cattle industry was developing, ranchers were acquiring land by having employees and relatives fraudulently file claims under their own names and later transfer title to the ranch owners after commutation. They were able to do this, not simply under the Homestead Act, but also under such settlement acts as the Timber and Stone Culture Act and the Desert Lands Act, which would later come under particularly critical scrutiny as avenues for land fraud.[51] While these abuses raised understandable criticism, they were merely indications of problems inherent in the homesteading principle itself and in the wider net of land laws. Most problematic was the 160-acre provision of the act, which many observers believed was a profound misjudgment of the amount of land required for successful homesteading in the semi-arid and arid West. In areas suitable for irrigation, 160 acres was more land than a family could successfully manage; in areas suitable only for grazing, where from 10 to 50 acres per head was needed, it was too little, and a family could not make a living on such small parcels.[52]

These problems contributed to Congress's appointment of a public lands commission in 1879, the findings of which, as E. Louise Peffer has noted, "constitute the most comprehensive study of the public domain ever made."[53] Among the members of this commission was John Wesley Powell, later head of the U.S. Geological Survey, who in the previous year had proposed radical changes to existing land policy. One of the most significant of these was allowing settlers 2,560-acre parcels of land (four sections) in areas that could only support grazing. But despite his much more realistic appraisal of range capacity, most members of Congress drew on the common bias against "cattle kings" and opposed Powell's proposal on principle, believing that it encouraged monopolies.[54] Creating workable policies for the remaining public lands was hindered by still larger hurdles than the 160-acre limitation. Fundamentally, land policy in the nineteenth century contained nothing that could encompass the needs of the range cattle industry. "Federal laws did not encourage . . . efforts to stabilize the livestock industry," Samuel Hays notes. "Under the homestead acts a settler could acquire sufficient land to raise hay and establish a farmstead, but he could not secure control of federal grazing for summer use. Those who depended on federal lands, however, could not exclude competitors who might obtain the lion's share of grass."[55]

By the late nineteenth century, many ranchers operated on a quiltlike pattern of land; they owned land outright to serve as a base for their outfits, but they might also lease or purchase land from railroads, as well as lease it from the states and individuals. This variety was further complicated when Congress authorized the president to create forest reserves, beginning in the 1890s. By 1900, nearly 47 million acres of forest lands had been reserved by presidential authority, over great opposition in the West, and by 1909 that number would increase to over 194,000,000 acres.[56] Despite the impression that they were tree-filled landscapes, the forest reserves also contained a great deal of grazing land, and although the reserves were set aside for the protection of timber and watersheds, at the start the most divisive battles over this land revolved around grazing. Since the lands were drawn from the public domain, the Department of the Interior was charged with their administration, and the department initially prohibited sheep grazing on the forest reserves, noting that it had "the right to forbid any and all kinds of grazing therein."[57] While the Interior Department administered the reserves, the work of forestry fell to the Department of Agriculture. This confusing division of labor confronted Gifford Pinchot when he took over the Division of Forestry in the Agriculture Department in 1898, when he also helped to broker a compromise between western sheep producers and the Department of the Interior that would allow regulated sheep and cattle grazing within the forests. By 1905, Pinchot would succeed in transferring the forests to his domain in what was then called the Bureau of Forestry, and that transfer, as we shall see in the following chapters, would have resounding effects on the grazing debates, especially as Pinchot further worked out the structures of grazing on the forests and established a political relationship with range users.

As historians have long noted, European forestry practices influenced Pinchot, and certainly his apprenticeship to French, German, and Swiss foresters shaped his ideas about extending governmental planning into timber production; American Progressives of every stripe were setting out for Europe to glean information about governmental reform efforts in such areas as workers' insurance and housing for the poor.[58] But like his Progressive peers, Pinchot also believed that European models had to be adjusted to American institutions. Recalling his opinion at the time he became head forester in the Division of Forestry in 1898, Pinchot argued that "[t]o do the work we had to do, a man must know about forests, of course, but he must also know about how people think, and how things are done in America."[59] In part, Pinchot understood this to mean working within a political system that required him to persuade politicians and citizens to accept his program. But like other young Progressives who sought to reform American politics and society, Pinchot saw opportunities for a kind of *American* governmental action that had not been pursued at the federal level before. "What we wanted was American foresters trained by Americans in American ways for the work ahead in American forests."[60]

Pinchot wanted, first, to put the government behind a forestry program that managed public and private lands for development; he distinguished his "practical forestry" from that used, for instance, in the Adirondack State Forest Reserve in New York, which did not allow the cutting of any trees. Rather, he saw forestry as a form of agricultural planning: "To grow trees as a crop is Forestry. . . . The forester gets crop after crop of logs, cordwood, shingles, poles, or railroad ties from his forest, and even some return from regulated grazing." [61] He clearly intended to have the government manage timber production, not timber preservation, which was a stance that put him at odds with some of the older pioneer foresters in the United States. These men were at best ambivalent about Pinchot's "practical forestry," and, from Pinchot's point of view, they did not want to see "the economic motives behind true Forestry." [62]

Holding the common Progressive belief that expertise could solve America's problems, Pinchot sought professional training for foresters, both in the government and in the universities. That training would differ from anything that had come before, he argued; while it would ground future foresters in scientific silviculture, it would also instill in them a sense of public duty and a passionate interest in the forests themselves. Given that forestry hardly existed as a recognized field in the late 1890s, Pinchot had the rare opportunity to build it from scratch, with government sponsorship. He "began to pick up youngsters," he remarked in his autobiography—mostly college graduates from Yale and Harvard—and he demanded that these young men have the "the physical hardiness" to become foresters. This demand proved deeply woven into Pinchot's conception of his mission; indeed, he does not hesitate to boast of his own physical exploits in detailing his maturation into the chief forester of the United States. "Incidentally," he writes in his autobiography about meeting Theodore Roosevelt in 1899, "T. R. and I did a little wrestling, at which he beat me; and some boxing, during which I had the honor of knocking the future President of the United States off his very solid pins." [63] Such boasts about physical strength are fairly common among turn-of-the-century Progressives—Roosevelt was himself perhaps the biggest boaster—and, like Roosevelt an easterner from a monied family, Pinchot found himself politically up against the men of the West. As Pinchot looked over his own professional life, he saw that part of his training came in testing his manhood in the mountains and deserts of the West. "I had to meet the Western men on their own ground or lose out," he wrote of having to confront ranchers about governmental policy toward grazing in the forest reserves.[64] And it is equally evident that he believed, not only that he had not lost out, but that he had created an organization of young men that ultimately would be able to earn westerners' respect. "These boys, wherever they worked, were the wonders of the natives for the hours they put in and the way they drove themselves," he noted. "That men on Uncle Sam's pay roll should work so hard was beyond local understanding." [65]

Pinchot also rejected the idea that the U.S. Army should manage "practical forestry" at the federal level, splitting on this issue with some older forestry leaders. As the youngest member of the National Forest Commission, appointed by Grover Cleveland, Pinchot opposed the commission's assertion that many of the "duties" of future forestry officials were "essentially military in character and should be regulated for the present on military principles"; forestry required "local cooperation," Pinchot argued, "and you can't get frontier people to co-operate on military principles." [66] Very likely, the failures in implementing Reconstruction shaped Pinchot's skepticism about army officers helping to get "practical forestry" off the ground in the West. But if Pinchot was skeptical of the report's emphasis on the necessity of military organization, he was very much behind its recommendation that forestry could "only be secured by a permanent Government administration." [67] Pinchot had grand hopes that all silviculture in the United States would come under government planning, and he saw the forests on the public lands as an obvious focus for government energies. These "public forests," he wrote, "held this enormous attraction for a forester—*they were under one and only one ownership and control,*" that is, the federal government's.[68] If Congress had the political will, it could establish "practical forestry" for these forests with a single act, enabling Pinchot to practice what he was preaching on a scale he would never be able to attain in dealing with private landowners.

The acts that created the forest reserves were remarkable in several respects. They gave enormous new powers to the president, and Grover Cleveland took advantage of those powers, creating thirteen new forest reserves in 1897.[69] The reserves also set in motion the bureaucratic wheels in Washington that would ultimately produce the Forest Service in 1905. As chief forester at the turn of the century, however, Pinchot was already transforming the Division of Forestry from an administrative backwater into a significant part of the Department of Agriculture; within three years, beginning with a staff of 11, he was employing 179 people in the division, and he increased the appropriations the agency received from $28,520 to $185,440. But I would also argue that the major significance of the forest reserves is that they gave the government real property to regulate—as Pinchot noted, a tremendous "attraction" to him. On the one hand, the public forests were attractive because Pinchot was concerned about land monopolies in the West, and he saw proper public administration and ownership of the western forests as ways to temper concentrated wealth in the region—a concentration he believed was vaster and more dangerous than in other parts of the country.[70] And government ownership and control of the western forests would, he hoped, repair the political and social damage caused by fraudulent exploitation of the land laws. On the other hand, as we shall see in much more detail in the following chapters, the attraction of owning the forest reserves also involved proprietary claims, as the government began to identify itself specifically as the owner of the public property.

But in 1898, when Pinchot became head of the Division of Forestry, little was known about the long-term ramifications of the forest reserves, and it would be some years before he and his staff would lay down a solid organization and develop a dependable set of regulations for those lands. The same year that Pinchot stepped into his new governmental role, a group of ranchers and civic leaders in Denver convened the first meeting of the National Live Stock Association (NLSA). Although western livestock producers had formed local and state associations in the past, and there had been several aborted attempts to form a larger organization of cattlemen, this attempt in 1898 actually got off the ground.[71] The first convention in Denver drew over 1,000 delegates and sought to include owners of horses and sheep as well as cattlemen (although there had been a national organization representing sheep producers since 1868, in the form of the National Wool Growers Association). From the beginning, however, the NLSA was largely dominated by cattle producers and their problems, bringing to public notice a remarkably active group of politically minded men who believed they were helping to inaugurate a new era of western ranching.[72] Rather than just glibly boosting the industry, speakers at the convention recalled the perilous ten years that had followed the disaster of 1886–87, although conceding that with beef prices now rebounding, livestock producers were back on solid footing. "For ten years, the raiser of stock has been almost an exile in those haunts," said Colorado Governor Alva Adams, "which for so many years he trod with such a lordly air, and where his name and his note were recognized and accepted as precious vouchers. But a change has come. Your maladies have been touched by the golden anointment of prosperity."[73] The early leaders of the association were indeed prosperous men; its first president, John Springer, had been mayor of Denver and was involved in a number of different money-making enterprises aside from ranching. Other prominent leaders included Frank Hagenbarth, who would go on to become a longtime president of the National Wool Growers Association; the Scotsman Murdo Mackenzie, manager of the enormous Matador Land and Cattle Co., which owned land across a number of states; and Henry Jastro, manager of several cattle companies in California and New Mexico. They were men who earned their money from the open range and yet believed that only through large-scale organization could the livestock industry of the West achieve financial stability. They were as nostalgic as Teddy Roosevelt was for the pioneer days of ranching, and yet they were also intent on shedding their reputations as frontier types and on being seen as part of a legitimate western industry.

With the creation of the National Live Stock Association in 1898, the range livestock industry would become politically involved in a panoply of issues, such as railroad rate regulation, sanitary laws, public relations, and, of course, public land policy. The latter proved controversial from the beginning. At its first convention, for instance, the association's program featured two speakers who took opposing sides on the public land question: Wyoming Governor William Richards argued that the lands should be ceded to the states, while Elwood Mead, also of Wyoming and the future head of the Office of Irrigation Investigations in the Department of Agriculture, argued that the federal government should lease the lands to ranchers and homesteaders.[74] Some ranchers in the organization were content with the status quo of the unregulated range, subject to the settlement laws already in place, but most recognized that one of the NLSA's primary political tasks as a new organization was to take a stand on the direction of public land policy, and that in so doing, they would have to make a political case for being allowed to have continued access to the public domain. Given the widespread antagonism to ranchers, both in the West and nationally, that followed the "Great Die-Up" of 1886–87, they understood that this would be a difficult task. At the same time, however, they were beginning to reconstruct their perceptions of their own industry and its relationship to the public range. The president of the NLSA, John Springer, opened the convention by announcing that a "new regime" had been instituted among western ranchers, which included using purer breeds of animals and taking better care of them. It was an implicit denunciation of the open range days when northern ranchers had left their cattle to fend for themselves.[75]

In their discussion of the public land question, Richards and Mead clearly worked from similar understandings of what ranching should look like in the West, for despite their specific disagreement over how the government should handle its lands, they both argued that western ranchers had to own irrigated land to produce feed for their animals, and that no public land policy could be constructed at either the state or federal level without securing the link between grazing land and irrigated land. "The man who would range cattle successfully must also be a farmer," noted Richards, in what would be a very common argument in future conventions, despite many ranchers' distaste at being associated with farmers. "The best results from either irrigable or grazing land require that they should be held and used together. The privilege of leasing [from the state] the grazing land should be reserved to those who own and cultivate the irrigable."[76] Similarly, Mead believed that the public pasture lands had to be used in conjunction with the greatest possible development of irrigated lands, that homesteaders who were willing to reclaim their land should be allowed to lease four sections of grazing land, and that large livestock operators must provide feed for their cattle and sheep. The public domain, both Richards and Mead believed, had to be tied to a homestead or a home ranch, a notion that would continue to take shape until it became an integral part of federal grazing administration.[77] But it was also a notion with deeply problematic implications for public land management, because it meant that the public grazing lands would be connected, through ranchers' use, to particular private properties. As ranching became a permanent feature in the landscape of the West, public rangeland would thus become more deeply embedded in ranchers' conceptions of their private property.

By the turn of the century, then, a complicated and uncharted set of legal, political, and social relationships had to be determined. The fledgling administration of the forest reserves would provoke several significant legal battles to determine the nature of government authority in grazing regulation on those lands. How far could the government go in setting rules and fees for ranchers to use that land? What was the nature of its authority over the unregulated public domain? And was that authority based on constitutional imperatives? As for the politics of the range, the new century saw the building of large political organizations on two fronts—among western ranchers and within the federal government, as the Division of Forestry expanded to become the Forest Service.

How much of a part would ranchers play in developing grazing policy in the Forest Service? Should the NLSA ally itself with the conservation program of Theodore Roosevelt and Gifford Pinchot? And, finally, the most basic of questions remained: should public land ranching continue in the West? What would it look like if it did continue? Did western states want ranchers to help make up the social fabric of their region? In the years to come, with Congress determined to reshape the nation's public land policy, these questions would come in for intense discussion and scrutiny. In the process, the country was reintroduced to a most perplexing and very powerful figure, who in the past had frustrated and thwarted ranchers' efforts to gain control of the range. Ironically, the homesteader—also known as the "home-builder," the "home-maker," and the "little fellow"—would do more political work for ranchers in the early twentieth century than they could ever have imagined.

CHAPTER 2

The Properties
of the Homebuilder

The great and boundless West may change, the cattle king
may become a memory, but in his place and in the place of
the measureless ranches which may be divided, will come ten
thousand homes of industry which will spring up where
happy children will play from morning to evening, and music's melodies will take the place of carnage and strife.

> —J. A. Reed at the 1903 National
> Live Stock Association Convention

"I have heard cow men and sheep men stand up and appeal for the rights
of the settler, and you would think the settler has no other friend,"
groused Sam Cowan in a speech before the convention of western cattlemen in 1907. "You fellows don't care about the settler. . . . There is
no use to mince words, and make false pretenses. What you want is to
get as much grass for your stock as you can." [1] Cowan (that is, Sam
Houston Cowan) was a Texas attorney who served as legal counsel and
lobbyist in Washington for both the American National Live Stock Association and the Cattle Raisers Association of Texas. In the capital, he
was known as one of the great railroad rate lawyers; in the ANLSA, he
was known for his plain talk and his long-winded speeches. [2] Used to
playing hardball politics, he was no doubt puzzled by the sentimental
paeans to the homesteader that were endemic at the ANLSA's annual
conventions in the early years of the century. Having undoubtedly observed that most political rhetoric masked economic self-interest,
Cowan tried to goad the cattlemen into talking about what was of
most interest to them: how to secure the public range for their ranching
operations.

But Cowan's attempt failed. If anything, the association increasingly praised the homesteaders of the West in the years before World War I, so much so that the ANLSA's president declared in 1916,: "I want to put myself fairly on record, at this time, as a believer at all times in the legitimate homesteader—the man who comes right out and drives down the stakes of civilization in the wild, and sometimes, desolate, country; the man who rears a family under adverse conditions; the man who makes a real home and puts up a permanent roof-tree." [3] Given that ranchers have typically been seen as enemies, and even bullies, of small settlers, such a homily to "the homesteader" seems strange indeed. Certainly, there was political pressure on organized ranchers to voice their support for settlers. But the fact that leaders of the association sustained this kind of talk for so long, and did so relatively unambivalently, suggests that their embrace of "the homesteader" did more than just hide their interest in gaining control of the range. It was, in fact, a central part of the transformation of ranching's identity and the politics of public grazing.

In this period, a conjuncture of events provided new social and political contexts for organized ranchers. For one thing, while many of the big cattlemen remained in the business, smaller family operations also emerged during this period, and both big and small ranchers employed different methods and principles in operating their businesses than did the frontier ranchers of the late nineteenth century. Western cattle ranchers began "breeding up" their herds—that is, investing in purer bred cattle—to meet consumer demand for higher grades of beef; these cattle were less hardy than earlier breeds and required better care, including feed during the winter. Ranchers thus now devoted more of their land to cultivating hay or other forage crops. What these changes indicated was that ranching was settling down, and although thousands of ranchers still used the public lands, their operations looked more like farming than ever before; indeed, their resemblance to farming provoked many a discussion at the ANLSA conventions. The changes in practice on the range were also both fueled and given political meaning by the renewed national interest in homesteading and, specifically, in altering the terms of the Homestead Act. Congress devoted more time to the public lands question during this period of less than twenty years than it had since the 1860s and 1870s, and the attention given to homesteading would have profound effects on both western ranching and the subsequent relationship between ranchers and public land agencies, as the "bona fide homesteader" became an inviolable and very popular figure in the political discourse surrounding the public lands. In both planned and unplanned ways, ranchers hitched their fortunes to the "homebuilder"; and in quite unpredictable and fascinating ways, this move established the terms in which ranchers and land managers would understand the public range of the twentieth century.

But if the homesteader was ascendant in this period, other events and trends moved the public land question in quite different directions—directions that tell us much more about the organization of politics and the power of the federal government. Perhaps most important, in several key decisions, the Supreme Court gave the federal government the green light to manage public grazing lands as it saw fit, and this go-ahead provided the Forest Service with the authority to develop and forge, sometimes with the help of ranchers, the policies that would govern grazing on the public lands until the present. The authority in and of itself was critical to the government, setting out the wide scope of its powers over the public lands. This authority, in turn, helped to build further the institutional structures for managing grazing in the national forests, and it provoked tremendous debate over the proper role of the government with respect to the public domain. Finally, if the federal government was becoming increasingly organized and mobilized around questions of the range, ranchers, too, were building impressive organizations to lobby for their interests, the most prominent ones being the National Live Stock Association (which early in the century became the American National Live Stock Association) and the National Wool Growers Association.

These two associations certainly did not represent the political views of all ranchers and of ranchers' smaller organizations: given how many of these there were—from county livestock associations to state-level ones—that kind of representation would have been impossible. But the coordination of national political activity is an important story to tell about the western livestock industry, because it would have such a profound influence on the formation of public land policy. That coordination brought the "national" livestock associations into a closer relationship with public land administrators than anything ranchers had known in the nineteenth century, and it opened the way for these two groups of actors to envision a new future for the public lands.

I use the word "envision" very deliberately, because this chapter explores two different visions about the West—and, specifically, two different stories about the public property of the West. In the early years of the century, one vision was dominant among politicians, many western citizens, some ranchers, and a good portion of the general public: the West needed to be peopled by homesteaders, and the land had to be divided and dispersed among small-scale property holders. For a variety of reasons, this projection left ranchers almost entirely out of the picture. But gradually, as politically organized livestock owners and federal land managers developed policies for the range, another vision emerged: the West could be filled with ranchers who would make their homes using large tracts of leased public land. Of course, we know the end of the story, that homesteading largely failed, and that by midcentury, the government managed hundreds of millions of acres for ranchers' use. But that story has some very peculiar twists, for although ranchers would later become infamous for their often brutal use of political force, in these years they were very decidedly the losers in almost every political battle of note. And because they were on the defensive politically for so much of this time, they appropriated the terms of their opponents, noting time and again that they believed the homebuilder would be best helped by government management of the public domain. How the homebuilder came to be such a popular presence at ranchers' conventions, and how he came to have a powerful influence on the politics of public grazing, is the focus of this chapter, for it was he more than any other figure that would change the course of policy for the public domain.

From the late 1800s through the early 1900s, the differences between ranching and farming were built into the categories people used to talk about western land use. Even though by the early twentieth century, ranchers were taking much better care of their animals and were actually cultivating forage and feed for them, ranching was not considered a part of agriculture. As late as 1914, a western livestock and loan manager noted, in a comment on whether the government should encourage further homesteading in the West, that "[p]assing laws to create 'agriculture' where nature planned a grazing or pastoral country does not relieve the situation any more than the efforts of the land locators, emigrant agents, or speculators to make the crops grow on the Bad Land Buttes of the Dakotas."[4] Like many other people associated with the cattle industry at the time, he did not believe that the government could make the semi-arid lands bloom with farms. But more important for our story, he did not see "grazing" as an agricultural pursuit.

This would have been self-evident to the cattlemen of the late nineteenth century, whose history seemed to distinguish them sharply from pioneer farmers. But these perceived differences from settlers also made ranchers politically unpopular, cutting them out from a widespread movement that sought to retain America's agricultural base. Proponents of this agrarianism argued that the nation could not continue to grow and develop without a stable population situated on the land, and that good citizenship stemmed from a man's owning his land and improving its value with the labor of his family. That the early 1900s saw a steep increase in migration from farms to cities created enough anxiety to spawn a veritable industry of publication on the "farm problem" well into midcentury. Such concern over how the United States would maintain its agricultural population produced an enormous amount of social commentary during the Progressive period and fueled the rise of both the country life movement, a mostly urban-based movement that sought to "uplift" the lives of farm families, and a brief back-to-the-land movement. Even President Roosevelt joined in investigating the problems of the American countryside.[5]

Encouraging homesteading was thus a response to a national concern over the country's agrarian base. But homesteading as a western phenomenon had other associations as well. By the 1890s, most of the fertile public lands had been taken up, and the 400 million acres left lay in the semi-arid and arid West. Westerners put their hopes initially in irrigation to reclaim the dry lands from rangeland and create a society of profitable homesteads. As the irrigation prophet William E. Smythe wrote in *The Conquest of Arid America,* irrigation was the key to opening up a new kind of society in the West. In this vision, ranching would fast become a thing of the past. "Civilization is driving barbarism before it," he argued. "The conflict is between the civilization of irrigated America and the barbarism of cattle ranching."[6] For Smythe, who was both editor of *Irrigation Age* and a popular writer for such magazines as *Harper's* and the *Atlantic,* agriculture was "the basis of civilization," upon which the nation had "hastened to erect the superstructure of a complex industrial life."[7]

But the argument that farming provided the only means for settling the West with homes and families also emerged with irrigation's flipside: the dry-farming movement. It too was fed by the notion that a stable society could only be rooted in a stable farm population, a belief that was especially profound because the movement claimed to be creating farms in semi-arid areas that seemed impossible to cultivate.[8] Throughout the early 1900s, boosters of the West maintained that dry farming was the only way to bring the vastness of the semi-arid public domain into the national polity, the only way both to utilize these lands productively and to sustain the country. Indeed, although Alva Adams had praised the newly organized cattlemen of the West as governor of Colorado in 1898, as the former governor in 1911, he declared at the Dry Farming Congress, "The best way to conserve the land is to use it, and it will be a fortunate day for state and nation when there are no great reservations and no public land; but when every quarter section will be the home of an industrious, producing American citizen."[9] The figure of the homebuilder thus emerged as the embodiment of *western* agrarian ideals—the man who, along with his family, would settle, and settle down, the country, who through his and his family's labor would cultivate and improve the region, transforming disordered public lands to orderly private ownership.[10]

By these standards, the turn-of-the-century livestock owner was seen as anything but a homebuilder, and before the early 1900s, ranching and homebuilding were culturally and politically viewed as antithetical categories in stories of western development. If the values of farming were seen to lie in the ownership of private property, agricultural improvement of land, family stability, and residential permanence, at the turn of the century ranching was still widely considered to be merely a temporary industry. Ranchers used vast amounts of land—the public domain—that they did not own, which they did not improve through cultivation, and on which they merely grazed their animals. And ranching was seen not to operate from homes with families. In what was a common rendering of late nineteenth-century ranching, Edward Everett Dale wrote in 1930: "Camps occupied by ranchmen and their employees and corrals for use in caring for the animals were of the most flimsy and temporary character. Under such circumstances homes and family life were virtually impossible. As a result the range area developed as a 'man's country' where women and children were seldom seen. . . . [Ranching became] entirely removed from the refining influences of home and civilization."[11]

Ranching's untempered masculinity contrasted starkly with the constructions of farming in this period, in which women and children were essential participants. Roosevelt played up the image of the "primitive" ranchman in his reminiscences, of course, and cattlemen also enjoyed boasting of their frontier pursuits. In none of their representations of the industry was the rancher depicted as an analogue to the family farmer, or the ranch as a semi-arid family farm. If "[t]he country home" was "the safe anchored foundation of the Republic," the western ranch was seen as a transient outpost for capital on the hoof and masculine heroism.[12]

Thus, despite the disappointing results of the Homestead Act in the semi-arid and arid West, it alone provided the framework within which Congress created the nation's public land laws during the Progressive period. For these politicians, and for officials in the Department of the Interior—which administered the Homestead Act through the General Land Office—the crisis of the public domain involved determining how much acreage was needed to support a family, and their ultimate goal was to transform the entire public domain into privately owned parcels. Such western politicians as Frank Mondell of Wyoming and, later, Harvey Fergusson of New Mexico were prime movers in popularizing legislation that increased the amount of acreage available under the principle of homesteading. The Kinkaid Act of 1904 was the first experiment in expanding these provisions, allowing settlers up to 640 acres in the Sand Hills of western Nebraska, with the idea that they would establish homesteads for small livestock operations. Although politicians and officials would argue about how successful this experiment was, as E. Louise Peffer points out, "the start made in creating grazing homesteads proved abortive." [13] With the emergence and initial successes of dry farming in the semi-arid West, the Kinkaid Act was followed in 1909 by the Enlarged Homestead Act, which allowed settlers to enter 320 acres on the public domain and was intended to encourage cultivation. However, in 1916 Congress went back to the idea embodied in the Kinkaid Act and passed the Stock-Raising Homestead Act, which allowed settlers 640 acres of the public domain and was specifically designed for small livestock operations.

These last two acts spurred the greatest run on homesteads since the passage of the Homestead Act (see figure 2), but two other points are equally important for our story. The first is that, given Congress's intense interest in getting the Homestead Act right, and given the clear popularity of homesteading as part of a larger agrarian discourse, the terms of the political debate about the public lands narrowed until few participants could speak about the public domain without voicing support for "the homesteader." However, within this constricted atmosphere of political discussion, there was a genuine struggle among politicians, bureaucrats, and ranchers to understand what form the homestead would take in the West, and whether it should involve ranching. Congress experimented with the idea of small ranch-homesteads in the Kinkaid Act, for example, then retreated to the notion of an agricultural homestead with

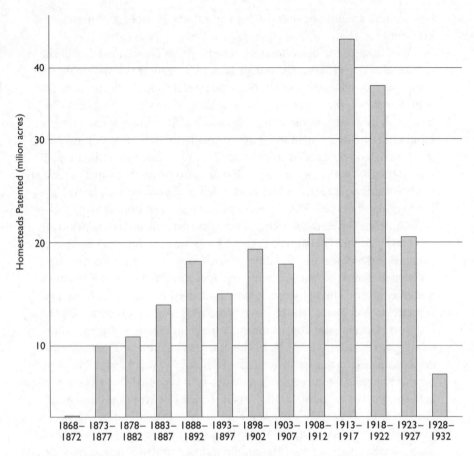

Figure 2. Homesteading expanded greatly through the teens and World War I, following changes in the Homestead Act, and then fell sharply in the 1920s as productive land became scarce. Source: U.S. Congress, Senate, *The Western Range: . . . A Report on the Western Range—A Great but Neglected Resource*, 74th Cong., 2d sess., doc. 199 (Washington, D.C.: GPO, 1936), 219.

the Enlarged Homestead Act, only to revise that again in 1916, allowing for small ranch operations. And that struggle would be echoed among cattlemen, who were also trying in these years to understand the relationship between homesteading and ranching. But as influenced as they were by the debates about homesteading, the western livestock associations had also entered a political relationship with officials in what would soon become the Forest Service, and that relationship would have a profound effect both on how ranchers envisioned their place in the

West—and more significantly, how their place would be established as policy by the federal government.

Leasing the public domain became a serious policy option with the presidency of Theodore Roosevelt because of his willingness, even eagerness, to open up the national dialogue about the public lands. In 1903, Roosevelt appointed a Public Lands Commission, made up of Gifford Pinchot (then head of the Forest Bureau) F. H. Newell (chief of the Reclamation Service), and W. A. Richards (commissioner of the General Land Office). Roosevelt's commission both harked back to the Public Lands Commission of 1879—which included John Wesley Powell's recommendations for the western public domain—and looked forward to a new era in public land management, favoring more federal involvement on the range.[14] The commission traveled throughout the West and met with 102 representatives of the National Live Stock Association; it also sent out a circular of questions to livestock owners across the West, receiving replies generally favorable to federal range control.[15]

Representing Roosevelt's political views, as well as its own, the commission recommended doing away with a number of troublesome provisions under the settlement laws, including the repeal of the Timber and Stone Act of 1878—under which many fraudulent claims had been filed—and the commutation principle of the Homestead Act. Congress acted on neither of these proposals and, in fact, passed only a minor point among the commission's recommendations.[16] But despite its failures in the realm of legislative action, the commission made important recommendations for the western livestock industry as a whole. It proposed that the remaining public domain be classified according to its agricultural possibilities, and that those lands that were only suitable for grazing should come under a loose form of government administration. The commission noted that livestock owners themselves wanted "government control of the ranges under reasonable regulations made to meet local conditions, and providing for a proper classification of the lands."[17] And classification had long been recommended within the government, John Wesley Powell having done so in 1879, for instance. As a way to order the vast area of land into manageable and productive units, classification was put forward as the solution to the endless disappointments of homesteading in the semi-arid region and as the means that would ultimately allow ranching to flourish. But the commission's report also indicated that it could only consider the future of ranching through the established principles of homesteading, especially the imperative that the government had to discover the correct amount of acreage that would support one family in ranching, just as it had settled on 160 acres as the correct amount to support one family in farming in the Midwest. For instance, the commission stated that "lands which could only be used for grazing should be so classified, and entry or settlement should only be allowed under such conditions as offer a reasonable assurance of the successful establishment of a home. New men engaging in the stock business should be allowed the use of enough land to support a home, the development of ranches suited to the support of a single family being the condition desired for the best use of public grazing lands." [18]

While the commission did not recommend "the immediate application of any rigid system to all grazing lands," it did propose a plan that would give the president authority to establish grazing districts, and the secretary of agriculture would be able "to make and apply appropriate regulations to each [grazing] district, with the special object of bringing about the largest permanent occupation of the country by actual settlers and home seekers." [19] This language, emphasizing that the object of leasing was home-building, would have long-lasting effects on the grazing debates. For one thing, it suggested that the ranching industry was still dominated by monopolistic cattle kings.[20] The commission's report would also contribute to the rather awkward fit between the support for leasing and agrarian ideals; thereafter, advocates of federal grazing control wedded proposals for a lease law to the notion that homesteading was the primary goal of western development, even though land leasing was anathema to American *agricultural* ideals of private ownership.

As other supporters of leasing would note in the future, the commission argued that leasing functioned like homesteading: it could attract settlers by proving that the lands were productive for grazing and by giving them more security than under the free-for-all of the open range. The commission noted, for instance, that the leasing of state lands in Texas had encouraged small settlers to come. But the example of Texas also worked against the commission's recommendations, for without proper regulations, the commission argued, the Texas lease law also spawned tremendous speculation in land, which was the specter that never went away for leasing bills during the Progressive period.[21] Any kind of government-run land program, it was argued, was bound to fall into the hands of speculators, not homesteaders. It was a charge made repeatedly against Roosevelt's conservation program, and one that he and Pinchot worked hard, and often unsuccessfully, to debunk. As Samuel Hays has noted, Roosevelt's and Pinchot's support of leasing "identified administration leaders with the large cattle corporations, so far as the West was concerned, and brought down upon their heads the wrath of farming groups and their representatives in Congress." [22] And while leasing bills were routinely drawn up in the years following the commission's report, they never left congressional committees, tainted as they were by the support of politically organized cattlemen in the West.[23]

The relationship between conservation leaders and politically organized ranchers cannot be characterized simply. On the one hand, in 1906, the National Live Stock Association officially split over whether the federal government should manage the range for grazing. It had previously been an association that encompassed both sheep and cattle producers, but the former now returned to the National Wool Growers Association, and the NLSA became predominately a cattlemen's association, but with a longer name: the American National Live Stock Association. For some years thereafter, the wool growers supported Congress's policy of expanded homesteading, suspecting that the Forest Service would privilege the demands of cattle owners over their own. It was not an irrational worry, given the exclusion of sheep grazing from forest reserves in the late 1890s. Conservation opinion was dead set against them: John Muir made his famous statement that he considered sheep "hooved locusts," and the American Forestry Association "vociferously opposed" the presence of sheep on the reserves.[24] Pinchot himself disliked sheep, although he would allow them in the reserves. But his own forestry program also included trying to oust the so-called "tramp herdsman," who roved over the public lands with his sheep, with no stable base of operations.[25]

Still, Pinchot's increasing influence over the forest reserves assuaged some of sheepmen's concerns. He understood that grazing in the reserves was "the bloody angle" and at "the center of the bitterest controversy," and in 1900, he traveled to Arizona to investigate the sheep problem.[26] This trip would prove a watershed event in several ways, orchestrated as it was by two leaders of the Arizona Wool Growers Association, E. S. Gosney and Albert F. Potter. Potter and Gosney led Pinchot and Frederick Coville—a botanist with the Department of Agriculture and one of the first government scientists to study grazing issues—on a strenuous trek through the Arizona backcountry, and Pinchot was convinced that "Potter deliberately set up this test of toughness for us Eastern tenderfeet." [27] Not only did Pinchot survive the test, but the trip also convinced him that grazing—even sheep grazing—should not be excluded from the reserves, only regulated. Pinchot also developed a friendship with Potter and eventually was able to bring him on board at the Division of Forestry as the head of the Branch of Grazing in 1901.[28] This would not be the last time that stockmen joined ranks with the foresters, and it was an important part of the culture of what would become the Forest Service; having former stockmen as officials gave the agency links to the associations, as well as a certain political legitimacy.[29] With Potter as head of grazing, no western stockman could say that the Forest Service was only a band of eastern-bred college men.

Potter's presence helped ease some of the tensions between wool growers and conservation leaders in Washington, and it certainly did not hurt the relationship between the latter and the ANLSA, which consistently supported the Forest Service throughout the Progressive period.[30] To begin with, the ANLSA enthusiastically endorsed transferring administration of the forest reserves to Pinchot's agency, a move that Pinchot had lobbied for since becoming chief forester, but which Congress did not accomplish until 1905. That transfer of the forest reserves to the Department of Agriculture bolstered Pinchot's agency: not only was the USDA a much larger department than Interior, and as Morton Keller has noted, perhaps "the most powerful and effective government department during the Progressive era," but Pinchot's conservation program also required a vast expansion of personnel to manage its timber, mining, and grazing interests.[31] The transfer expanded the powers of Pinchot's agency, and it also gave the livestock industry more secure access to grazing lands in the national forests, compared with Interior Department administration. It was this security—that under Forest Service administration, ranchers who used the national forests could depend on being able to graze their animals there—that the ANLSA sought. At the same time, however, Pinchot had to engage the ranching industry in policy controversies; to institute grazing regulation in the forests, the Forest Service established grazing districts, requiring an enormous range of administrative decisions over who would or would not receive a permit, how many animals they would be allowed to graze, and how long those animals would be allowed to graze that particular allotment. While these decisions involved the Forest Service in a host of local conflicts, the agency also became embroiled in a larger political conflict over grazing fees, which Pinchot decided to institute in 1906. All these conflicts, as we shall see below, would have formative effects on how ranchers and Forest Service officials understood the land that lay at the heart of their political relationship. But suffice it to say that, at this moment in the early 1900s, the ANLSA was committing itself to a future of range management, both within the reserves, and, the association hoped, in the un-reserved public domain, and it was committing itself politically to the Forest Service.

Reasonably enough, that alliance suggested to many westerners that cattlemen and the Forest Service did not support the cause of home-steaders, that they wanted to shut small settlers out of the reserves and keep them off the range. Even at the ANLSA conventions, a number of delegates in the early years of the century stood, at least rhetorically, for the homebuilder, as against the interests of their own association. In what was one of the more common versions of this perspective, one del-egate to the convention in 1900 argued that federal leasing of the range would keep "all public lands from entry. The homesteader will have no place to go and locate and establish a home for himself and for his chil-dren. . . . Great corporations within a few years will own the major part of this grazing land." [32] That these corporations included the ANLSA men, whose hearts might not truly be with the homesteader, was a com-ment often made by members of the association. "[T]here is one class of people that are conspicuous in this meeting for their absence," began one delegate from Arizona, who spoke at the association's conference with members of the Public Land Commission in 1904:

> I refer to the small stockman and farmer, the home seeker, the pioneer of the West, who is, for the most part, to-day following occupations in blissful ig-norance of what is taking place here, which is of more vital importance to that man than to any of us. In many instances it involves his home, the future of his family, and, whatever is done, we must bear in mind that it has been the policy of this country . . . to keep in view the humbler settlers of the coun-try and to preserve the public lands for the home seeker. [33]

He went on to worry that, if the government instituted a leasing law, "we will build up a system of serfdom, of peons, as we have in our sis-ter Republic, Mexico," and that these small settlers would "feel that the Government is against them and that stronger and more powerful people are against them." While large landowners and cattlemen might gain from government control, he argued—and while it might "add to our individual bank account"—such control "strikes at the root of so-ciety, at the foundation of all that is best and most sacred in our Gov-ernment." [34] The very livelihood of the West depended on keeping gov-ernment control out of the public domain. As one delegate from Iowa put it, maintaining the homestead principle "means whether or not the States that are sparsely settled today shall be literally covered over with a hardy race of small farmers and raisers of cattle, shall be covered with school houses, churches and little towns, that shall pay into the treasuries their taxes to help maintain the country . . . or whether it [sic] shall be thinly populated by a few cattlemen, as it has been for the past years." [35]

But several speakers questioned, as Sam Cowan had, such devotion to the cause of homesteaders, given ranchers' traditional antipathy toward them and need to control as much grass as possible. "[T]hough on the face of it the cause of the settlers appeal [sic] to our sentiments and to our sense of justice and right, yet such a view is only a superficial one," noted one member. And a judge from Colorado, reminding his audience that a farm family could not exist on 160 acres in the West, remarked that "there is a great deal of demagoguery in the clamor that has been made here relative to the homesteader. (Applause) Who is the homesteader? Who has been the homesteader in this arid region in the past?" [36] These and other speakers attempted both to unmask the ranchers' rhetoric and to explain the support for homesteaders as a simple case of interference with ranchers' interests. However, they often seemed resigned to what they saw as the settlers' inevitable encroachment. The same Colorado judge who opposed the rhetorical grandstanding about homesteaders also saw social benefits in the homesteading movement: "The cottage upon the plain, the little school house upon the hill, the church steeple at the cross roads, all go to admonish us that the higher plan of civilization has invaded the West, and to convince us that the mother, the baby and the hearthstone are here to stay, and demand of us honest, careful and candid consideration." [37]

The judge's obvious ambivalence (the *invasion* of "civilization") highlights that ranchers' exhortations of homesteaders had a strategic purpose, of course, and did not always express cattlemen's economic interests on the range. Nonetheless, ranchers' appropriation of the homesteader occurred at their own conventions and was not simply a rhetorical device to win favor from politicians or popular support. Rather, these conventions show the organization in an extended discussion over the relationship between the figures of the rancher and the homesteader. One can see from the above statements, for instance, that ranchers saw little relationship between themselves and the "home-seeker." Whether they supported the government's homesteading policy or not, the cattlemen distinguished themselves in their speeches at the early ANLSA conventions by stressing that they were engaged in business, not agriculture, and did not grow crops; that they dealt with the wilder forms of nature;

and, by implication, that ranching was not an occupation that involved their wives and children.[38]

But the way these ranchers conceived of the homesteader was also shifting during this period, particularly around the time of the Kinkaid Act. As Congress turned, in a very limited way, to the "grazing homestead" to solve the crisis of settling the public domain, the definition of who could be a homesteader began to expand. And both in and outside of the ANLSA, the "public domain question" came increasingly to involve how the government could best encourage homebuilding on the range. Some of the attempts to get cattlemen recognized in these terms revolved around the familiar evolutionary argument that the cattle or sheep rancher had helped to settle the West as much as the homesteader had.[39] Occasionally, too, ranchers claimed a rather paternalistic ground about their status as real homebuilders. For instance, at the 1907 Public Land Convention, which showcased western anti-conservation sentiment, the longtime president of the Wyoming Wool Growers Association, J. M. Wilson, grew vexed that only small-time settlers who came out West to take up lands were seen as homebuilders. Noting that he himself was considering settling two hundred families on his "irrigation enterprise," he declared: "When the representatives of the government say that they are trying to hold [the public domain] for the homebuilder, they certainly cannot mean that the people of the West are not the homebuilders, the people who have come here from the beginning and have withstood the privations of frontier life. . . . If they are not the homebuilders I would like to know in the name of Heaven where the homebuilders come from."[40]

Speakers at the ANLSA conventions tried explicitly to include ranchers in the category of homebuilders. At the 1904 ANLSA convention, for example, J. M. Wilson showed the same interest in allowing a small rancher to be a homesteader as he would three years later in allowing a large rancher to be a homebuilder: "I notice most of the men here are sheepmen and cattlemen, and the general idea I got in regard to the homestead was that the homesteader was a farmer, similar to back East, and was to plow his land. . . . Now the homesteader in the arid West is not a farmer. He is the best type of citizenship that there is in the West; he is the small stockman."[41] In a more sentimentalized rendering, a delegate in 1903 maintained that stockmen were like "pilgrim fathers" on the range: "[O]ut of this gigantic range evolution the old dug-out has disappeared before the model American home, with books, music, comforts, luxuries and happiness. All hail the home-builders of the American Union!" [42] But there was evidently a good deal of confusion over ranchers' relationship to the terms "homebuilder" and "homesteader." For instance, at the 1904 Public Land Conference between organized ranchers and the Public Lands Commission, one Colorado delegate explained: "[W]hen I say that homesteaders have taken up homes, I don't mean the man who wants to raise corn, wheat and oats. I don't mean the homesteader that mortgaged his farm and ranch, and went back East with the money. . . . I mean the cattle farmer of to-day; the man with a little herd of 40, 60, 80 or 100 head." [43]

That this delegate spoke of the "cattle farmer" indicates just how much more ranching had to do with agriculture than in the open range days. But most significant here is that in their political discourse, members of the association reconstructed the image of their industry by arguing that ranching, like agricultural homesteading, could build permanent *homes* in the West. Indeed, one of the more prominent opponents of federal range control acknowledged this shift in 1914 when he noted that the Kinkaid Act of 1904 "was an evolution in homestead law, in that it recognized grazing as the basis of the homestead rather than farming." [44]

The small stockman was therefore given room to become a western "homesteader." But another shift in language was also under way, because throughout the Progressive period, leaders of the ANLSA argued that it was not a homesteading policy that would produce homebuilders on the range; it was federal leasing. As Congress considered the terms of what would become the Enlarged Homestead Act, the ANLSA as an organization put its faith behind government range control. Speaking of a congressional proposal to counter an expanded homestead act, the ANLSA's Committee on Resolutions argued that "[a]bove all, from the standpoint of the public good, [government leasing] will encourage the establishment of homes upon the public lands." [45] Or as former senator Joseph Carey of Wyoming argued before the convention in 1908, about the same bill to provide for leasing the public domain, "It is popular to talk about the homesteader and homebuilder. If the bill under consideration should become law, it would give a great impetus to home building, to ranch development and ranch improvements." [46]

To whom were the ANLSA leaders speaking when they supported leasing as the way to make homes on the range? The assumption among historians has been that they used this language to address Congress or some notion of the American public (or easterners) to win them over to their political goals. No doubt this was true. But politically organized livestock owners were generally suspicious of the reception they received outside their community, feeling that the rest of the country was biased against ranchers because of their late nineteenth-century reputation as "cattle kings." In fact, the most important conversation the ANLSA was having was with administrative representatives of the federal government, such as Theodore Roosevelt and officials in the Forest Service. For one of the most striking things about meetings of the ANLSA was the annual presence of foresters—first Pinchot in the early years, and later, grazing experts—who explained the benefits and regulations of public grazing in national forests.[47] What we thus see in the changing language of cattlemen is an emerging discourse that paralleled the highly articulated policies of Roosevelt, Pinchot, and, institutionally, the Department of Agriculture. Between the early 1900s and World War I, both the ANLSA and the Forest Service supported a leasing bill for the public domain, and that support was phrased primarily in the language of homebuilding. This shift worked effectively to change ranchers' positions in visions of the developing West. If ranchers were homebuilders, then they were certainly not just a phase in the social evolution of the West. By publicly voicing its support for the "bona fide settler," the ANLSA remade its own image, giving it a cultural and political currency that it had not hitherto had nationally, and established cattle production as a legitimate form of homebuilding.

This parallelism between the ANLSA and the architects of conservation is evident when comparing statements by Roosevelt and Pinchot with the speeches of leaders at the ANLSA conventions during the middle years of Roosevelt's administration, when Pinchot was a ubiquitous presence in the West. Even before the establishment of the Forest Service in 1905, Pinchot established institutional ties with the ANLSA, and the association's conventions gave him yet another platform from which to explain the administration's emphasis on homebuilding. In 1904, for instance, he noted to the National Live Stock Association that he had "only one speech for this convention, and I have already delivered it once before to the wool growers." That speech, which he maintained Roosevelt had asked him to give to the western livestock owners, was "a sort of text" of the president's policy for the forest reserves, and particularly for grazing therein:

> He was talking about the policy of home-making and he said that it was the primary object of our Government; that everything else is secondary; and that the object of the forest reserves . . . is absolutely the making of homes.

(Applause) . . . The whole effort of the Government in dealing with foresta-
tion must be directed to this end, keeping in view that it was not only necessary to start homes prosperous, but to keep them so. The way to keep a home
prosperous is to keep the forests yielding wood, water and grass, and keep
them at it permanently.[48]

In other words, the relationship between "homes" and the resources
needed to develop them was not simply natural, in the sense of not requiring mediation by public authority. The only way to build stable
homes in the semi-arid and arid West was through governmental management of natural resources.

This single "text" was continually reiterated by federal officials, particularly by Roosevelt and Pinchot and officials in the Department of
Agriculture generally, to the point of becoming an administrative man-
tra. One of the major reasons for this repetition was Congress's passage
of the Forest Homestead Act in 1906, which opened up the forest reserves to homesteading. But this would not be the homesteading of the
past, as the Forest Service was in charge of deeming whether particular
parcels of land had sufficient agricultural value to be open for entry.[49]
Such bureaucratic mediation in the homesteading process sparked understandable fire from many westerners and put Roosevelt and Pinchot
on the defensive about their commitment to "home-building." For instance, in a letter to the 1907 Public Land Convention—which was organized in part to protest the Forest Service's power over homesteading
in the reserves—Roosevelt argued that "[o]ur whole purpose is to protect the public lands for the genuine home-maker. . . . [I]f the administration's policy is upset[,] the one man who would be irreparably injured
would be the settler, the home-maker, the man of small means, who has
taken up a farm which he intends himself to work and on the proceeds
of which he intends to support and bring up his family." [50]

But if the homebuilder here was a farmer, he was beginning to take
on other shapes elsewhere. Roosevelt himself blurred the categories of
rancher and homesteader/farmer when he announced to Congress in
1907 that the government's "prime object" in settling the public domain
was "to secure the rights and guard the interests of the small ranchman,
the man who ploughs and pitches hay for himself." [51] And Gifford Pinchot noted in the 1908 convention of the American National Live Stock
Association that "[t]he men who are employed in caring for the cattle,
as a rule, are owners of the cattle and actual home-makers." [52]

It was not self-evident to many others in the West that ranchers could
be described as homemakers, and certainly large-scale livestock pro-

ducers continued to be unpopular figures. For instance, in the last Progressive-era struggle over the public domain—the hearings that preceded the Stock-Raising Homestead Act of 1916—livestock industry leaders felt themselves very much on the defensive. As the secretary of the National Wool Growers Association, S. W. McClure, argued in hearings before the House Public Lands Committee in 1914, the livestock industry was routinely vilified by advocates of the expanded homestead acts: "It has been my construction, based on what I have heard, that Congress feels that every man who is engaged in any way in the livestock industry of our country is a criminal and that he is of no importance or of no consideration in the West." [53] McClure correctly read the charged atmosphere of the hearings, for he and other stockmen were up against powerful boosters of homesteading. "Iowa is the greatest farming State in the Union, and is second in raising meat, and my State will be settled up like Iowa, except instead of 160 we will have 640 acre farms," argued Congressman Harvey Fergusson of New Mexico, the sponsor of the Stock-Raising Homestead Act, who was perhaps the era's best agrarian spin doctor.[54] (Admittedly, his audience responded to this claim with some astonishment.) Fergusson was not alone in expressing this agrarian vision. Most of the other congressmen on the committee also supported an expanded homesteading act in the West and had no compunction about publicly attacking the sheep and cattle industries and their supporters. McClure's defense of the industry, for instance, went nowhere. At one point making the inestimable mistake of referring to the parts of the public domain as "our range," he was reminded by the committee's chairman, Scott Ferris, that he "ought not to say 'our range,' or impugn the good faith of the homesteader who is seeking a home, because nothing strikes as high a chord as the man who is trying to get a home." [55] Ferris made it clear at another point in the hearings that the western states needed "people, many of them with a few cattle each, not a few people with a large number." [56] Even the ANLSA's president, Dwight Heard, argued that "[t]here is no question in the world but what the agricultural homestead, properly developed, is better than grazing." [57]

Again, such comments should indicate the general level of skepticism, and even hostility, to the idea that ranchers were proper settlers of the western public lands. But there is evidence of some resistance to the terms with which the public domain question was discussed. At the 1915 meeting of the American National Live Stock Association, Congressman William Kent of California, an advocate of leasing, vented his wrath

in describing the hearings that had preceded the Stock-Raising Homestead Act:

> First and foremost, our opponents stuffed some abandoned overalls and
> gunny sacks with straw, and painted across the bosoms of the scarecrows the
> magic word "homesteader."
>   They would have homesteaded the Mojave Desert, all the mountain-tops,
> and the alkali flats with "splendid, sturdy American tillers of the soil. . . ."
>   The discussion brought out the theory that Uncle Sam, in so far as he is a
> landowner, is a most malicious malefactor, and, in so far as he seeks to con-
> trol his property in the public interest, the pillory stocks and whipping-post
> are too good for him.[58]

Especially in a Congress thoroughly under the spell of homesteading,
Kent was one of the very few people to allow such a statement to go
on the public record, although he was simply articulating in an angrier
manner what ranchers had long contended of the homesteading policy:
that the homestead laws were not successfully transferring the public
lands into small homesteaders' hands. His lively reaction is important
because he provided a devastating critique of the discourse that revolved
around the figure of "the homesteader," as opposed to simply criticizing
Congress's actual policymaking. At the same time, however, Kent
was unable to provide or even have access to an alternative discourse
about the public domain; like those who opposed government leasing,
he too had defended his recommendations for federal range control by
arguing that leasing would settle homebuilders more permanently on
public lands. And Kent missed one important fact: by passing the Stock-
Raising Homestead Act, Congress now accepted ranching—albeit on a
small scale—as a legitimate occupation for settlers on the public domain. Although the hearings pitted the proponents of homesteading directly against proponents of leasing, these hearings highlighted just how
close both sides had come in publicly expressing their support for "the
little fellow." The ANLSA had transformed itself from an organization
that exalted its frontier exploits and business acumen into one that consistently supported the presence of both homebuilders and government
administration on the range.

    Although the stockmen appropriated the figure of the homesteader in
support of their interests, this strategy turned out not to be politically
expedient. The ANLSA did not get the leasing bill that it had been seeking since 1900, and had to wait until 1934 to get the Taylor Grazing Act,
by which time the association was quite ambivalent about federal grazing management. The significance of this discourse about the home-

steader therefore lies in its practical political applications. First, it played a role in shaping the organizational identity of politically active ranchers. It reconstituted their own image of the industry, shearing it of its nineteenth-century qualities. No longer was ranching an occupation just for virile, adventurous men; like agriculture, it would settle people and homes permanently on the land. The ANLSA's very different relationship to the federal government than at the turn of the century went hand-in-hand with this changed image. The talk of homebuilding gave the ANLSA and Forest Service and USDA officials a language in common, helping create an alliance between a formerly frontier industry— now turned modern organization—and an active government agency. This alliance was hardly unusual in Progressive-era America, an era of organization in which businesses, manufacturers, farmers, and academics (to name just a few groups) joined together in associations, which then established ties with specific government agencies. In the case of the western cattle industry and the Forest Service, the ties involved an accord that government leasing of the range would best stabilize land use and make possible more permanent settlement.

"Never in the American past had so much been demanded in the name of so many whom so few could locate," Robert Wiebe observes of the Progressive concept of "the people," and much the same might be said of these homebuilders.[59] Indeed, whether the "bona fide settler" existed ceased to be the important point. Rather, he was, for want of a better metaphor, the *frame* that shaped the view of the public lands for all the participants in these political debates. This framing had political, cultural, and legal significance. It helped create a public alliance between the ANLSA and the Forest Service, permitted ranchers to be popularly seen as potentially legitimate settlers in the West, and contributed to the passage of the expanded homestead acts between 1900 and 1916, which conversely also reinforced it.

The public grazing lands—both in the national forests and on the unreserved public domain—made up an enormous amount of property owned by the United States; vast as it was, vast beyond most people's comprehension, it nonetheless was tangible to the people most interested in settling the public land question. It was, to draw on the property theorist Carol Rose's work, property that people *saw,* and through their sight, it was property about which people developed certain stories. Its general aridity, its grasses, its contours—all these things went into how people saw and envisioned the future of those lands. But as Rose also reminds us, "seeing property . . . reflects some of the cultural

limitations on imagination. Different people see the signals of the sur-
roundings through very different imaginative lenses, and they put those
signals together in different property stories."[60] And it is important to
pause here to explore what meaning those different visions, those different stories, had and the foundation they laid for the institutional future of the public grazing lands.[61]

When ranchers, politicians, and bureaucrats looked at the public domain in 1900, what they saw was failure all around: first, a market failure (the land had not been divided into privately owned parcels, and
therefore was not able to circulate and assume value through the market); second, a social failure (there was still no clear sense of whether a
permanent population had been established on those vast lands); and,
finally, a legal failure (these lands existed in a gray area of statutory authority, where the government chose to exercise very little police power,
but technically only allowed grazing by "sufferance.") To these, one
might also have added a *political* failure, as they caused constant political tension with no foreseeable road to resolution. When ranchers, bureaucrats, and legislators tried to envision the future, to envision the resolution of all these failures, they imagined both similar and different
pictures. All three groups imagined that property rights had to be established for that land. When ranchers envisioned their future on the
range, for instance, they imagined a legal structure that would provide
them with secure and exclusive access to particular lands. Whether
they imagined metaphoric or real fences bounding off these rights is unclear, but they saw the public domain as a land divided among individual ranchers who had legally enforceable rights to specific parts of the
range.

But if the three groups shared a general vision of private property
rights ruling the range, one vision alone was politically and culturally
dominant at the turn of the century, and that was of the settler, "who
goes into the wilderness to carve out a habitation and a support for himself and his family." As a group of anti-conservationists wrote in 1907,
on the occasion of holding a convention showcasing their views, "In the
administration of our public laws and in the making of new laws it must
never be forgotten that the bona fide homestead settler is *the central
figure* around which the public land system is and should continue to be
maintained."[62] It was through the homesteader and the homestead that
politicians saw the public domain, and that is just one of several reasons
why the forest withdrawals had produced such a volatile backlash: of
course, timber magnates wanted access to the forests, and of course,

many ranchers wanted continued free use of that land for grazing. But it was not simply the political influence of powerful economic interests that shaped congressional politics. To reserve such areas, to make them unavailable for settlers, also went deeply against what many people—especially many westerners—had imagined that land would look like and be used for.[63]

Given the context of agrarianism in the early twentieth century, as well as the political activity around expanding the homestead act, the range of political discussion about the public domain came down to that one sight—to what had really become a metaphor—the homebuilder attached to a specific piece of land. From our standpoint today, one can imagine other visions, such as of a group of small ranchers successfully cooperating around a commons. But this alternative was simply not available to legislators in the Progressive years. The imperative was to transfer the public domain into small parcels of privately held land. I would argue, however, that that picture of the homebuilder, so absolutely dominant in the public land question, was appropriated to signify something else. That is, ranchers and land managers in Roosevelt's conservation program used the image of the homebuilder to articulate a different institutionalization of property in the West. Compared to the politicians who supported expanded homesteading, these men used "different imaginative lenses" when they looked at the public lands; they kept the ever popular homesteader as "the central figure" of that vision, but instead of attaching him simply to a privately owned parcel of land, they also attached him to leased land, and specifically, to land owned by the United States. In other words, they used the same picture as congressional partisans of homesteading did, but they used it to tell a different story: a story where the government did not go away, as it did in the homesteading tale, or more generally as it did in the classic story of the creation of property rights, but where it stayed to adjudicate and secure the rights of ranchers, large and small.

And that story began to stick. If ranchers and land managers were politically unsuccessful in getting a leasing bill passed, they were eventually successful in changing politicians' "imaginative lenses" for western public land use. What may seem surprising to us, given the degree of public animosity between ranchers and federal land managers today, is that the ANLSA leaders and conservation officials told this story together, for they had become allies in the fight against an expanded homesteading act. But while they agreed on the broad outlines of this "story" of property—that ranchers could be legitimate homebuilders while using government land—there were also disagreements over the specifics in the story that would explode in later years. First, ranchers and Forest Service officials were working out the very structures of their property relations during these years. Although the ANLSA leaders supported leasing the public domain and lobbied to have the Forest Service take it over, what the Forest Service was actually doing in the national forests was developing a *permit system*—a distinction with a great deal of difference. What ranchers had in mind when they imagined leasing was like leasing in the private market: a rancher would pay a given rent for a particular area of land and in exchange would acquire a fair degree of control over how to use that land. The permit system devised by the Forest Service, however, put the agency squarely between ranchers and the land. While it fully accepted and even encouraged grazing in the national forests, it also very quickly established a set of rules for its administration.[64]

For instance, the Forest Service had to decide who would be allowed to graze their animals in the forests, and here, the agency followed principles of occupation and priority rights. It would institute three classes of grazing permits, it stated in its first *Use Book:* Class A permittees would be those ranchers who had "adjacent property" to the reserves; Class B permittees would be those ranchers who owned property, but not adjacent to the forests, and who had used those ranges in the past; and Class C permittees would include those "transient herders" who owned no property at all. Typically in most forests, the demand on the reserves was so great that only Class A and Class B permits were issued. And if this system weeded out the "tramp herdsman," it also institutionalized the notion of "commensurate property," of which we saw an inkling in chapter 1: that is, the Forest Service now stipulated that the greatest priority would be given to those ranchers who owned enough private land to support their animals when they were not on the forest ranges.[65] The rule of "commensurate property" would guide grazing policy for the rest of this century, and we shall therefore examine it in much greater detail in later chapters. It should be noted here, however, that while the leaders of the ANLSA, and, to some degree, of the NWGA, accepted the principle as a basis for management, ranchers would lock horns with grazing administrators over what constituted "commensurability"; and while the principle encouraged livestock owners to take care of their animals, especially in the winter, it also tied ranchers' allotments in the forests to their own property. This connection between ranchers' private and public land had enormous ramifications. First, ranchers conceived of the public land they used as part of their entire operation and increasingly folded the public grazing land into their notions of their private property. Second, from the start the grazing permits had a property value, as the Forest Service allowed them to be transferred from one rancher to another along with the sale of the commensurate property. Often the grazing privilege would increase the value of the base land substantially, and it would not be long before bankers, in issuing loans, privileged those ranchers who had permits to graze their animals in the national forests.[66]

Those ranchers who made it into the forests were happy enough to get permits. But the Forest Service also intended to manage the use of that land. Forest supervisors had the power to determine both how many animals ranchers could graze on their allotments and when those animals should be put on and taken off those ranges. In doing so, the service set both a "protective limit" on the number of animals in the allotment—that is, the minimum necessary for a permittee to stay financially afloat—and a "maximum limit" of animals that any one owner could graze. As the Forest Service's administration got off the ground, many ranchers found their numbers being reduced to their protective limit, especially as the agency made it a policy to allow room for small ranchers on the forests.[67] Other contentious issues remained, as well, such as how long the ranchers could securely hold grazing permits and how much they would pay for that privilege.

From the ANLSA's perspective, the matter of grazing fees was relatively unconflicted in the beginning. Soon after Pinchot decided to institute a fee in 1906, the association passed a resolution approving it.[68] But the association's views did not represent those of all ranchers. Many, in fact, saw the fee as a wedge that would drive small ranchers out of the forests, a prospect that stood in contrast to the Forest Service's stated goals of encouraging the homebuilder. Other westerners thought likewise. The 1907 Public Land Convention, which convened largely anti-conservationist westerners, railed against the fee, seeing it as a tax, as the first link in a chain that would bind ranchers to the federal government as tenants, and as the government's attempt to gain commercial value from the range. That the Forest Service had the authority to implement fees, as well as even to arrest people who violated its regulations, set the stage for a never-ending struggle over what this property meant—what sets of rights it conferred on the ranchers who used it and on the government who administered it.

But what rights did the government have? What was the relationship of the government to that land, now that that the national forests had largely been excluded from settlement? These questions were as troublesome to answer as were those about the rights of ranchers to public grazing in the national forests. Gifford Pinchot, for one, was quite clear about the rights that the government garnered in public land management. Years later in his autobiography, he commented bluntly on what powers were granted to the Forest Service after the transfer of the forests to the Agriculture Department. "Before the transfer," he noted, "we were limited to peaceful penetration. . . . After the transfer the situation was radically changed. While we could still say nothing but 'Please' to private forest owners, on the national Forest Reserves we could say, and we did say, 'Do this,' and 'Don't do that.' We had the power, as we had the duty, to protect the Reserves for the use of the people." [69] Pinchot clearly saw his power as constituting the means for discharging his public duty. But he also articulated, if unwittingly, that the Forest Service now stood in a very different relationship to the property of the United States.

It is important to put this power in perspective, because the federal government was saying "Do this" and "Don't do that" to more people and corporations than ever before, and with greater frequency. Starting with interstate commerce, Washington had by Roosevelt's administration taken on a limited number of regulatory functions over property, as had the states themselves; American government, in other words, was now involved in negotiating the limits of private property. Just as Pinchot had gone to Europe to study forest practices there, young Progressive economists traveled across the Atlantic, and particularly to Germany, to imbibe the ideas of European economic theorists, who sharply criticized America's weak state and laissez-faire policies. Although these men returned, also like Pinchot, hoping to avoid the dominating state presence found in Germany, they were intent on asserting public authority over certain forms of private property. And their ideas did not float in a vacuum on their home shores. Throughout the last decade of the nineteenth century, the most important political questions at both the state and national levels concerned the degree to which government should become involved in the economic and social transformations set in motion by the phenomenal growth of industry. By Roosevelt's administration, federal regulatory power over property was still limited, when compared, for example, with the New Deal, but it was certainly present and certainly a focus of conflict. If such bodies as the Interstate Commerce Commission did not have much bite to them, the

Progressive-era interest in such regulatory bodies in general signaled the prevalent political concern with distinguishing property imbued with public interest from that which was merely private.[70] But for Pinchot, a fundamental claim of private property served as the foundation for the regulatory functions of the Forest Service. That foundation not only protected the public interest, Pinchot realized, but bolstered the government's proprietary interest in the national forests.

How did this transformation happen? The answers lie in both specific legal texts and a more general reading of the political and cultural atmosphere at the time. In the most important Progressive-era case relating to Forest Service grazing land, *Light v. United States* (1911), the court upheld the government's authority to establish rules and regulations for the forest reserves.[71] The case involved a Colorado cattle owner named Fred Light who had turned 500 cattle out to range on the unreserved public domain. The cattle ended up, however, on the nearby Holy Cross Forest Reserve, and the Forest Service charged that, in fact, Light had known full well that they would graze on the reserve and that this constituted trespass on U.S. property, because Light had no permit to graze his cattle there and did not intend to get one. Light's lawyers argued that "[t]he Government holds title to public lands, not as sovereign, but as a proprietor merely," meaning that the United States's use of these lands was subject to the police power of the state of Colorado. Under Colorado's fencing law, which, like other fencing laws in the West, privileged open range grazing, individuals had to fence their property if they wanted to collect damages from stray cattle; and likewise, the lawyers argued, the United States ought to have fenced its reserve if it were to recover damages from Light. The court's decision dismantled this last argument, however, noting that, even if it were incumbent on land owners to put up fencing to keep out stray cattle, this did not mean that the Colorado fencing law authorized intentional trespassing.

But of more interest to our narrative is how the Court answered Light's claim that the United States was "a proprietor merely." Quoting from an earlier case, *Camfield v. United States* (1897), the court agreed with the metaphor of individual proprietorship: "The Government has with respect to its own land the rights of an ordinary proprietor to maintain its possession and prosecute trespassers. It may deal with such lands precisely as an ordinary individual may deal with his farming property."[72] It was a neat analogy, except there were complicated layers to it. First, the United States does not hold an actual title to the land, in the same way that an individual owner of land would gain title to land. The

closest approximation to a title can be found in the treaties that authorized the United States to buy or gain control over the land, as well as the
land cessions by seven of the original thirteen states after the Revolutionary War. More difficult still, however, is that technically the public
lands belong to the United States as a whole. Congress acts loosely as
the trustee for the people in legislating for those lands, and this includes
delegating administrative powers over the public lands to the executive
branch.[73] Indeed, right before the decision in *Light,* the Supreme Court
decided in a case involving California sheep owners that it was constitutional for Congress to delegate power to the Department of Agriculture to set rules for the forest reserves. While acknowledging that it was
"difficult to define the line which separates legislative power to make
laws, from administrative authority to make regulations," Justice Joseph
Lamar argued in *Grimaud v. United States* that the acts that established
the forest reserves achieved the latter.[74] One final problem was that the
reserves also lay in a kind of netherworld of property: they were public
property, but did "public" refer to the rights of all American people or
to the rights of the federal government to manage that property as a
"public trust"?[75] Clearly, in *Light v. United States* the latter interpretation held, as it would fairly consistently in Supreme Court decisions.[76]

The "public" largely meant the government, which was not only
analogous to a private proprietor; it was also, in the court's decision,
simply *sovereign.* Its authority over the forest reserves trumped that of
the state. Yet this begged the question, where did the federal government
get this authority? The Constitution seemed explicit on this issue, because it states that "Congress shall have power to dispose of and make
all needful rules and regulations respecting the territory or the property
belonging to the United States."[77] But two things are evident in *Light v.
United States* that call into question the strength of this claim. First, the
court admitted that "the full scope of this paragraph has never been defi-
nitely settled," although it accepted that this was "a grant of power to
the United States of control over its property."[78] But while this was a
constitutional grant of power, one could also argue that the argument
about sovereignty and the argument, by analogy, about property—that
the United States could administer these lands because it owned them,
like an individual proprietor—collapsed into each other. Proprietorship, which entailed an individual's sovereignty over the land he or she
owned, and sovereignty, which entailed the state's rule over its territory,
looked very much like each other.

This point would not have come as a surprise to Morris Cohen, who wrote a groundbreaking essay in 1927 on "Property and Sovereignty." While property and sovereignty have traditionally been studied as separate categories of law, Cohen notes, the distinction is a false one because property accords to the owner certain degrees of power over other people: a property right "is always against one or more individuals," and ultimately gives the owner of the property "the right to exclude others." That power is inherently a political power, Cohen argues, and therefore justifies the intervention of government to regulate property as it sees fit to maintain the welfare of society. In Cohen's mind, then, property *is* sovereignty.[79] But in the case of the public lands, was sovereignty property? Did the sovereignty of the government over these lands rest on its ownership of them?

On the one hand, this proposition seems, on the surface, patently wrong. The sovereignty of the United States government lies in the consent of the people, not in its owning property. And in writing the *Light v. United States* decision for the court, Justice Lamar was careful to note that the United States could not "hold property as a monarch may for private or personal purposes." [80] On the other hand, the issue of the national forests dramatically called into question the classic liberal view, stemming back to Locke, that the role of the government is largely to protect private property and not to encroach upon property rights. Even if this is not wholly accurate, given that the rights of property ownership have been restricted in all sorts of ways by the U.S. government, the starting point of this argument envisions the government as divesting itself of property. And to say that the government's sovereignty over the public lands derives fundamentally from its owning them is merely to underscore what a number of property theorists, Cohen included, have argued—that owning property confers upon the owner a political sovereignty over that property; that property is itself a political relationship between the owner and other people. Again, this is not to say that all private property confers unlimited rights on the owner to use that property however he or she wishes, because government has always imposed certain limits on property use. But what is so striking about the case of the Forest Service is that the government had the power to make regulations and establish limits over its own property rights. And with that power came a narrowing notion of property ownership in the public lands. *Light v. United States* gave the Forest Service a wide range of powers to make regulations for its lands, and it would also provide the opening for the government to see itself increasingly as the proprietor of the national forests, to make claims on the public lands as an owner of private land would.

This shift would become more important to the public land debates after World War I, but it is important here for this reason: just when the government came to see itself as analogous to a private property owner, ranchers and bureaucrats were also reenvisioning the property relations of the range. Although expanded homesteading continued to be the popular political answer to the problem of disposing of public domain land, proponents of leasing had used the "homebuilder" construct to reimagine the range as a place where ranchers would stake out their private claims to land, claims that depended on grazing animals on the public range. The Forest Service was the first experiment to adjudicate and negotiate the competing claims of ranchers to public lands, and this experiment involved ranchers and federal bureaucrats in creating a new institution for property rights in the West. It was, of course, not *outside* the institutions of private property in the United States, but fully enclosed within them, for the terms of private property ownership informed all sides of the public land question, and therein lay the problem: at every level, the expansion of federal authority over the public lands was structured and given meaning by property ownership. By World War I, ranchers saw their use of those lands through their private real estate; that private real estate, in turn, served as the institutional foundation for their access to public lands; those public lands were owned by a government, whose ownership was understood to be like that of an individual. After the war, these competing private claims on the public lands would come into explosive conflict and once again change the politics of the western range.

CHAPTER 3

The Lessons of the Market

The World War from which we have just emerged has
brought about, and is bringing about, a readjustment of our
entire economic life. Never before were we as a nation so disposed to base our actions and conclusions on a cold-blooded
examination of facts and figures, rather than on precedent
and tradition. So, with this old recurring problem of the public domain and stock industry, what we have done in the past
is in no way controlling as to what we should do in the future, except as we may profit from the experience of the past.
—Clay Tallman, commissioner, General Land Office

The most striking thing about the public land debates of the early 1920s
is the absence of the homebuilder, and the obvious reason for this shift
was the war. Coming on the heels of the last major homesteading act in
America, World War I fundamentally altered the terms of the struggle
over the public domain by mobilizing government agencies, businesses,
and industries on an enormous scale. After the war, in the homesteader's
wake, western cattle and sheep owners achieved a new legitimacy, which
was largely founded upon their relationship to the government in the
form of the Forest Service and the Department of Agriculture. As we
have seen, the Forest Service had recommended grazing control over the
public domain for years, arguing that since it ran a grazing system in the
national forests, it should do so on the western range too. In contrast,
the General Land Office in the Interior Department had successfully argued that inasmuch as homesteading remained a viable policy, the public domain lands should remain under its jurisdiction.

However, the war changed the relationships between range users and public land agencies, because beef production became a top priority. Under the leadership of Herbert Hoover and a vastly mobilized USDA, food production and administration became, next to armament production, the area in which the government was most involved.[1] This was certainly an economic boon for ranchers and raised their expectations of federal economic encouragement in the future. But by centralizing governmental activity, the war also opened the door for increased regulation, and ranchers' expectations of government encouragement then clashed explosively with the expanded role of federal authority over grazing lands in the national forests. It was a clash that could not have been anticipated on the eve of the war, when the ANLSA held the Forest Service in rather high regard—with some complaints, of course— and the woolgrowers had finally come around reluctantly to the idea of a federally administered range, having grown dismayed at the effects of enlarged homesteading on their ranges. Livestock owners generally expressed the opinion that the Forest Service had been fair in its development of a grazing system in the national forests, and that this would also be the case if the public domain were handed over to it. By the Hoover presidency, however, livestock owners were beginning to embrace a states-rights' position—advocating that the federal government give public domain lands to the states—and did not recommend that the Forest Service take on the public domain.

The foundation for this reversal was laid in the early to mid 1920s, a period that can be said to have inaugurated the pattern of political conflict that is familiar to us today. Until the war, the policy debate over the public domain was polarized between enlarged homesteading and federal control of the range. But after the war, when homesteading was no longer a popular policy option, the alliance between organized ranchers and the Forest Service no longer revolved around a shared political opposition to congressional policy and a shared vision of a new property regime in the West. What was left was simply the relationship itself, a relationship structured around the public property of the national forests. Because ranchers and land managers had to negotiate that relationship of property through politics, and not primarily through the courts, a political struggle quickly developed between the two groups both over how to interpret the property relations of the range and over how to draw the lines of federal authority over range use.[2] That they emerged on different sides of these questions may not seem surprising to us today, but it was not a foregone conclusion, especially when viewed from the starting point of World War I.

Without a doubt, the most important material effect of the war on ranchers was that the Department of Agriculture encouraged them to step up beef production, which meant that the Forest Service allowed a 10 percent increase in the number of cattle and sheep in the national forests.[3] It stocked the ranges to the limit, hoping, in Will Barnes's words, "to secure the fullest possible utilization of every nook and cranny of the forests."[4] These were flush times for ranchers, and although the end of the war found forest supervisors trying to reduce the swelled ranks of livestock, they continued to emphasize the importance of encouraging the livestock industry's *productivity* and *utilization*. Indeed, these would be the watchwords of the 1920s.

But the war was also important for bringing together government officials and business leaders throughout the United States to mobilize the country's resources. This "war corporatism," as Ellis Hawley calls it, revolved around quasi-public agencies, staffed by both private and public leaders, whose administration was intended to bring about an orderly system of providing food and matériel to American and foreign troops, to overseas markets, and to consumers at home. Hawley's characterization fits the experience of organized livestock producers during the war well, as American National Live Stock Association and National Wool Growers leaders were actively involved in questions of food administration. For instance, in the midst of the war, during the ANLSA's twenty-first convention, Frank Hagenbarth noted that leaders of the livestock industry had been in a number of conferences with the secretary of agriculture and the Food Administration to discuss how best to supply meat for the war effort. Out of these conferences was formed the United States Live Stock Committee, made up of representative producers and feeders, whose job it was to meet with government officials and "pass on matters pertaining to live stock." And this was no small job, because among other things, the committee "directly" influenced the government's decision to supervise large packing plants and to set prices on hogs.[5] Others also spoke on Washington's livestock policy and urged even greater cooperation between the West's producers and the Food Administration.[6] And, in an unusual move, the convention proceedings for 1918 featured a photograph of the country's food administrator, Herbert Hoover, although he did not attend the convention.

The nature of associational activity changed, in other words, during the war, as business and government combined to serve the goals of winning the war. But leaders in the western livestock industry were also very concerned, in Frank Hagenbarth's words, about how to "preserve" their industry, given that the war was creating a tremendous amount of market fluctuation for all agricultural products.[7] Their concerns about what would happen to their markets after the war were not ill-founded, of course, as ranchers and farmers were confronted by a postwar depression that lifted only slightly before the Crash. This depression coincided with problems in administering the Stock-Raising Homestead Act. As part of the act's stipulations, the GLO had to classify the remaining public domain according to whether different tracts were suitable for grazing or for dry or irrigated farming, and this process initially tied up the land. Although settlers filed claims on over 105,000,000 acres by 1921, the results were gloomy, particularly because of the economic fallout in agriculture. By 1923, Will Barnes of the Forest Service argued that the Stock-Raising Homestead Act had produced mostly suffering and overgrazing, and chastised the government for deluding potential homesteaders about the character of the land. By the early 1920s, the USDA also publicly stated that the act lured people into an "extremely hazardous" endeavor.[8]

Some observers at the time might have argued that being engaged in livestock producing was itself a hazardous endeavor, and a sense of crisis filled the pages of the livestock industry's trade journals. Beef prices, for instance, had peaked during the summer of 1919, reaching $16.45 per hundred pounds, but by the summer of 1921, they had fallen to $8.50, and they bottomed out by the end of the year at $7.00.[9] Getting the industry back on its feet was a clear priority for both organized ranchers and federal land managers, and this shared interest gave them a common language, as it had done during the Progressive period. However, instead of emphasizing their support for the homebuilder, the ANLSA and NWGA leaders and Forest Service officials spoke about the need to "stabilize" the range livestock industry, to put the industry on a "business basis." We can hear this shift from the homebuilding discourse of the teens to the vocabulary of business in the speeches that Forest Service officials made before the American National Live Stock Association. On the eve of his resignation in 1920, for instance, Associate Forester A. F. Potter still spoke of the need to reduce the number of animals grazed by large permittees in favor of smaller landowners. The reductions were required "to make room for the little homesteaders, the fellows who are trying to raise a family, improve their homesteads, and become an asset to the community. For such a policy I have no apology to make." [10] A year later, Will Barnes spoke on the same subject to the National Wool Growers Association, but with a somewhat different and telling angle:

> Primarily, of course, the struggling settler should be given every opportunity to build himself up in livestock as an additional source of income to his little farm. I am sure we would be going against the general public sentiment in this matter if we refused to recognize the claims of these men up to a certain limit. . . .
>
> It goes without saying that the large owners are more interested in their stock and the use of the range, give their stock far closer supervision than do the little men, obey our regulations much more willingly, and in every way make what may be considered ideal users of National Forest range. [11]

Barnes here acknowledged that "public sentiment" was partially responsible for the Forest Service's preference for small ranchers and argued that larger landowners helped it run more efficiently. This striking new public claim about the value of big ranchers would have been politically suicidal for land managers before the war, when bigness was synonymous with monopoly. Unlike many of his cohorts, Barnes also publicly questioned the very category of the "small man": "What rule or measurement will we apply so as to determine the exact point above which all men are sheep barons and below which they are poor settlers struggling to make an existence?" he asked. [12] By 1923, Chief Forester William Greeley would state rather baldly that it was the Forest Service's duty to encourage the most efficient and productive ranches. [13] While the homesteader would reemerge in the early 1930s as a figure in the dialogue about the public domain, the ideals of business now overwhelmed the agrarianism of the teens.

This shift away from agrarianism was significant because, as we shall see in more detail below, it marked a changed conception of what goals were involved in Forest Service policies. Throughout the Progressive-era debates about public grazing, the homebuilder had stood in for the public interest in the public lands. That is, by instituting a permit system for grazing in the national forests, the service had argued that it was protecting the public interest in those lands by making it available for settlers, by assuring that the permit system was open to newcomers. Although Forest Service officials also argued that conserving the rangelands was in the public's interest, it was the agency's emphasis on homebuilding that signaled that it had not been created simply to serve big ranchers' needs. The Forest Service's embrace of the homebuilder also provided a powerful, moral justification for the structure of property relations it was building on the range, conveying the message that its policies would carry on America's long tradition of settling "empty" areas with small and productive landowners—only, this time, those owners would be supported by their use of federal land.

The federal government's turn away from the homebuilder thus closed the book on nineteenth-century settlement policies. Even Agriculture Secretary Henry C. Wallace argued that the era of agricultural settlement had passed.[14] Although Western historians have tended to identify that passing with the Taylor Grazing Act of 1934, it is clear that by the early 1920s, neither Congress nor the executive branch remained committed to creating policies for the small settler and both were trying out other arguments to frame their goal of protecting the public interest in the western range. Nothing signaled this as clearly as the shift in the Department of the Interior's position on public domain policy. This switch changed the terms of the already sizable jurisdictional feud between the departments of Agriculture and the Interior, which before World War I had revolved around whether the government should continue its homesteading policy and also around administrative rivalries over such bureaus as the National Park Service and the Forest Service.[15] Moreover, it highlighted the most significant categories that the two departments used to differentiate themselves.[16] In an address to the ANLSA in 1919, for instance, Secretary of Agriculture David F. Houston noted that he was pleased that the Interior Department, "at this late day," finally supported the regulation of the public domain. But Houston strongly opposed the interior secretary's suggestion that the regulation be given to the Interior Department on the grounds that it held title to that land. The Forest Service regulated the grazing of the national forests, he argued, although the title to the forests remained with the Interior Department. What was in fact more important was handing over regulatory authority to the agency with the most expertise: *The control of grazing should not follow the location of land title. It should follow the location of expert agricultural and successful experience. Grazing is an agricultural problem, and should be handled by agricultural experts.*[17]

This is a curious argument, because as we saw in chapter 2, there was no actual title to the land in the public domain; that the Interior Department's claim to that land was metaphorized as such suggests how deeply land managers saw the public lands as property of the federal government—and more specifically, that they connected an agency's regulatory authority with "owning" particular lands. But Houston's statement also unveils his understanding of his department as a modern bureaucracy: clearly, for Houston, everything about the western live-stock industry fell into the category of "agriculture," from the control of predatory animals to reforestation and marketing, "and the Depart-ment of the Interior could not properly deal with [these agricultural problems], unless it took over the Department of Agriculture or built up a duplicate of it." [18] To Houston's mind, the latter two proposals were not viable, because to run an efficient and modern federal government required specializing and differentiating tasks so that there would be no overlap. Finally, however, Houston's articulation of the jurisdictional struggle over administering the public domain involved a much more complicated process than simply "modernizing" the state. The struggle to *categorize* the problem was paramount, and how the government defined that problem would determine the agency to handle it.

Of course, officials in the Department of the Interior saw things much differently than did those in the Agriculture Department. They argued that their department had been in charge of homesteading the public do-main since 1862, and that its extensive network of land agents and its scientific wing—especially the Geological Survey—were fully qualified to administer grazing regulation on the public domain. The first assis-tant secretary of the interior noted in a government hearing in 1925, for instance, "We are closely in touch with the western people through ad-ministering [the public land laws] as well as the reclamation act. We have, as you know, local land offices, we have field division offices, agents of various kinds, and geological survey officers throughout the West." [19] The Department of the Interior had perhaps the most localized bureaucracy in the West, given the historic presence of land offices, and its officials emphasized that grazing control on the public domain would be more a matter of land administration than agricultural production. This categorical dilemma perfectly captured a long-standing quandary over what grazing lands were, and the Interior Department represented a widespread view that grazing was not agriculture, as it did not require cultivation. Because the department was not involved in agricultural re-search and was not at this time proposing to do so, it also offered to administer grazing control on the public domain "without any appre-ciable expense in the way of increased force," using its "existing facili-ties." [20] This argument would be used again by Harold Ickes in 1934 in the drafting of the Taylor Grazing Act in 1934, although it was a goal that the department ultimately could not meet.

But officials at the Department of the Interior had had relatively little to do with the two national associations of western range users, the American National Live Stock Association and the National Wool Growers Association. In contrast, following the transfer of the Forest Service to the USDA in 1905, Forest Service officials regularly spoke at livestock association conventions and wrote pieces for western livestock journals.[21] Their familiarity with the associations and their leaders emerged repeatedly in their speeches, particularly in the case of Will C. Barnes, who had left the ranching business when the Forest Service began taking up grazing issues in the early 1900s. During his long career as head of the Grazing Branch, Barnes was remarkably successful in remaining loyal both to his department and to western livestock owners; ever faithful to the goals of the Forest Service, he also represented the humane face of the agency, consistently avoiding the bureaucratese of his fellow officials. As we saw in chapter 2, Associate Forester A. F. Potter, who was in charge of grazing policy between 1910 and 1920, was also a former rancher. Although he did not always pursue the course advocated by the livestock associations, he was well regarded as an administrator. The interaction between Forest Service officials and livestock industry spokesmen was thought notable even by the participants themselves. "I believe you will agree with me that of all the different interests, public or private, concerned with the handling of the National Forests, the livestock interests of the West have been the outstanding ones in their friendship and support of the Forest Service," Barnes remarked to the Forest Service's chief, William Greeley, in 1925. "I know of no other interests that have ever come to Washington in numbers to appear before Congressional committees in our behalf or to endorse plans which we were advocating."[22]

Barnes's easy way with the livestock associations, particularly the ANLSA, emerged in all his speeches. "Coming to these live stock meetings gets to be something of a habit," he said in 1921. "[I]t is a very pleasant thing to come here to these conventions and meet the old-timers. Even if they don't attend all the sessions, you meet them at the hotel, and rub noses with them, and make plans for the future."[23] This informal interaction simply was not the case before the 1920s with the Interior Department. For one thing, it held steadfastly to a homesteading policy until 1920, and as late as 1918, Secretary of the Interior Franklin Lane commented that federal grazing control was "a revolutionary policy." [24] The Interior Department was therefore in conflict with the stated ANSLA position. And although their interaction was more contentious, the NWGA and the Forest Service still had to engage each other. Although the NWGA officially favored homesteading until 1916, and opposed many Forest Service policies, sheep owners could not avoid dealing publicly with the Forest Service, because it regulated sheep grazing in the national forests.

Officials from the Interior Department did not regularly attend ranchers' meetings until after World War I, and when they did so, they had none of the rapport we see between Forest Service spokesmen and the livestock industry. For instance, the commissioner of the General Land Office, Clay Tallman, began his speech to the cattlemen in 1919 by admitting that he had at first thought that the organization was composed of both cattle and sheep owners, although the cattle interests had united in the ANLSA many years before, in 1906.[25] While Tallman smoothed over this admitted misperception, the fact that he noted it at all indicates a general lack of familiarity with western livestock interests. Only when Farrington Carpenter, a western rancher, became head of the Grazing Service after the Taylor Grazing Act did Interior Department officials evidence a familiar relationship with the ANLSA.

The Interior Department's switch to supporting federal grazing administration has been only fitfully interpreted by scholars, and the standard works of public land history offer little explanation. While devoting a fair amount of attention to the prewar jurisdictional disputes between the Interior and Agriculture Departments, E. Louise Peffer merely notes that the change of presidential administration in 1921 produced the Interior Department's new policy position. Paul Gates, too, leaves this shift little understood. Both imply simply that the Interior Department wised up to the failures of the Stock-Raising Homestead Act, saw the reason behind grazing control, and began drafting bills that naturally gave it control of grazing administration.[26] A much more forceful account is given by the political economist Gary D. Libecap, who argues that the Interior Department's shift, while in reaction to fewer homesteading claims, also occurred because "after 1920 the secretary [of the Interior Department] and the commissioner [of the General Land Office] viewed central management of federal land as providing a greater source of advancement and growth." [27] Federal bureaucracies do not simply react passively to Congress and voters, Libecap argues. Rather, bureaucrats seek "to expand the administrative role, budget, and staffing of their agencies. A growing agency provides an environment for advance-

ment to positions of greater authority and higher salaries."[28] Within a
few years of the Forest Service's transfer to the USDA, Libecap notes, it
was receiving much larger appropriations than the General Land Office,
which was in charge of administering the homestead acts. By 1920, for
instance, it was appropriated $6 million as compared to the GLO's
$3 million. Although the Interior Department profited from home-
steading up to 1920, it switched to a policy of federal grazing management in order to win funding and increased administrative girth like that
put on by the Agriculture Department via the Forest Service.[29]

Few would disagree that officials in both Interior and Agriculture were deeply interested in regulating the remaining public domain
as a way to bolster their administrative positions, and indeed the long-
standing rivalry between the two departments exacerbated bureaucratic
tendencies toward proprietariness over public lands, as officials in neither of them ever concealed their desire to have the lands under their
control. But while individual bureaucrats may have had self-interested
motives, the vying for administrative control also involved other
changes that are more important, I would argue, than whether federal
agencies were attempting to garner higher appropriations. One indica-
tor is that the Interior Department's shift to supporting range control
did *not* happen before the end of the war, even though the Forest Service had been receiving more appropriations than the General Land
Office since Theodore Roosevelt's second administration. Before 1920,
in other words, appropriations and potential advancement were not
enough to force a shift in the Interior Department's position vis-à-vis the
public domain. Rather, the Interior Department's shift signaled that the
public domain was no longer seen as a staging ground for individual settlers, but rather as rangeland for well-established ranchers. This transformation included a change not only in how the land was to be used,
but also in how the public property would be understood by the government and ranchers alike. And while the Interior Department would
sit on the sidelines of the major debates about public grazing during the
1920s, those debates would shape the department's political relationship with ranchers within the next decade. For at the heart of the conflicts were questions about what constituted appropriate administrative
control of public property, as the Forest Service asserted itself publicly
in more powerful ways than it had before. And it was Chief Forester
William Greeley who stood behind this new public face, who neither
shied away from controversy nor was able to deflect the heavy criticism
lobbed at him by western livestock producers.

   William Greeley (or Colonel Greeley, as he was also called, because of his participation in the war effort) was an earnest bureaucrat, and he worked hard to earn the approval of politically organized ranchers. In the contemporary ANLSA convention *Proceedings,* his youthful face and prominent, owlish glasses contrast starkly with the photographs of cowmen. It was an image he sometimes played with, joking at his own expense and making fun of his role as a government official. He began his 1923 speech before the convention, for instance, by saying, "It always does me good to get away from Washington and up against the real men of the West—the men with whom we are working so closely in the administration of our national forests. I very often get reactions—comebacks—from the straight-speaking men of the West that are good for my immortal soul." [30] Simultaneously reifying the distance between himself and the national forest users and attempting to break it down, Greeley positioned himself as a Washington bureaucrat (what we might now call a "policy wonk") as opposed to the "real" practitioners of range use. But while he superficially made fun of himself, the distinction between wonks and real men also signaled the political relations of the range, for while the ANLSA and the NWGA could and did exert their powers over the Forest Service, Greeley continued in this speech to explain how the government aimed to control the national forest rangelands more authoritatively. It is a speech well worth pausing over for a moment.

   Greeley often noted, as he did here, that "the open range live-stock industry of the West has got to be re-built." [31] This rebuilding, directed by the Forest Service, was to take place in several different areas. First, Greeley argued, the government should work more extensively on scientific studies of range management. This concern was part of a widespread move within the Department of Agriculture in the 1920s to discover the most efficient means of running farms as businesses, particularly in terms of marketing and distribution.[32] The activist stance the department was taking in expanding its research into agricultural questions was spelled out in a wartime statement by Agriculture Secretary David F. Houston to the ANLSA. "[I]t is essential," Houston noted, "that the government have power to secure all pertinent facts. Then we must have a careful analysis of them, an impartial and intelligent interpretation, well-founded conclusions, and the courage and determination to apply the conclusions, no matter where they hit or what prejudice they run counter to." [33] A similar desire to know more facts about public land ranching produced a number of rangeland studies in the

1920s.[34] But range management differed from purely agricultural research in that the Forest Service also had the power to enforce some of these new ideas. Not only was it shifting the onus of research into land use from the individual to the federal government, as was evident throughout agriculture during this period, but it had the means to control actual practices.

Politically organized ranchers agreed that the government should fund more studies of livestock raising. Although they scoffed at "eastern college men," ranchers had few qualms during this period about the Agriculture Department spending money on and training people in range science and management; if anything, they believed their industry was underfunded. They argued, for instance, that they could use more information about improving the breeds of their range cattle, in preventing animal diseases and eradicating poisonous plants, and also in management techniques. At this point, however, ranchers did not explicitly link the investigative wing of federal involvement with the imposition of regulations they clearly did not like, as they would in a decade or two. They thus retained a certain faith in the Department of Agriculture as a disinterested—and certainly well funded—institution of experts. That there was no other source of scientific knowledge about the range left ranchers with little choice. However, when range experts tried to mandate how many animals a given allotment could hold without danger of overgrazing, the resulting regulations were often unpopular.

Such regulations, which involved the Forest Service directly in ranchers' business decisions, represented a second area in which the agency asserted its authority in rebuilding the range and which often implicated the property relations between the two sides. The most prominent example of this connection was Greeley's argument that the Forest Service should take over the construction of range improvements such as "division fences," which helped keep cattle and sheep from drifting. Greeley noted that private users had built these improvements in the past and acknowledged that this had "been a desirable thing. But I believe the government should take the obligation to itself of installing the more expensive and permanent range improvements. It can thereby, at one throw, increase the value of its own property and contribute materially to the well-being of the live-stock industry."[35]

Greeley understood many livestock owners' point of view—that the improvements they made gave them a greater sense of security and permanency on their range allotments. "I believe thoroughly in stability of tenure on national-forest range allotments," he argued, "but that ought to rest upon the general grazing policy, rather than the precarious foothold of privately owned improvements on government land." [36] In other words, allowing privately constructed improvements on the range opened up a space for private control, which threatened the nominally public nature of the national forest grazing lands. Moreover, Greeley wanted the Forest Service to have the authority to decide the terms of ranchers' stability on these lands, and he understood that when ranchers constructed improvements, which are the very things that indicate a property is *owned*, these structures increased ranchers' sense of having a property right in their allotments. But if Greeley was intent on keeping ranchers from believing they were the proprietors of their allotments, his language indicated a similar slippage to that in the Supreme Court decisions of the teens, where the public ownership of the national forests became lost in the articulation of the government's authority over those lands. In this case, Greeley implicitly identified the government's position as being like that of a property owner, arguing that the government should invest in improvements in order "to increase the value of its property." He never explained, however, why the government would want to increase that value, since presumably those lands would never be sold on the market.[37]

But how the Forest Service should regulate such infrastructure in the national forests was a relatively tame dilemma compared to two other issues: herd size and priority use. Both problems had continually hounded Forest Service officials and forest users since the early 1900s. As for herd size, organized ranchers and land managers fought briefly during this period over how the Forest Service should charge for its grazing lands, and in particular, whether it should move from charging on a "per capita," or "per head" basis, to a "per area" basis: the former would entail a fee for each head of cattle (or, in the standard formulation, for five sheep), while the latter would require a fee for a certain amount of allotted land. Ranchers largely supported the latter, as it would mean that they would pay for the use of the particular land and be able to determine themselves how many livestock they could run, giving them much more control over their business. Not surprisingly, for reasons similar to Greeley's in opposing privately constructed improvements in the forests, agency officials argued that a "per area" charge would quickly increase a rancher's sense of proprietorship over a given piece of land, making it harder for the government to assert its administrative authority over that land.

The second issue, whether present users would have "priority" or "preference" over newcomers, was, next to grazing fees, the most steadily and eventually successfully fought battle for ranchers. This battle brought together, like no other one, the conflict between the government's former commitment to homesteading and its current commitment to ranching's "stability." It was leavened by ranchers' increasing sense of their rights to certain public lands and land managers' countervailing sense of their own right to administrative authority over the government's land. While this concern with newcomers would continue past the Taylor Grazing Act, the "preference" given to established ranchers was erasing the notion that the public land should be saved for future settlers. Greeley articulated this clearly in his 1923 speech to the ANSLA, arguing that the "efficient live-stock unit—as a business enterprise—should, I believe, become more and more the key-point in the grazing management of the national forests, including the ranch property and equipment needed to supplement public range allotments. The government should encourage such well-established and well-equipped live-stock enterprises." [38]

At this point, Greeley advocated a five-year permit, but by the following year, under pressure from livestock producers, he advocated a ten-year permit, which was then put into place. This long-term permit was the closest thing a rancher had to a legal right to grazing lands in the national forests: it provided for secure tenure on the allotment, albeit with some insecurity about how many animals the rancher would be allowed to put on the land. In legal terms, its closest analogue was a license, meaning that the permit could be revoked and did not create a property interest for the rancher. But while the ten-year permit did not give away any of the government's rights to the public property, it produced a thorny problem for the Forest Service, because it took the government one step away from the view that the public lands were "open" to settlers. Since that "openness" had served as one of the major ways that the Forest Service understood the "public interest" in the forests during the Progressive years, the agency's distancing of itself from such a justification left a hole in defining what the public's interest would be in the lands. And whereas the agrarianism of the prewar era privileged settlers, the emphasis on "the efficient live-stock unit—as a business enterprise" made the more stable large ranches the exemplary livestock operations, even if the Forest Service claimed it was encouraging smaller permittees.

Yet even the conflicts over Forest Service rules paled in comparison to those that erupted in the third arena in which Greeley sought to "rebuild" the range—conflicts that brought the greatest storm of protest of the decade and that would change the politics of public grazing thereafter. This was the matter of grazing fees.

"I hardly know whether I am standing before you for the purpose of making a speech or of receiving a sentence." [39] So began William Greeley in 1924, who had the unenviable task of explaining to members of the American National Live Stock Association why the Forest Service sought to increase their grazing fees up to 100 percent in some forests. This proposal spawned the bitterest fight between range users and Forest Service officials during this period and ultimately meant that the service would not gain control of the unappropriated public domain: the actions of the Forest Service, in other words, served as a kind of bureaucratic touchstone against which ranchers evaluated the drafting of public domain policies, and it is telling that the movement to give the rangelands to individual states came hard on the heels of the grazing fee controversy. That William Greeley became the primary victim of the fight indicated both the ANLSA's growing political influence and its powerful opposition to the very terms the Forest Service used to describe their political relationship and the property entwined within it.

Although most of the leaders in the western livestock industry would soon forget, Congress was as much to blame as the Forest Service for the drive to raise fees. After the war, the House Agriculture Committee, which was dominated by midwestern representatives, sought to raise grazing fees on national forests up to 300 percent,[40] arguing that by charging only nominal fees, the Forest Service was subsidizing the western livestock industry at the expense of livestock producers in other regions of the country.[41] The Forest Service at the time argued *against* the increase: having just approved giving livestock owners five-year (as opposed to annual) permits on the forests, it was reluctant to institute higher fees for that length of time. As a compromise measure, it arranged to do a lengthy evaluation of grazing fees in the national forests and to devise a fair system of bringing these fees closer to the "true value" of the forage. Assistant Forester Christopher E. Rachford was put in charge of the study, which took nearly four years to complete.[42]

Western livestock associations greeted the prospect of the study with guarded optimism and argued that such a survey was long overdue. Moreover, the Forest Service appeared to be reaching out to the users of the rangelands, as its officials held over 400 meetings with livestock owners across the West.[43] But as news of the report began to filter out near the end of 1923, the wrath of these ranchers—and especially of the livestock associations—quickly rained down upon the Forest Service.[44] By the time it was actually issued in November, 1924, the report manifested the bitterness of the struggle as much as it described the new fee policies of the Forest Service.

Although receipts for grazing fees amounted to three times the administrative costs of grazing management in the Forest Service, Rachford's appraisal argued that those fees should be set higher, at a "fair and reasonable rate" and based on the leasing fees charged for private land. This was a position the Forest Service could justifiably take, he wrote, not only because it was fair, but also because the policy reflected the original intentions of the Department of Agriculture when it took on the national forests in 1905. At that time, Secretary of Agriculture James Wilson noted that, although the fee would initially be kept very low, it would "be gradually advanced when the market conditions, transportation facilities, and demand for reserve range warrant it, but the grazing fee will in all cases be reasonable and in accordance with the advantages of the locality."[45] The history of the policy was also buttressed by the Forest Service's newly articulated conviction that "[n]ational forest range is a commodity the same as any other forage sold or traded in by livestock operators." This had a kind of corollary; that is, Rachford noted, the "question has been repeatedly raised as to whether the Government should follow the practices of an ordinary business concern and secure a fair compensation for the commodity." The answer, with some restrictions, was "yes."[46] The problem, however, was to establish a "method of equalizing fees," because the Forest Service was currently using a flat rate for range allotments of widely varied character.[47] The method chosen—to compare representative tracts of private leased land with national forest grazing land—meant comparing not only rates but also such qualities as availability of water, carrying capacity, topography, and accessibility to market. In addition, it meant trying to understand how much Forest Service restrictions (on such things as herd size and when ranchers could put their animals on the range and take them off it) brought down the value of national forest range. By evaluating the character of both public and private lands, Forest Service officers then calculated the ratio of the fee to the quality of private lands to arrive at the new fees for forest lands. For Rachford and other Forest Service leaders, this method of structuring fees was the closest thing yet to discovering the "true" value of range forage on the national forests.

If these points made up the basic argument of Rachford's appraisal, in no way do they accurately describe the tenor of the document. Rachford's report was primarily a defense against the already mobilized western livestock industry, and the latter third of the piece takes on the arguments of ranchers directly—setting down the fifteen different "claims" that ranchers made against the appraisal and providing rebuttals. These claims, along with the arguments presented in the *Producer* and the *National Wool Grower,* covered a large territory, but can be roughly categorized.

The first criticism that the livestock industry made was simply that it was the wrong time to institute fee increases. As a frequent contributor to the *Producer* would write in 1925, bemoaning the Forest Service's relationship to livestock owners: "There is, of course, a real economic conflict in the matter of fees. Personally, I feel that if the Forest Service had requested a reasonable increase in fees at a time when stockmen were prosperous, it would have but little opposition. . . . Looking at the matter solely from the standpoint of the Forest Service, I can imagine nothing more stupid than the attempt to raise fees in the face of the present financial condition." He went on to note that the controversy was particularly damaging because the Forest Service, "by long years of hard and conscientious effort, [had] finally won over the support and goodwill of the stockmen" by the end of the war. Its intention to raise fees thus "destroyed all the good work of many years, and the feeling between the stockmen and the Forest Service is now probably the worst in its history." [48]

Whether livestock owners would have accepted Rachford's increases in better financial times is impossible to know, of course, but certainly the postwar depression made the proposed increases seem that much more unpalatable. Time and again, in their conventions and in their journals, livestock owners and those associated with the business articulated what can only be described as a sense of betrayal that the Forest Service would countenance fee increases when meat and wool production was under financial pressure. Rachford did acknowledge the severity of the depression in livestock production, but he responded in his report simply that the Forest Service thought the fees were reasonable and, moreover, that it would put the increases into effect gently. [49] Rachford also disagreed with the notion that the increases would put livestock owners out of business. Most livestock owners had to pay the higher rates on private grazing lands, and, he claimed, grazing fees were in any case only "a small part of the operating expenses of the business." [50]

Another major objection was that *on principle* the Forest Service should not "commercialize" the fees at all. Some in the industry argued that commercialization was illegal at worst and at very least simply went against the mandate given by Congress to the Department of Agriculture; if any change in the grazing fee were to be made, it had to be decided at the level of Congress. It was, in other words, not simply an administrative decision but a matter of national policy.[51] Both the National Wool Growers Association and the American National Live Stock Association also argued that the Forest Service's comparison of public and private lands simply did not yield "true" information. As the ANLSA's secretary wrote in one of the early responses to the Rachford Appraisal, Forest Service officials never did discover the real "commercial value" of the national forest ranges: "It might rather be said that . . . they have determined the market prices of grazing during recent years. . . . [I]t is apparent to every student of the western live stock situation that the going prices of grazing have been higher than warranted. There is a great distinction to be made between market price and true value. The former is much the easier to determine."[52]

Finally, other livestock producers responded directly to the Forest Service's claim that, in Rachford's words, the "fact that [the forage] grows on government land rather than on land owned by individuals does not change its value to stockman," and they argued that there was a vast difference between government and private ownership.[53] First, they routinely claimed that the restrictions placed on them by the Forest Service, as well as higher than normal losses, justified lower fees than on private lands.[54] But they also developed a more principled opposition.

The most boldly and clearly articulated of these responses appeared in the *National Wool Grower,* where a 1924 article argued that the government should not commercialize fees because the government was not analogous to an owner of private lands: "[T]he owner of private lands owes allegiance to his dollars. He must, if he can somehow manage, show a profit of his investment. His interest is an entirely selfish one and reaches no farther than his pocket book. Fortunately, the Forest Service is under no such obligation. It was not conscripted into financial servitude through some unfortunate investment; it stands in the position of trustee of the country's natural resources, and owes allegiance only to the people."[55] Although the writer did not expand on who "the people" were—the American public or simply the range livestock producers—like other spokesmen who argued that the federal government should provide livestock producers with "cheap feed," he went on to maintain that without livestock owners in the national forests "there would be no market for the grass; it would simply dry and shrivel on the range." [56] As it stood, the livestock industry made the grass productive, and by getting cheaper feed in the national forests, ranchers were able to return those gains to their community whenever they hired extra labor, paid taxes, or made improvements to their land.

This writer did not directly dispute the Forest Service's claim that the grazing fee was lower than the "actual" value of the forage. But his argument reflected a widely held belief among organized ranchers that they, not the government, should capture the difference in that value. "The country risks nothing with its grass," he added, whereas the rancher should be "compensate[d] for weeks and months spent under all sorts of skies, pounding saddle leather, eating out of tin plates, [and] going hungry at times." This characterization was a variant of a long-running story told by ranchers: that they took real economic and sometimes physical risks by running livestock on the public range; that such risk and initiative should be rewarded—whether, in this case, with a lower-than-market-value grazing fee, or, as in the past, by privileging ranchers in land policies—because without livestock on the range, the grass would produce nothing and have no market value whatsoever. It was an argument about the rancher's role in creating national wealth, but it was also one that privileged the rancher's *labor* as that which gave the range value, meaning that there was a moral imperative for the government to return that value to him.[57]

However, the Forest Service argued that ranchers who had forest permits had a very different relationship to the market than this characterization, that in fact they were much more cunning about market forces than this rather innocent picture portrayed. As we saw in chapter 2, grazing permits had gained market value since the establishment of the permit system, because the permits were transferable along with the sale of either the dependent ranch property or of a rancher's cattle.[58] Ranchers often made a profit on that transfer, a fact that indicated, to Rachford's mind, that "this question of commercialization is not so abhorrent to stockmen if they themselves are permitted to do the commercializing." [59] But if Rachford's comment hit the right chord—for, indeed, ranchers with permits could gain profit from the transfer of those privileges—he and other Forest Service leaders also understood the private market in simplistic ways. On the one hand, the private rental value of grazing land was, in Rachford's words, "determined by the old law of supply and demand." Once the range survey was completed, it was "an authoritative source" to which "private landowners could go and ascertain what their grazing lands were really worth." [60] Here was a notion that the real value of private grazing land could be known absolutely for the entire West, and that it indicated a smoothly operating set of "laws," despite the tumultuous fluctuations of the postwar years. Ranchers' understanding of the market stood in stark contrast to this: in their eyes, the laws of supply and demand for both cattle and sheep had been completely disrupted.[61] But Rachford also contrasted his abstract picture of land valuation with another, where it was "the stockmen themselves [who] create the price for range lands," suggesting that the market values of private ranges were entirely in their hands, and that even an authoritative survey could not change that. Consider, for instance, his response to ranchers who were concerned that private landowners might merely increase their rents if the government increased the cost of a Forest Service permit. Rachford answered that stockmen "pay whatever [the] conditions justify, but oftentimes do not consider the real value of the tract as they could consider it. If the Government increases the rates and the stockmen permit an increase on private lands, that is their own responsibility and not the Governments [sic]." [62]

Several things are remarkable about this statement. First, while Rachford acknowledges that the system of supply and demand revolves around what ranchers in a particular area are willing to pay, he sees no external forces shaping ranchers' economic choices. To be fair, Rachford did not have the economic tools that would later be available for land managers to understand the peculiarly difficult matter of range valuation.[63] As the Bureau of Land Management's director, Marion Clawson, would write in 1950, "The market for range land is imperfect. In a given locality, there may be only a very few ranches that could effectively use a particular tract of land." In other words, the pool of ranchers wanting to rent a given piece of private land was often relatively small, and because of the distances involved and the labor costs of transporting cattle, ranchers could easily be exploited by being made to pay inflated rents for pastures close to their home ranches.[64]

Second, much as in the Supreme Court decisions we saw in chapter 2, Rachford constructs the government here as acting like an individual landowner, trying only to get fair compensation for the use of his or her land. But in absolving the government of any responsibility for potentially raising private land rents along with increased fees, Rachford ignored the fact that the government would be deciding to raise fees as a matter of *public policy;* it would not do so only in reaction to market trends, the way an individual might. And while the Forest Service embraced the truth value of the private market, it also rejected the method of setting grazing fees that would have best allowed the market to function outside of government rate-setting, which would have been a competitive-bid system. The agency refused to go down this road, however, because while it embraced the large, efficient ranchers in its postwar management, it was also still haunted by the specter of land monopolies. The effects of such a system, Rachford maintained, would be "to inject a speculative feature into the business which would seriously interfere with, if not preclude, efficient and permanent management of the range." [65]

But, finally, most remarkable of all is the fact that nowhere in Rachford's report or in the public utterances of Forest Service officials was there any acknowledgement that the existence of federal lands affected private land rents. "Rentals of private lands were relatively high," Clawson wrote twenty-five years later of this period in the 1920s, "because grazing fees on Federal ranges were low; all that [Rachford] did was measure the discrepancy." [66] At this time, the Forest Service simply did not admit that ranchers' complicated patterns of land use created real obstacles to understanding the economic values of different grazing lands. In contrast, by the middle of the 1920s, organized ranchers were arguing back forcefully that the Forest Service could not separately differentiate the values of public and private land, because the two types of land were so closely involved in ranchers' year-round operations.

William Greeley himself conceded to the ANLSA that ranchers made "intermingled" use of private and public lands. [67] But that characterization only scratched the surface of the problem. Again, Marion Clawson's 1950 text on the range livestock industry is instructive on this point, for he notes, in a typically understated way, that "[w]hen one attempts to value separately the different types of grazing land used by a ranch, one often runs into trouble." Where ranchers depended on different ranges —such as Forest Service permit holders who fed their livestock during the winter and put them in the national forests during the summer, and possibly on the public domain in the spring and the fall—each type of land had no value without the rancher's access to the other. Grasping for an analogy from the manufacturing world that would make sense to readers, Clawson writes: "It is exactly as if one manufacturer made Ford Engines, another Ford bodies, and still another made Ford chassis. If there were no other manufacturers of any of these and if there was no use for any of them except on Ford automobiles, then the value of the combined product might be known, but not [the values of] the separate products." [68]

The Rachford report did not establish the "true" value of the forage in the national forests, but it did bring to the surface this fact: that private ranch properties and the public property of the United States were deeply intertwined—in geography, in valuation, and in the ways that ranches had to operate, using different pastures (with different legal boundaries) at various points in the year. And the report highlighted the difficulty the Forest Service had in making the argument that the private rental market could serve as the basis for a sound public policy on grazing in the national forests. Politically, it confirmed many ranchers in their belief that the commercialization policy was meant merely to fill government coffers and bolster federal administrative authority over public grazing in the forests. Even more important, the Forest Service never successfully articulated why it was in the public's interest to have it charge a market-based fee, except that it would put the livestock industry on a "business basis" with the government, which would "command public confidence." [69] Even this argument was ambiguous, however, because Forest Service officials asserted alternately that it was the *public* that deserved full value and that it was the *government* that received it. It was a critical distinction, because it called into question again the nature of who owned the national forests. Of course, the legal understanding was that they were the property of the United States, and that it was the government's responsibility to safeguard the lands in the public interest. And yet, in the grazing fee controversy the Forest Service also positioned the government, implicitly and explicitly, as a proprietor —implying that, in its role as trustee for the American public, the government deserved to capture more of the value of public grazing lands. Moreover, it was incumbent upon the agency to make sure that ranchers did not capture that value, because the property right did not adhere to them but to the government. Thus, the Forest Service's turning to the market as a basis for grazing fees was not simply about the exchange of money between permit holders and the government; it also served as a property marker. The commercialization policy was understood by ranchers to mean that the government wanted to assert its ownership more fully over the national forests, and that in doing so it had the authority to control ranchers' property. Indeed, the grazing fee battles quickly moved onto the terrain of property rights, as the livestock industry and its allies in Congress responded by seeking more security in ranchers' grazing permits.

This movement was already afoot by the time Rachford's report came out, because Rachford specifically rebuts ranchers' demands that they be given greater legal recognition in their use of national forest lands.[70] But their demands emerged with more vigor in the aftermath of the report. In the spring and fall of 1925, hearings on public grazing were held by a subcommittee of the Senate Committee on Public Lands and Surveys, headed by Senator Robert Stanfield of Oregon. These "Stanfield hearings" (as they were informally dubbed) reflected a new era in governmental hearings on public grazing. Whereas previous ones had been limited affairs, consigned to Washington, D.C., the Stanfield hearings traveled all over the West, after beginning in Washington, and ultimately encompassed over 6,000 pages of testimony. They also established a new pattern, because the last extensive set of hearings on public grazing—the hearings before the passing of the Stock-Raising Homestead Act in 1916—had largely showcased western politicians' animus against organized ranchers and their desire to encourage homesteaders. In contrast, Stanfield himself was a prominent livestock owner and, along with Senator Ralph Cameron of Arizona and Senator Tasker Oddie of Nevada, used the hearings "to play up the grievances of the stockmen."[71] Stanfield and Cameron in particular, along with the committee's attorney, George Bowden, questioned witnesses relentlessly on every imaginable particular having to do with public grazing. They unabashedly saw themselves in a "fight" with bureaucrats over everything from the grazing fee to priority rights to grazing on the public domain and Indian lands. At times, in fact, the sheer multitude of complaints so overwhelmed the witnesses that even their supporters, the cattlemen and sheepmen of the West, were left groping for an opinion.[72]

The influence of the hearings in bolstering organized ranchers' opposition to the Forest Service emerged quickly. Although the ANLSA and the NWGA had published stinging attacks on the grazing fee proposal, those attacks were largely confined to the economic questions involved in range valuation. Some months after the hearings began, however, in late summer of 1925, representatives from the western livestock associations held a meeting in Salt Lake City to air their grievances about the government's public land policies; one might even call it an advance attack, because it was deliberately planned to precede the holding of the Stanfield hearings in Salt Lake City. While divisions existed among the organizers about what recommendations to make—the representatives from Wyoming, for instance, rejected the notion that the public domain should come under any federal regulation at all—the meeting hammered out a list of resolutions for both the national forests and the public domain. Leading the list for national forest policy was the group's belief that "by law there [should] be a recognition, definition, and protection of rights to grazing upon national-forest ranges upon an area basis," and, among other things, that "such rights be definite and transferable, without penalty." [73] Its recommendations for the public domain bore the marks of dissension, as the group noted that conditions on this land were so varied across the West that no single policy could be developed for it. But the representatives were able to articulate at least general principles for determining a new government policy toward the public range, which included "the necessity for definiteness of control in the operator"; a fee that would not lead to a depreciation in the "investment values in privately owned properties dependent on the use" of the public domain; and the granting of range access to those ranchers who had prior use of the lands. [74]

The *Producer* commented that the meeting unfairly emphasized anti–Forest Service sentiment, but clearly both the ANLSA and the NWGA were shifting to a more forceful demand that ranchers be given greater "stability and security of tenure" in national forests—and, ultimately, in the public domain. [75] The holding of the Stanfield hearings obviously emboldened them to articulate a language of rights that they had not employed before, because Stanfield and Cameron tirelessly argued that the government should construct ranchers' use of public lands as a right, not just a privilege, and that every safeguard should be put in place to protect ranchers' property from any government policy that might depreciate its value. But the importance of the hearings lay not only in a much more public articulation of rights; they also highlighted a larger discourse about the law that was emerging during this time, which itself had connections to ranchers' quest for recognized rights to public grazing. [76] One of the thorniest and unresolved issues concerned defining how far the service's administrative functions could go before they became "legal" issues. By 1925, representatives of the livestock associations were arguing that the Forest Service wanted, and exerted, powers going far beyond simple administration, and that the service had both taken over legislative functions and made decisions that should have been left up to a court. Some of these leaders turned to Progressive models of regulation and argued that a separate commission or board should be established, outside the Forest Service, to hear ranchers' complaints about decisions that affected their permits or property. Others looked to the established system of law. As the president of the Idaho Wool Growers' Association argued, the permit holder should be able to protest the decisions by Forest Service personnel by appealing to the federal courts, and he represented Colonel Greeley's position in the following way: "Colonel Greeley says that the Forest Service must have all three functions: It must have the legislative function—make the rules and regulations; the administrative, which is its proper function; as well as the judicial function—that is, be judge, jury, and prosecutor concerning any infraction of its own rules and regulations." He did not want to see the Forest Service abolished, but, like other leaders in the livestock associations, he attempted to whittle down the extent of its administrative authority.[77]

At issue, of course, was trying to define the difference between an "administrative" and a "legal" problem. On the one hand, Greeley acknowledged the murkiness between these two categories. In the Stanfield hearings, for instance, Greeley noted that while the department had taken cases of trespass—where a permit holder allowed his or her animals to range beyond the given allotment—to federal courts, the federal judges had advocated that such cases be handled within the department "by administrative action." "That is a rather unusual position for a court to take," he said, "and a position that we do not like to be put in the position of judge and jury." [78] On the other hand, Greeley had a quite different view than some of the representatives of the livestock associations. He did not agree to establishing a separate "tribunal" that could supersede the authority of the secretary of agriculture. The question of what separated "the law" from departmental rules lay at the heart of the debate, however, as evidenced in this exchange during the hearings:

> *Greeley:* . . . [Y]ou are dealing here with administration. You are not dealing with matters of law. If you were dealing with matters of law the cases would get into the courts, but you are dealing with matters of administration.
>
> *Senator Cameron:* Under the regulations?
>
> *Greeley:* Under the regulations of the Secretary.
>
> *Senator Stanfield:* Of course your rules and regulations really become the law.
>
> *Greeley:* . . . When an appeal is made on one of these cases it deals with an administrative decision. A supervisor decides that he will allot a certain range to Mr. A rather than Mr. B, and Mr. B appeals. There is nothing about that that is a of a legal character to be decided by a court.[79]

On the contrary, argued some leaders of the livestock industry: because their property was at stake, they were entitled to have their cases heard by either a court or a commission outside the Forest Service's administrative structure. And, indeed, the hearings helped to solidify this larger critique in the livestock associations that Forest Service officials had assumed the mantles of judges. As we shall see in much more detail in chapter 4, this argument would lead organized ranchers to take an additional step—that is, to argue that such assertions of federal authority were in violation of the western states' sovereignty.

But increasing hostility to federal land management was not simply fueled by the political theatrics of the Senate Public Land Committee; the grazing fee battle had changed the tenor of the positions staked out by the livestock associations on the question of administrative authority. Of the two, the NWGA has been viewed by public land historians as the less progressive association. After all, it had supported enlarged homesteading on the public domain until 1916 and was a continual thorn in the side of the Forest Service. Up until the late teens, representatives of the NWGA tended to see all legislation for federal grazing control as a plot between the government and large cattle owners to steal their rights to the public domain, and even after the association backed a federal leasing plan, it was only partially on board.

In fact, articles in the *National Wool Grower* about public land administration were consistently pitched higher on the scale of outrage than those in the *Producer,* and sheep producers were generally skeptical that federal bureaucracies could administer land fairly. Even small signals manifested the bad feeling that the sheepmen felt toward the Forest Service—for instance, that the NWGA's president, Frank Hagenbarth, rarely referred to the agency by its proper name, instead calling it the "Forest Bureau," its pre-1905 title. The NWGA's responses to the grazing-fee controversy displayed the depth of its wariness of the Forest Service, for they quickly went beyond the mere matter of fees to larger questions about the development of the American regulatory state.

In 1925, for instance, Frank Hagenbarth said in his annual address to the NWGA that "[t]he issue involved in this matter is not, as many suppose, the increase in fees that is now proposed to be made by the forest bureau, but it is decidedly the principle involved." The principle, on the one hand, was that the western states in which the forests were located were "deprived" of development and settlement that the rest of the states in the country were allowed to enjoy. This was a standard argument by western critics of the Forest Service, but Hagenbarth also went further, saying: "A bureaucratic form of government has been set up with unlimited and confiscatory powers from which there is no right of appeal. Though today we are on most friendly terms with the bureau that administers the forests and the unusual powers which it possesses to date have not been abused, yet the power is there and who can tell, under different conditions, what the future may have in store for us and whether or not this power will not be abused." [80]

Hagenbarth's concern was not simply that bureaucracies held certain powers beyond their electoral or judicial mandates, but that the use or abuse of such powers was entirely dependent on the officials who ran those bureaucracies. As supposedly impartial institutions, charged with public service, they were at the mercy of personnel changes, and those changes could, in this view, lead to the loss of property. Ranchers might be forced to reduce their herds or even be excluded from certain ranges. Hagenbarth was apparently convinced that without proper controls, the federal government might destroy the livestock industry. During the Stanfield hearings, for instance, he argued that as grazing regulations then stood, "the Secretary of Agriculture, prompted by the Chief Forester of the United States, and he in turn prompted by his advisers, has the right and the power under the law to deprive us of our property." [81] This inflammatory claim represented the core of Hagenbarth's political beliefs: that an unchecked regulatory state had the potential power to take ranchers' property, and that the rightful arbiters of any matter having to do with their private property were the courts.

Much more so than the ANLSA, the NWGA put its faith in Congress to counterbalance the bureaucratic weight of the executive branch. Where the ANLSA often worried about the "politics" of legislation, the NWGA saw an avenue for hemming in bureaucratic power. "Time has shown the error of Congress in abdicating its power and shifting its responsibilities to the bureaus and commissions," one editorial read. "Congress must make the national policies and define the limits within which the bureaus shall function. The autocracy of bureau administration is more to be feared than the possible errors of legislative action." [82] The NWGA raised more hell about the Forest Service than the ANLSA did, and it was much less clear about what it wanted for the public domain. As early as 1920, Hagenbarth began backing away from his recent support of grazing control, advocating instead that the public domain be sold at very low cost to livestock owners. Articles in the *National Wool Grower* continued to argue for this course, particularly as the battle over grazing fees worsened. As one author noted in 1925, "It

is perhaps fortunate that the Forest Bureau decided to put grazing permits on a commercial basis at this particular time. It gives stockmen an
idea what to expect when the entire bureau is administered by a similar
bureau," and under such conditions, he argued further, "[y]our right to
the proud boast that you are an independent American will no longer be
true."[83] Another observer wrote: "The more I study this problem of
range control the more convinced I am that the Government has no
business with the public domain beyond providing a system of control
during the period necessary for securing a satisfactory transfer from
public to private ownership." He went on to argue that "the Government's proper function in relation to the range is that of teacher rather
than landlord"; that is, "[t]he Government, through the Bureau of Forestry" produced worthwhile scientific knowledge about grazing and information about range management, but such knowledge could not help
livestock owners if they did not have control over the land they used.
The government's role should thus be restricted to "educating stockmen
in a proper system of range management and [guarding the period of
transition from public to private ownership." Instead of relying on "government compulsion" to accomplish good range management, "the focus of individual enterprise and energy must be liberated" to develop the
range livestock industry.[84]

Such criticism was not confined to the conservative group of western
wool growers but could be heard across American society, particularly
given the Republican-dominated government, as public and private
leaders turned away from what they saw as heavy-handed models of regulation of the Progressive years. This skepticism did not mean that they
turned away from regulation entirely, because the 1920s saw a burst of
what Ellis Hawley has termed "associational" models of managing economic problems, bringing together leaders in both private and public
sectors. But the skepticism about federal administrative power did include a more widespread fear that the grant of broad, discretionary
powers to government agencies was a genuine threat to constitutional
checks and balances. Indeed, the degree to which administrative rules
could become rapidly woven into bureaucratic structures was remarkable to some in administrative circles. When Ray Lyman Wilbur, the
president of Stanford University, became secretary of the interior under
Herbert Hoover, he was frankly amazed at the power of bureaucratic
rules. "Only a short residence in Washington is sufficient to make any
administrator fear the bureaucrat and bureaucracy," he later observed

in his *Memoirs.* "It is so easy to get rules established and then, with the power of the government, put them into effect and keep them there." [85]

We shall hear more of both Wilbur and Hoover in chapter 4, but Hoover's presence in Washington was already important in the public grazing debate. As an ambitious public servant at the head of the Department of Commerce in these years, Hoover was also at odds with a great deal of Agriculture Department policy, particularly when Henry C. Wallace stood at its helm. Hoover believed that the department was seeking to expand its bureaucratic power, and he actively concerned himself with its direction, taking a leading role in helping Calvin Coolidge select William M. Jardine as the next secretary of agriculture after Wallace's death.[86] In fact, Hoover also had his hand in the politics of public grazing. The secretary of the NWGA, F. R. Marshall, was a friend of his, and that connection gave him the opportunity to weigh in on the political alignments that were taking new shape during the 1920s. Hoover and Marshall clearly discussed which department the NWGA should support to administer the public domain, because in late 1924, Hoover communicated in a confidential letter to Marshall: "I understand that the policy of the Department of the Interior is to make leases on such terms as will simply cover the cost of administration, whereas the policy of the Department of Agriculture is to make leases that will secure the maximum possible return. It would appear to me therefore, much more desirable for your organization to support the policies of the Department of the Interior rather than to see that they are transferred to the Department of Agriculture a[n]d incorporated in their line of thought." [87] Marshall gave every indication that "the present thought of Western stockmen is quite favorable to having it done by the Department of the Interior." [88]

But the depth of the struggle between ranchers and the Forest Service stemmed from more than uncertain or even unraveling political entanglements: the controversy over fees and the growing call by organized ranchers for greater legal recognition of their right to use the forests put a tremendous strain on the patience of the Forest Service, and William Greeley both went on the attack and wound up discredited in the livestock associations. This was partially a result of bad timing. As an editorial in the *Producer* acknowledged when Greeley resigned in 1928, "It was Mr. Greeley's misfortune to have been placed at the head of the Forest Service at a period when the stock men had to count their pennies." Nonetheless, what organized ranchers saw in Greeley's behavior was simple "bad faith." The grazing-fee controversy caused "a wound" that was "still festering," and they believed that Greeley "was the man . . . who not only inflicted it by his stubborn adherence to a wrong principle, but who would have had it within his power to heal it, when he saw the mischief he was doing—and refused." [89]

Greeley was in a difficult political position, but he also "wounded" the livestock industry in what was considered a public betrayal of its relationship to his agency. In November 1925, he published a lengthy article in the *Saturday Evening Post* on "The Stockmen and the National Forests," and while stock growers had come to expect attacks on their industry from eastern conservationists groups like the American Forestry Association, Greeley's article clearly caught them off guard.[90] On the one hand, his representation of the industry's political positions was accurate, as he explained that at the heart of stock owners' politics was the desire to gain legal rights to the range. But the tone of the article caused a tremendous rift, for he made the inestimable mistake of falling back on stereotypical treatments of both western livestock owners and their political goals. If these owners got what they wanted, Greeley wrote, it would mean "the complete legal intrenchment [*sic*] of past range usage. The big sheepmen who pasture ten to twenty or fifty thousand woolies in the national forests—and there are still a few of them— would each be given perpetual control of thousands of acres of public land. The cattle barons counting three or five or seven thousand in their herds would be ensconced far more securely on their hundreds of square miles of the nation's common property than ever in the old days, when their reign depended upon custom and the six-shooter." [91]

Greeley's claim that it was only the "active few" among livestock producers who objected to Forest Service policy, and that these "flockmasters" wanted to trample the rights of homesteaders, provoked immediate reply. As one cattle grower from Washington State wrote: "If Greeley had been fair enough to state that in the forest reserves of Washington and Oregon the average herd size of the licensee numbers only about fifty head, and that the meetings of the Senate committee were attended by these small owners, who kicked as hard as it was possible for them to kick, the article would have conveyed an entirely different idea to the average reader." [92] A yet more powerful response came from E. L. Potter, professor of animal husbandry at Oregon Agricultural College, who argued that Greeley was "denying the policy of his own bureau," saying: "[A]nyone who is at all familiar with the present policy of the Forest Service knows that it is doing all in its power to prevent the dividing-up of the ranges among the homesteaders and other newcomers who have not demonstrated their ability to handle stock properly and cannot stay in the business with a reasonable degree of permanence." [93]

Potter's point was well taken, for even publicly the Forest Service contradicted itself on the extent to which its policy favored smaller land and livestock owners. Christopher Rachford himself got caught in this contradiction while trying to argue both for "commercializing" grazing fees and against ranchers' claims that they should get a break because they were pioneers in the country. He noted that "[w]hile approximately 85 per cent of the owners of cattle who use national forest range are small operators, they graze only 31 per cent of the number of stock on the forests." This fact alone represented a disjunction in Forest Service policy, but Rachford unwittingly drove home Potter's point more by adding that "[69] per cent of the cattle grazed on national forests are owned by comparatively large operators. These men are in a commercial enterprise just the same as the lumber or power companies, and have no more relationship to pioneering in the West than other commercial interests of Western states." [94]

But the animus directed at Greeley's article was not so much about what he had said (although certainly the term "cattle barons" raised ranchers' hackles), but that he had written it at all. In a published reprint of a letter E. L. Potter sent to Secretary of Agriculture William Jardine, Potter explained that "the stockmen very bitterly resent the fact that skilled and trained writers in the Department of Agriculture put out articles inimical to their interests," when the western livestock industry had "no one with sufficient skill as a writer to reach the national magazines." [95] Potter made stockmen out to be much less articulate than they were, of course, but what he conveyed was that the western livestock owners were not producing articles for "national [read eastern] magazines," not having the contacts to do so. Moreover, western livestock owners had for decades seen themselves vilified in the eastern press. As Potter wrote to Jardine, "The stockmen and farmers have looked largely to the employees of the colleges and the Department of Agriculture to fight their battles in the press; and then when these turn against them, they feel that they have been betrayed." [96] The depth of that betrayal was evident when, as late as 1932, a rancher angrily referred to Greeley's article in a letter to the *Producer*. [97]

It is tempting here to metaphorize the relationship between the Forest Service and the range livestock industry as strangely familial—that by going to the eastern press, Greeley broke a tacit agreement not to

take the range problems outside the western ranch family. But even
without the help of this metaphor, the conflicts regarding whom the
Forest Service served are apparent in the response to Greeley's article.
This was an acute problem for all clients of the increasingly bureaucratized American state and was experienced acutely by many different
groups in the American West. In California, for instance, irrigation
farmers and ranchers battling with the city of Los Angeles over water
rights sought a client relationship with state and federal agencies. As
John Walton has written of the rebellion by Owens Valley farmers in the
1920s, "[a] new kind of struggle developed as constituents of the state
fought from within over their political rights and the question of whom
the bureaucracy should serve." [98] Likewise, the Forest Service had to mediate between different private clients—loggers, miners, and ranchers—
and "the public" or "public interest." As recreation in particular had increased throughout the teens and the early 1920s, Forest Service officials
found themselves under pressure to mediate between local users and
campers, anglers, and sport hunters. Although it was not yet an official
policy of the Forest Service, the agency clearly operated under the framework later described as "multiple use," seeking to accommodate all the
different uses of the national forests. This framework meant that, rather
than resolving the tension over who the forests served, the battles over
public grazing were sure to flare up any time stock growers believed that
their use of the forests was up for renegotiation. After the grazing fee
conflict, a latent volatility would forever define the relationship between
public land ranchers and the Forest Service, as the stock growers increasingly believed that both their political rights and their property
were at stake in the debate over public land policy.

With the end of the Stanfield hearings in the fall of 1925, the furor over
the Forest Service died down somewhat. The hearings had mustered the
political strength of western ranchers, bolstered by allies in Congress,
and the next few years brought Forest Service policy more in line with
what western livestock owners wanted. After Secretary of Agriculture
Henry C. Wallace died in October 1924, the acting secretary, How-
ard A. Gore, and then the new secretary, William Jardine, rejected the
notion of "commercial value" in analyzing grazing fees. To resolve the
impasse created by the Rachford appraisal, Jardine appointed a Kansas
stockman, Dan D. Casement, to do his own appraisal of grazing fees in
the national forests. Not unexpectedly, his results were a compromise
between the Forest Service's and the industry's proposed figures, and

they were still contested by the livestock associations, although in a much less urgent manner.[99]

In January 1926, Jardine published a revised set of grazing regulations, which contained three major changes: the elevation of the ten-year permit to the status of a real contract; minimal new distribution of grazing preferences, thus giving more stability to current users' grazing privileges; and finally, a "reemphasized" role for local grazing boards in helping settle local disputes.[100] In the same month, as a direct result of the hearings, Senator Stanfield introduced a bill seeking "to force the Forest Service into full retreat on its grazing policies."[101] Of its specifications, the most important was recognizing more fully the right of livestock owners to graze their animals in national forests, for as it currently stood, grazing was not written into the original set of functions assigned to the national forests. Both the cattle and sheep associations wanted the security of a legal recognition of their right to graze their animals in the national forests—a recognition with which the secretary of agriculture was sympathetic. But Jardine was wary about granting a place for grazing equal with the other reasons for which the national forests had been established—timber conservation and watershed protection—and he refused to approve the change.[102]

Although the Forest Service did not meet the largest demands of the livestock owners, the grazing fee controversy did finally end. In January 1927, Secretary Jardine announced the final fees, arrived at through conferencing with the industry, which the livestock associations publicly accepted with relatively peaceful resignation.

With its rather anti-climactic ending, the battle over grazing fees has appeared to public land historians as a product of overwrought—if not fundamentally irrational—cattle and sheep owners. If only 25 percent of western livestock producers used the national forests, and if many participants acknowledged that the great unresolved problem of western range use was the unappropriated public domain, why did the livestock associations spend so much energy and time on the grazing fee controversy? Was it a case, as Greeley maintained, that a radical few were pulling along the rest in their organizations? And why such heated language? The answers lie at a number of levels. Perhaps the most obvious and important one is that the Rachford Appraisal appeared to western livestock owners to go against a fundamental principle of federal grazing control in the national forests. Both prongs of the western livestock industry held that the basis of forest fees, established along with the Forest Service's grazing program in the early 1900s, was to provide for

cheap forage, and that it was explicitly not to equal private fees. The
Forest Service disagreed, saying that it had intended all along to increase
the fees gradually until they reached market value. The cattle and sheep
industries were never won over by this argument, and to them it made
them question both its commitment to providing them with fair grazing
administration and, more generally, its bureaucratic powers. It is important to emphasize again that neither the ANLSA nor the NWGA
wanted to dismantle the Forest Service, for they recognized the benefits
they received from the agency. Rather, the grazing fee controversy represents the moment when the livestock associations began to articulate
a much more cohesive opposition to administrative expansion, and that
opposition would consolidate in the following years as association leaders focused increasingly on how public land regulation was grounded in
property ownership.

However, the contours of the livestock associations' critique were already emerging in the 1920s, because the grazing fee controversy also
marked the point at which the Forest Service found itself caught between seeing itself as both the guardian of public interest in the national
forests and a manager of government property. It was in the latter capacity that it chiefly sought to justify raising grazing fees, especially in
Rachford's report, and that justification helped to erode the political
trust that had been built between organized ranchers and the Forest Service. Unfortunately, both sides were locked so tightly into this battle that
they paid little attention to the fact that the controversy over grazing fees
had parallels in other governmental areas. The most clearly analogous
case was state and federal attempts to set "reasonable" rates of return
for public utilities. Here, the problem also hinged on the relationship of
the "public" to the "private": as one liberal writer at the time noted, the
Supreme Court affirmed "that the private owner of public utility property should be given the same value for his property that it would possess if it were being used in private business." [103] Had such parallels been
seen, perhaps the debate might have been cast as a part of a *national* argument about the role of an expanded state in economic regulation, as
opposed to simply a western problem. And yet it is worth noting that
there was a critical difference between the problem of grazing fees and
the problem of utility rates. The Forest Service was attempting to set
"fair and reasonable compensation" for government-owned land. The
Rachford appraisal was thus not analyzing the fair return to the private
user; rather, depending on how the Forest Service articulated the project, it was analyzing the return either to the public or to the government

itself. Again, the elusiveness of the distinction confirmed many ranchers in the belief that the government was no better than a landlord, raising rents to maximize its return.

The intervention of the Senate Subcommittee on Public Lands and Surveys also had an enormous effect in publicizing the grazing-fee conflict, sanctioning livestock owners' complaints and fanning the flames. By holding such extensive hearings, Stanfield and his committee helped bring the controversy to national attention, but perhaps more important, they literally brought the issue to the West by holding their hearings throughout the public land states over a period of six months. Clearly a public relations coup for the western senators involved, the hearings helped to renew livestock associations' faith in the congressional process, which had reached a low point with the House Agriculture Committee's proposal in 1920 to increase grazing fees. Congress now assumed the role of mediator between public land users and the federal bureaucracy, as the legislative brake on potentially "arbitrary" federal agencies. Polarizing the users against the bureaucracy ultimately functioned, then, as a kind of governmental theater, in which the Senate subcommittee was both actor and director. The staging of these hearings across towns and cities of the West helped make the grazing-fee controversy part of a larger drama about the state's role in society.

Politically, the struggle over grazing fees also seemed to contain the shadow presence of the public domain. Whether explicitly stated or merely implied, the livestock industry saw the resolution of the public domain debates as hinging on the direction of the grazing-fee controversy. For one thing, Stanfield's 1926 bill attempted to resolve problems with both the public domain and the national forests and was a culmination of hearings that discussed the two public land categories in tandem. Stanfield's proposed legislation for the public domain incorporated a highly decentralized bureaucracy, with more powers and rights given to western livestock owners compared with previous bills. And the bill also lodged public domain administration with the Department of the Interior, a direct result of the industry's disgruntlement with the Department of Agriculture. The shadow presence of the public domain, in other words, raised the stakes in the grazing-fee controversy, changing the shape of the contest so that it did not simply concern grazing areas in the national forests but also the future administration of all federal grazing lands. As soon as the grazing-fee controversy was settled by Secretary of Agriculture William Jardine's announcement of the revised fee structures, an editorial in the *Producer* immediately reminded its read-

ers, "While grazing on national forests may be nearer an amicable settlement, the question of sane regulation of grazing on the remaining unappropriated public domain seems about as far off as at any time since
it was first broached, thirty years ago." The editorial added that "[i]n
certain western public-land states the opposition to this legislation
seems more formidable than in previous years," a casualty of the grazing-fee battle.[104]

It was an accurate statement, and by the following year, a louder opposition to federal control over public grazing could be heard within
both the American National Live Stock Association and the National
Wool Growers Association. But ranchers' voices were not the only ones
to be heard; as ranchers, bureaucrats, and politicians all turned their attention once more to the public domain and to the vexing connections
between public property and political sovereignty, the highest office-
holder of the country also joined in the chorus.

CHAPTER 4

Sovereignty of the State, or the States?

The whole process of Regimentation with its enormous extension of authority and its centralization in the Federal Government grievously undermines the State jurisdiction over its
citizens; State responsibility, and in the end State's Rights. It
thereby undermines one of the primary safeguards of Liberty.
                    —Herbert Hoover, *The Challenge to Liberty*

Although the grazing fee fracas of the mid 1920s ostensibly revolved
around the issue of money, it became a watershed for a western critique
of administrative expansion and federal land ownership, and by the late
1920s, this critique took on the shape of states' rights, which had become an important national force. But the western states' rights movement also gained momentum through policy shifts at the very upper
reaches in the American state, for the Hoover presidency marked the
only time in this century when a president advocated giving the remaining unappropriated public domain to the states. At no time before this
period was such a radical departure from standard public land policy
considered at the federal level, nor would it ever be again until James
Watt became secretary of the interior in the Reagan administration.

   This chapter of the grazing debates, leading up to the passage of the
Taylor Grazing Act, is undoubtedly the most puzzling of all. For twenty-
five years the Department of Agriculture and the American National
Live Stock Association had supported federal grazing control, and the
Department of Interior had lobbied recently to gain control over the public domain. Now, however, President Hoover aimed to alter the terms of
the struggle completely. In 1929, Hoover appointed a public lands committee that endorsed his own view that the government should, with cer-

tain restrictions, hand over the public domain to the western states, although recommending that federal administration of the public lands
be retained in some other contexts. In 1932, the House and Senate
committees on public lands held hearings on bills based on the committee's recommendations. Nonetheless, within two years, the Taylor Grazing Act passed with relatively little trouble through both chambers of
Congress.

Brief and anomalous though this period was, it had resounding effects on the debates surrounding the public domain. First, it brought to
the surface unresolved questions of administrative rule, most specifically, questions of *where* the public domain would fit as a management
problem within state structures. This emphasis on administration stood
in contrast to the public land policies of Progressive-era administrations,
because, while the latter certainly addressed the issue of administrative
location, they did so within the ideological arena of agrarianism and the
policy constraints of enlarged homesteading. Recommendations for
public domain policy were framed as a geography of the individual, and
a very particular individual at that—the "homebuilder." By the Hoover
presidency, the debates had shifted to whether the public domain would
be administered by the Forest Service or the Department of the Interior,
or even by the western states.

The much more striking effect of this period was the mobilizing of
states' rights sentiment among organized ranchers, a shift that has been
little understood by historians. That ranchers appeared simply fed up
with the Forest Service is one explanation, although not to my mind a
sufficient one, as the critique of federal power was too large and too sustained to reflect mere irritation with Forest Service regulations. It is
tempting, too, to explain the livestock industry's anti-federal agenda as
a product of "traditional" western individualism, erupting out of the
West's increasing dependence on the federal government. Certainly, individualist strains inflected the struggles over the public domain, but
this, too, does not fully explain the nature of the livestock industry's political discourse in this period. As it turns out, the "individual" was mentioned surprisingly little during this time, and I would argue that to the
degree that "individualism" influenced the debates over the public domain, it reflected the ways in which private property relations structured
people's responses to public domain policy and the ways some observers
understood the states' relationship to the federal government.

The emphasis on states' rights during the Hoover years, in other
words, was far from a frontier remnant. Not only was it a theme

throughout national political discourse, but it was also an explicit policy directive from the Hoover administration. Its purest articulation
among Wyoming states' rightists held to long-standing themes in states'
rights discourse, but it also was very much a product of post–World
War I rethinking of federal power. This rethinking was not simply a blip
on the political screen before the advent of the New Deal: as we shall see
in the chapters ahead, it deeply affected the construction of range policy
in the Taylor Grazing Act and the political discourse about the range for
years to come.

Herbert Hoover went to work quickly on the public domain question.
Several months after his inauguration in 1929, his new secretary of the
interior, Ray Lyman Wilbur, suggested the possibility of an astounding
departure in federal land policy. Speaking in Boise, Idaho, he argued
that it was "time for a new public land policy which will include transferring to those states willing to accept the responsibility the control of
the surface rights of all public lands not included in national parks or
monuments or in the national forest." He even suggested that at some
point in the future, the national forests themselves could be handed over
to the states.[1]

Hoover's recommendation to turn over the public lands to the states
arose, not as a matter of western states' rights principles per se, but out
of administrative and bureaucratic concerns. While Hoover did show
real interest in giving the western states more political autonomy, this
concern was rooted in ideas about appropriate federal governmental
administration. The president's first statement outlining his ideas about
the public domain—a letter read to the Western Governors' Conference
in August 1929—actually offered several reasons for his proposal to
turn over the lands to the states. First, Hoover noted, the western states
had evolved to such a point that they would be able to handle the administration of the public lands; they had "long since passed from their
swaddling clothes and are today more competent to manage much of
these affairs than is the federal government." While he did not explain
why they were more competent (and even many westerners disagreed
that they were), he maintained that "we must seek every opportunity to
retard the expansion of federal bureaucracy and to place our communities in control of their own destinies." To do so would be to "obtain better government."[2] However, Hoover was contradictory about why state
rather than federal ownership of the public lands would create more
efficient government. If anything, the reason appeared to be that Hoover

simply wanted to unload the grazing lands: "They bring no revenue to the federal government. The federal government is incapable of the adequate administration of matters which require so large a matter of local understanding. Practically none of these lands can be commercially afforested."[3] Hoover thus believed the federal government should rid itself of the lands both because they were not a productive property and because administering them from Washington was too difficult. On both points there was considerable disagreement.

Hoover then began appointing a public lands committee to investigate how to settle the problem of the unappropriated lands; he was only the second president, after Theodore Roosevelt, to organize such a commission (the first public lands commission of 1879 having been brought together by Congress). Creating a national committee to investigate a problem is a significant statement of presidential will, and that Hoover called for this so early in his presidency indicated that he saw the issue as having national importance. But like the two earlier commissions, it utterly failed to effect any real change for the public domain. The most stunning suggestion in the 1879 report, John Wesley Powell's proposal to sell off 2,560-acre parcels of the semi-arid and arid lands, never became politically feasible; Roosevelt's commission advocated immediate land classification and a loose system of federal control of grazing leasing, neither of which were implemented; and the proposal of Hoover's committee—to cede the public domain to the states—ultimately lost, of course, to the Taylor Grazing Act.

But presidential commissions are as important for their membership and what they say as they are for how effectively they can get their proposals through Congress. The comparison between Roosevelt's commission and Hoover's committee is instructive. Roosevelt appointed only three members to the 1903–5 group: Gifford Pinchot, then head of the Forest Bureau in the Department of Agriculture; Frederick Newell, head of the Reclamation Service in the Department of the Interior; and W. A. Richards, commissioner of the General Land Office. They were all federal bureaucrats at that moment, and at least Pinchot and Newell were point men for Roosevelt's conservation program, emphasizing public land ownership of nonagricultural lands, which at that time meant bringing grazing lands under federal management. As Samuel Hays has noted of the report's principles, public ownership of lands was seen as the only way to a "rational development" of the West.[4] In contrast, Hoover's commissioners came both from within and outside of government. Hoover initially intended to appoint about ten members, but that number ballooned to twenty appointees (plus two ex officio members, the secretaries of the interior and agriculture).[5] The committee—which included William Greeley, now head of the Western Lumberman's Association, representatives of every public land state in the West, and public figures who had little or no relationship to the grazing question, such as the mystery writer Mary Roberts Rinehart—eventually took the name of its chair, James R. Garfield, a former secretary of the interior. Although in the end it endorsed the president's position, given its size and varied makeup, it spoke with many voices. Not all of its members were happy with its stance. Indeed, the Wyoming member on the committee understood that he represented different interests with different voices. Introducing himself to the House Public Lands Committee in the 1932 hearings about cession, Perry Jenkins noted that he represented the state of Wyoming, the American National Livestock Association, and was also "incidentally" a member of the Garfield Committee. But, he emphasized, "in that connection I do not wish to speak."[6]

Jenkins's effective disavowal signaled deep divisions within the committee, which largely centered around the terms on which Hoover offered the states the public domain lands. That offer, as it turned out, included only the surface rights to the land, and he was adamant that the federal government would not relinquish the subsurface rights under any circumstances. Hoover and other officials maintained that giving states mineral rights would not help build their treasuries, arguing that, as it then stood, western states already benefited from federal mineral leases, which put over 30 percent of the royalties into the reclamation funds of the respective western states. However, Hoover's (and the committee's) resistance to handing over all rights in the public domain to the states became a rallying cry for those who supported western states' rights—further evidence to them that federal bureaucracy would remain ensconced on western public lands.[7] To many westerners, including those on the committee, Hoover appeared to be giving with one hand while taking away with the other. And in the western press, there was no dearth of metaphors to describe the offer of only the surface rights: "[I]t would be like giving the states 'skimmed milk' after all the cream has been extracted," the Idaho *Statesman* quoted Senator William Borah as saying. It was "like handing [the states] an orange with the juice sucked out of it"; or as if the "federal government has taken the corn and is handing the states the husk." In the words of the *Denver Post*, "You wouldn't consider an apple as a gift if you were allowed to eat nothing but the skin." [8]

The question quickly became one of whether the surface rights that the Hoover administration was offering to the states had much value or not, and whether they would be worth accepting. How to understand the value of grazing land was a question that had, of course, already been raised by the battle over grazing fees only a few years before, and it had clearly become a great concern for western livestock producers in this period. As we saw in chapter 3, this concern emerged in part because it was generally recognized that assessments were too high on private ranch lands at a time when ranchers were confronted with low prices for their products. And as it had during the grazing fee battle just a few years before, the problem of value proved profoundly complicated.

At the broadest level of policymaking, an apparent contradiction marked the debates about the public domain. As one prominent rancher in Colorado, Joseph Painter, articulated the problem sarcastically in a letter to Garfield, the lack of legislation for the public domain arose out of "a deeply implanted impression in the national mind that mysterious treasures lay hidden" within it. "Consequently it became a sacred duty [of the government] to jealously guard the ownership if not the grazing privileges of its grazing lands." But echoing Hoover's argument, Painter then argued that "[t]he surface or grazing rights of the public domain as we know it to day in its deteriorated condition is of comparatively little value." And noting that the area remaining had not been homesteaded, Painter asked, "If these lands as they exist at present are of no substantial value to the individual, how can they possess an intrinsic value to the state?" [9]

Painter's comments are incisive, on the one hand, because the public discussion about grazing lands had revolved to a large degree around the suspicion that ranchers wanted to make a land grab, that ranchers would gain tremendous riches if allowed to get control over public domain lands. But Painter did not get the equation quite right, for the surface rights to the land had both great *and* little value. To an individual rancher who had customarily used a certain tract, that land was essential to the overall ranch operation, even if it did not produce copious forage. But because of its low productivity, it was considered not to have a high monetary value, and ranchers and land managers widely acknowledged that, were the land transferred to the states, many ranchers would not be able to afford to buy acreage unless the price were set very low.

In fact, some even doubted whether ranchers would want to buy public domain land at all, because it would require more capital to maintain and improve the property than it would return.[10] Secretary of Agriculture Arthur Hyde was one of the few people to note publicly that no one, least of all the members of the Garfield Committee, had attempted to define what "valuable" meant when assessing public grazing lands: did it mean "monetary value or current land rental value or permanent economic value or social value"?[11] The answer, of course, was that its definition changed according to who was doing the assessment and what purposes that assessment served. Ironically, for instance, despite Hoover's statement that the lands brought no revenue to the federal government, his administration was publicly optimistic that the states would see some return if given these lands. Secretary of the Interior Wilbur argued, for instance, that certain western states might garner up to $500,000 in extra "rental and lease money" if they accepted the transfer.[12] Even Hoover implied that the states could somehow figure out how to produce revenue from them, but he was vague at best: the lands, he argued, "could to the advantage of the animal industry be made to ultimately yield some proper return to the states for school purposes and the fundamental values could be safeguarded in a fashion not possible by the Federal Government."[13]

Hoover and Wilbur were by far in the minority, however. Most westerners believed that without the subsurface rights, the lands could not produce substantial revenue for the states. Even so, the question remained whether the states should accept them for what might be called their political value, as a way to avoid federal administration. This political value was noted in the Garfield Committee's report, which displayed a skepticism about federal control that stands in stark contrast to the principles of the 1903 Public Lands Commission. The report concluded, for instance, that "as to agricultural *and grazing lands,* private ownership, except as to such areas as may be advisable or necessary for public use, should be the objective."[14] That agricultural lands should *not* be leased was a mainstay of federal land policy, but there had been no consensus in the thirty years of discussion over whether grazing lands should be privately held.[15] This was clearly a new articulation, although one not ultimately pursued by the federal government.

Perhaps even more noteworthy is the assertion in the Garfield Committee's report that it believed in the "principle" that whatever conflict involved "two or more States, but not that of the other States of the Union, all questions arising therefrom should be settled by agreement and compact so far as possible and not by Federal intervention, save an appeal to the courts where necessary." [16] This recommendation reflected Hoover's experience as the facilitator for the Colorado River Commission Compact of 1922, in which he helped forge an agreement among the western states about dividing up use of the river and created what was considered a model of interstate cooperation without federal intervention.[17] Significant, too, was the committee's belief that disagreements among western states, if not solved by compact, should go to the courts and not to federal administrators—a position that paralleled the concern by ranchers that conflicts involving public land use required the intervention of the law, not of federal administrators. Again, the committee's recommendations are striking compared to the discussions about the public domain in the Progressive era, as the report gave unprecedented authority to the *states*. That this was a remarkable departure from previous policy may be seen in the committee's restrictions on how states could dispose of these lands. While they were charged with the "rehabilitation" of the public domain lands, the states could also choose to sell them. If they did so, the committee maintained, the sales had to "be made only at public auction after previous advertising." In other words, the public domain could now be sold off to the highest bidder, overturning the homesteading principle as soundly as would federal range management.[18]

The committee recommended that the federal government should retain its authority in some areas, especially in high-profile reclamation and irrigation projects like the Boulder (later Hoover) Dam, which were sacred cows for the Hoover administration because they were of such obvious benefit to the West's economic development. "[T]he right of the United States as the proprietor of public lands to improve them by reclamation and irrigation" was "fully recognized," the Garfield Committee's report stated.[19] In contrast, it gave only a tepid account of the Forest Service's work. Acknowledging that the agency had done good work in the area of timber protection, the report also noted that "the extent . . . to which the activities of the service should be enlarged beyond areas valuable chiefly for forest cover or for reforestation raises a controversial question." [20] In fact, the committee's recommendations for the national forests were its most controversial: it proposed that a board consisting of five members be established in each state to evaluate the national forests within the state's boundaries; while the board could increase the areas of federal withdrawals, it would also be empowered to recommend "the elimination of lands from existing reservations, withdrawals, and classifications when such action is deemed proper by the board." [21] And it was this proposal that drew the greatest fire and contributed to William Greeley's decision not to sign on to the report. Indeed, especially coming from a committee concerned with the effects of arbitrary *federal* power, this recommendation struck many as sanctioning autocratic power at the state level. An editorial in *American Forests* noted that by taking power away from Congress and the president to determine national forest boundaries, the state land boards would be given "unlimited authority to alter the boundaries of public property of incalculable value and of interstate and national importance. . . . This is too much power to place in the hands of a few men. It is inconceivable that Congress will consider such unlimited delegation of its authority." [22]

While Greeley protested this specific proposal, his opposition to the report stemmed much more from his disagreement with its general position toward the Forest Service. He noted both privately to James Garfield and publicly to the press that he believed that lands only valuable for grazing should be granted to the states; but lands that had any other value, such as for watershed protection, should be added to the national forests. Not only should grazing land in the national forests remain under the Forest Service, he further argued, but the service's range management should be expanded where it would be efficient to do so. "I believe that we should deal with these public lands in national terms," Greeley said, in clear contrast to the tenor of the report, and from his point of view, the only way to do that was through the land management of the Forest Service. Greeley's opposition to parts of the report was not surprising, another member of the committee observed in a letter to Hugh Brown, the secretary of the committee. It was, in I. M. Brandjord's words, a "mongrel report," and while his own sympathies lay primarily with the majority of the committee, he also saw some virtue in the different voices captured by the report:

> As you are fully aware, it is a two headed hybrid; one head looking toward land and land improvement from the old fashioned standpoint of the individual farmer or peasant, and the other gazing with great admiration in the direction of public management, control, conservation and development.
>
> Trust that Chairman Garfield will succeed in convincing Colonel Greeley of the admirable qualities of this "mongrel critter." Hope, however, that the Colonel will not induce the Chairman to further "twistification" of this peculiar critter. If it should turn entirely in the direction of the delectable mountains where grows the manna of the Forest Service, I am ready and willing to leave its company. [23]

But if the report appeared to go in a number of directions, calling for a national plan of conservation in water reclamation, but autonomy for western states in range conservation, it did essentially capture Hoover's "associational" ideas about the role of the federal government in managing the public domain. The looseness of these ideas in terms of governmental structures was perfectly articulated in how the report framed the goals of conservation:

> [T]here is a distinction between wanton waste and that which is not voluntary and results from imperfect and inefficient methods of production. . . . The first can be remedied by invoking the police powers of Nation and State; the second, only by the education of our people under an enlightened and courageous leadership. In the latter field *the usefulness of the Federal agencies is not measurable by, nor dependent upon, nor confined to, the ownership by the United States of a relatively limited quantity of natural resources appertaining to the unreserved, unappropriated public domain.*[24]

This articulation of conservation goals fits the characterization of Hoover's policies and practices by Ellis Hawley, who argues that Hoover and his administration's leaders were not, as often depicted, "unimaginative proponents of laissez-faire," but were rather "engaged in imaginative processes of state building and bureaucratic expansion," based on cooperative alliances between the public and private sectors.[25] Given his profound faith in "associational" activity, Hoover's proposal to turn the public domain over to the states (in contrast to the Department of Agriculture's desire to put it under its own control) was in fact analogous to his earlier disputes with the USDA as secretary of commerce. During the agricultural depression of the mid 1920s, he struggled with Secretary of Agriculture Henry C. Wallace over how to provide economic relief for farmers. While Wallace urged that the government intervene in the agricultural market by establishing a federal export corporation that would buy up surplus crops and sell them abroad at prices lower than the domestic ones, Hoover sought to organize farmers in voluntary marketing cooperatives, which he hoped would create a better balance between farmers' production and the nation's consumption.[26] As Joan Hoff Wilson has noted, both secretaries hoped to solve farmers' problems in distribution and marketing. But they disagreed fundamentally over "whether federal power should be used *to force cooperation* from independent farmers . . . or *to elicit voluntary cooperation* from them in following federal guidelines."[27] Hoover rarely wavered in his belief that the federal government should not interfere with the workings of business. "No one can sit in the middle of the Federal Government," he remarked in 1927, "and watch this operation of bureaucracy . . . and have any confidence whatsoever as to its ability to buy, sell, and distribute commodities and services."[28] The Forest Service's administrative authority was, of course, combined with the government's property ownership, and Hoover was clearly skeptical that that ownership was a necessary element in regulating public grazing.

However, Hoover would not have had to stretch his philosophy of governance very far to have envisioned a system akin to that which was eventually enacted by the Taylor Grazing Act, one that gave sizable control to local livestock associations and afforded the states a degree of autonomy, and one that hired as the first director of the Grazing Service a livestock owner.[29] For many livestock owners themselves, the prospect of ceding the public lands to the states represented the worst kind of inefficiency, given that they often grazed their animals across state lines; that each state would develop different and perhaps incompatible policies; and that state grazing politics would likely be more capricious and inequitable than if the federal government took over administration. There was also already an example of associational administration of public grazing, currently being put into place in southeast Montana. In 1928, Congress passed a bill authorizing the establishment of the Mizpah-Pumpkin Creek Grazing District, an area consisting of private, state, and public-domain lands, and that thus set up a cooperative arrangement between the local livestock association and the Department of the Interior. Although critics complained that it aided only large-scale ranchers, in fact most who joined the district were smaller owners, grazing between 100 and 500 head of cattle, and while the Interior Department still held ultimate "supervisory authority," the stockmen's associations were given a great deal of responsibility for actually administering the district.[30]

This system, then, would have seemed an attractive policy choice to Herbert Hoover, and it is curious that Hoover, the consummate engineer and systematizer, should have advocated legislation devoid of any unifying conservation plan or goals and that could only produce a mishmash of land policies. And why did he not turn to local and state livestock associations in developing a cooperative land-use program that would be analogous to his work in agriculture, where, throughout the 1920s, he encouraged marketing and credit organizations to work with federal agencies? The answer, I would argue, lies in his views on federal land ownership and economic productivity. The difference between livestock marketing and credit organizations, on the one hand, and setting up a truly "national range," on the other, was that the latter would involve federal ownership of the land, and Hoover's administration had deeply ambivalent views of such ownership when it came to controlling western grazing use. The recommendations of the Garfield Committee echoed Hoover's belief that the government's role should be to educate the public about conserving the public lands, and that education and conservation did not require land ownership. This principle stood in direct contrast to the kind of statist management, arising out of Rooseveltian progressivism, practiced by the Forest Service, which Hoover wanted to avoid in the administration of the public domain. The Forest Service thus figured in the Garfield Committee's report as the bad child of the federal conservation program. Its large (albeit decentralized) bureaucracy, its own autonomy within the USDA, and the animosity that had built up between it and the forest permit holders, signaled too much state direction to Hoover. As in the early 1920s, the Forest Service was the touchstone for anti-bureaucratic sentiments and served as the example against which public land recommendations were made.

What emerges from the Hoover era, in other words, are the contradictions that had bedeviled the resolution of the public domain problem since the turn of the century. The western livestock industry, with its reliance on public lands, had always fallen somewhere in between agriculture and business in the ways that federal officials categorized the political economy. By appointing the Garfield Committee, Hoover indicated that managing the public domain was an important issue, but by advocating cession of those lands to the states, he revealed his unwillingness to see control and ownership of the public lands as the responsibility of the federal government, particularly if it brought little revenue to the government. Hoover's program for the public domain stood, then, at a kind of crossroads, allowing "those states which want[ed] the responsibility" of administering the range the chance to do so; it argued further that "the Central Government has failed to enact adequate legislation for protection of these areas, and should now allow the States to protect themselves." [31] But Hoover's attempt to redirect public land policy resulted in just one of several bills that emerged from Congress in the early 1930s, and at the same time that legislators were considering cession, Congressman Don Colton of Utah introduced a bill advocating federal range control that would be the prototype for the Taylor Grazing Act. That the Interior Department actually endorsed both the Colton bill and a bill that advocated cession suggests that even though the Garfield Committee articulated the principles of private ownership and anti-federal regulation, the Hoover administration was nonetheless casting about for a workable administrative response to the problem.[32] In other words, although Hoover's policy directives sanctioned certain states' rights principles, they should not be conflated with the western states' rights movement of the time, which deeply influenced the views of the western livestock industry.

If the Garfield Committee offered lukewarm support for the Forest Service, western states' rightists abhorred it. In the words of one of the most insistent voices, the former Wyoming congressman Charles Winter, "I know of no department within the Government and no bureau which has so consistently, persistently, and insatiably demanded and secured expansion and power as the Forest Service."[33] Winter roundly attacked any provision giving the Forest Service an opportunity to expand its authority. Other political figures from Wyoming joined in the critique, which fluctuated from the quotidian to the monumental. In one of several government hearings between 1932 and 1934, for instance, livestock industry spokesmen expressed both ends of this spectrum. Thomas Cooper, then president of the Wyoming Wool Growers Association, commented that the stockmen protested against the Forest Service, not because of grazing fees, but "on account, as I get it, of a great deal of what seems to the stockmen as petty aggravating regulations."[34] Perry Jenkins provided a much larger perspective on the relationship between the western states and the federal government. "The effect which the nationalization of the West has had upon the West has not been fully appreciated by the people who have lived east of the Mississippi River," he noted. "The most fruitful yield of expansion of departmental government has been the public lands and the open territory of the West." The number of federal offices and employees were multiplying across the West, and would only continue to increase, he argued; it was thus "in the interest of the National Government that the States be allowed and be called upon, and . . . have it made imperative . . . to take care of the lands within their borders."[35]

Both of these stockmen represented Wyoming livestock interests, which, along with Nevada ranchers, had by the early 1930s developed the most virulent states' rights strain in the West and within the livestock associations. As we shall see below, what was particularly significant about the movement was that it took a different angle on the question of cession than did Hoover and the Garfield Committee; in contrast to their emphasis on the western states' *ability* to administer the public domain, western states' rights proponents believed that cession was the only way that the western states could achieve true sovereignty. However, western states' rights never became a strong or coherent enough political movement to win the cession of the public domain. As the *Producer* noted, "Unfortunately, there is far from agreement in the West as to just what is wanted. Conditions differ so much that what is suitable for one state does not fit the situation in another." [36] In fact, the livestock associations were tremendously divided over the proposal to cede public lands to the states. This division is perhaps the more remarkable in the case of the ANLSA, which had so steadfastly sought a federal leasing or permit system between 1900 and 1920. And up until the very last months before the Taylor Act was passed, the associations remained as concerned about forest-grazing fees as they were about the fate of the public domain. After Wilbur and Hoover made their initial recommendations for cession, the *Producer* noted that the ANLSA had supported federal leasing for many years, but, in an unusual gesture, admitted that "[t]hese resolutions . . . have never been passed without dissenting votes." [37] By the 1930 ANLSA convention, the association endorsed Hoover's proposal to cede the public domain to the states, adding that the federal government should not retain the mineral rights. [38] Despite the mounting resistance to the Garfield Committee's recommendations, because of the worsening conditions of the Depression, the association echoed this resolution in 1933, but added that each state should have the option of accepting or rejecting the lands.

By the early 1930s, the *National Wool Grower* was paying greater attention to the public domain problem than the *Producer,* which was in keeping with the journal's deeper examination of issues related to federal land management. We saw in chapter 3, for instance, that the wool growers provided both a more extensive and a more penetrating critique of the Forest Service during the grazing fee controversy. Their resentment of the agency did not abate, however. In his 1932 annual address, two years before he died, Frank Hagenbarth noted: "It is difficult to review with patience the treatment which has been forced on the producer by the bureau controlling the national forests. Injustice, sophistry, inconsistency, exaggeration, browbeating and breach of contract, are perhaps mild terms that may be used in discussing this situation." [39] The focus of the association's wrath still fell on the matter of grazing fees, which it felt were too high given the increasingly depressed condition of the industry. But the association also continued to take up what it considered the excessive power of the Forest Service, particularly in relation to the Department of Agriculture. A 1932 article stated that, since the grazing fee controversy, the Forest Service "clique" had been too powerful to be opposed by a cabinet officer. It noted further that the intervention of President Hoover in that year—he directed Secretary of Agriculture Hyde to reduce the fees on national forests—had "cut the Gordian knot" whereby livestock producers had lived under "eight years of unbridled, autocratic and unsympathetic domination by a strongly entrenched government bureau."[40]

But in terms of the resolution of the public domain issue, the wool growers were as divided as the ANLSA. The 1932 report from the National Wool Growers Association's Committee on Public Lands presented three different options for the resolution of the public domain standoff: "first, private control by lease or purchase; second, public control by Federal agencies; third, voluntary combinations of both under the supervision of some Federal department." The report went on to note that the first could best be effected by giving the lands to the states (along with the subsurface rights); the second by a similar administration to the Forest Service's; and the third by local combinations like that in the Mizpah-Pumpkin Creek Grazing District. "In such instances in the future," the report maintained, "supervision over voluntary combinations should be, and remain, in the Department of the Interior."[41] The presentation of these options was also laced with states' rights rhetoric, because the report proposed that each state should be allowed to decide what kind of land control it wanted. "To contend otherwise would be to deny that our public land states were admitted into the Union on an equal footing with the original thirteen. We refuse to admit such a Constitutional heresy."[42] This final stage of the debate over the public domain thus effectively split the NWGA so fundamentally that it could not speak with a single voice at the national level. At hearings in the spring of 1932, for instance, the NWGA did not even send a representative, "as the affiliated state organizations that it represents in such matters were not in agreement as to whether the bill should be favored, or as to the points upon which it should be amended."[43]

This indecision about what legislation to pursue would finally end with the Taylor Grazing Act, but not before the political discourse around states' rights had come to shape organized ranchers' sensibilities about what constituted a just grazing policy. We must therefore dig deeper into the ideas behind the western states' rights movement during this period, because they will help to explain why the relationship between ranchers and the federal government continue to be so fundamentally embattled. The power of states' rights as a set of ideas emerged from the way it encompassed both long-standing critiques of federal land ownership and opposition to the rise of the administrative state; it thus drew its inflammatory character both from the nineteenth-century language of western states' sovereignty and from opposition to federal management and expertise.

One should begin with a cautionary note in speaking of a "states' rights *movement*" in the West at this time. First, many westerners did support federal management of western natural resources and continued to believe that the range should come under federal administration. Second, although the states' rights proposals of both the ANLSA and the NWGA coalesced into a fairly coherent program in the early 1930s, the fluidity of their thinking is striking. By the time of the Taylor Grazing Act, for instance, one could find people and local livestock associations that advocated both ceding the lands to the states and establishing federal control of the range, arguing that the latter should be merely an interim solution pending the final disposition of the public domain. It is thus perhaps more useful to think of states' rights as a movement of ideas, of certain tenets between the Hoover administration and the livestock associations; between states' rightists not associated with ranching and organized ranchers; and within the associations themselves.

That the western livestock industry began advocating that the federal government should take the public domain out of its ambit is a striking story in the history of business-government relations. As Robert Wiebe has noted, businessmen in the Progressive era wanted business removed from politics; in particular, they wanted business out of state politics.[44] Both the American National Live Stock Association and the National Wool Growers Association made this one of their early precepts as well, in contrast to their state legislators and federal representatives, who regularly voiced political support for "the bona fide settler" and resisted encouraging ranching interests. As noted earlier, officials in the Roosevelt administration were the first federal administrators to attempt an alliance with the western cattle industry, which they did at great risk to their stated support of homebuilders. The cattle industry turned to the federal government because it was the only locus of political support, and second, because, like businessmen involved in interstate commerce, cattlemen believed that "one national regulatory law served them better" than a panoply of state laws.[45] Like other businessmen, once certain regulatory functions were lodged in the federal government—in ranchers' case, the Forest Service—they lobbied extensively to create the kind of administrative rules they wanted: low fees and a high degree of security and autonomy in land-use decisions. However, such lobbying to garner more local control, which most trade associations did at the time, was certainly a very different political agenda than trying outright to remove the public domain from federal control both as a problem and a property and hand the public domain over to the states. While this turn was very significant, it was not unique, of course: states' rights arguments emerged in connection with other issues in the mid 1920s. But that states' rights came to play a role in the Taylor Grazing Act and continued to do so in other "sagebrush rebellions" in the West gives the movement particular significance on the eve of the New Deal.

But one also cannot discuss the issue of western states' rights without addressing its relationship to perceived notions of western individualism. Especially with the rise of the new western history, scholars have delighted in the apparent ironies of western self-sufficiency: westerners seem to be the hardiest of individualists—whether in terms of political opinions or voting behavior—and yet, because the federal government owns over half of the lands in the West, westerners appear more dependent on the federal government than any other regional group in the country.[46] Scholars have argued that that very dependence exacerbated western individualism, which represents a kind of exaggerated response to the daily presence of the federal government. In the battle over grazing fees, however, ranchers' access to the grazing lands in the national forests did not push them to act from a stance of dependence so much as from a stance of political empowerment. And more specifically, while westerners' political beliefs have often been expressed as grounded in self-reliance and opposition to government interference, the term "individualism" tends to smother all other analytical categories found in the political discourse of the American West—or, for that matter, any other region.

As a description of at least twentieth-century political discourse, "individualism" may, in fact, be a projection of scholars' own constructions of the West, for with regard to the public domain debates, the concept of individualism only awkwardly describes the mix of western reactions to federal activity. Significantly, even the political leaders whose language most resembles a stock individualist's—for instance, the organizers of the 1907 Public Land Convention or the Wyoming states' rightists of the late 1920s and early 1930s—rarely even used the term. This in itself does not mean that they were not concerned with individuals' freedom, but it is an indication that the debates over government activity were couched in a wealth of other categories.

Consider simply one example, the closest thing to a pure individualism that can be found in the transcript from the 1907 Public Lands Convention, in a speech by Senator Clarence Clark (R-Wyo.), a former attorney for the Union Pacific Railroad, who had long opposed leasing the public domain. Like Wyoming Congressman Frank Mondell, Clark was particularly agitated about the effect of national forests on the settling of his state, and he emphasized the roadblocks faced by individual settlers trying to enter on lands in the national forests under the Forest Homestead Act. "I do not believe it is a good policy for this republican form of Government to interfere in any way with the free exercise of my rights in my home, in my business relations or in my private affairs, as long as I keep the law," he declared, to audience applause. In contrast to homesteading on the public domain—where the settler decided for himself what land to use—in the national forests the homesteader's "judgment counts for nothing and the inspector sent to look at it is the man who tells this farmer whether or not that land is good farming land." [47]

At the same time, however, Clark clearly was not just simply concerned about the individual homesteader's freedom; he worried about his family, for one thing. Homesteading in the national forests, although technically allowed, was made difficult by the fact that a forest reserve simply could not spawn community institutions. This was one of the meanings embodied in the western complaint that the government was "locking up" lands. In Clark's words: "Is there a man in this house that would go out fifty miles from the nearest settlement and build a home if he thought he could not have neighbors? Is there a man, a good citizen of the United States, with a family to rear, that would rear that family in a place where it was impossible for him to have schools? Now the practical effect of forest reserves is to isolate man and to isolate the home." [48]

Even in the most individualist language, then, there were concerns not simply about unfettered economic or social freedom but also about the individual's relationship to other community structures. This was equally true of the states' rights discourse that emerged in the 1920s: the rights of individuals to own the public lands and the rights of states to have public lands ceded to them were intricately connected.

To explore this connection—between notions of individual property ownership and notions of state sovereignty—we must first take a glance at the historical relationship of the states to the public lands. It had long been very clear that Congress alone had the power to decide what to do with the public lands; even one of the more politically active states' rightists from Wyoming in the early 1930s acknowledged to a congressional committee that "we are assured by the Constitution, that it was within the realm of your province to dispose of the public lands." [49] But two competing principles clouded this principle about Congress's power. On the one hand, when the original states ceded their claims to western lands to the federal government, Congress assured the states that these lands "would be disposed of for the common benefit of the United States, thus making it clear that the public lands belonged to all the people." [50] However, under the Northwest Ordinance of 1787 and the U.S. Constitution, Congress also pledged that "the new States shall be admitted on the same terms with the original States." [51]

Not surprisingly, then, the history of conflicts over the public lands centered on what "common benefit" and "equal terms" actually meant, and during the nineteenth century, older eastern states often complained that they were not receiving their fair share of the public domain. As new states emerged out of the old Northwest in the early 1800s, and as Congress gave them hundreds of thousands of dollars in grants to build roads and millions of acres to build schools and other public buildings, the eastern states demanded that they receive some of the "common benefit" assured to them by their original acts of cession. As the Maryland legislature stated in a memorial to Congress in 1821, the public lands could not be given "to the use and benefit of any *particular* State or States, to the exclusion of others, without an infringement of the principles upon which cessions from States are expressly made, and a violation of the spirit of our national compact." [52] Western politicians saw the problem in a very different light, however. The governor of Illinois insisted in 1828 that the newer states had not achieved real equality with the older states, because the federal government continued to exercise control over the public lands even after the states had been admitted to the Union. And in language that remarkably foreshadowed that used by Wyoming states' rightists, a memorial from the Indiana legislature from the period argued that "[t]his State, being a sovereign, free, and independent State, has the exclusive right to the soil and eminent domain of all the unappropriated lands." [53] Only if Congress ceded the lands to the state could Indiana achieve "equal footing" with the original thirteen states.

Politicians from the eastern states continued to assert throughout the

nineteenth century that they were seeing little of the benefits of the public lands, and what with the draw of the western lands, would in fact see
their section decline in strength—both economically and politically. As
Paul Gates noted, the eastern states garnered "direct benefits" from the
public lands in only a handful of acts, primarily those that established
and supported the agricultural colleges and experiment stations between
1862 and 1887.[54] Nonetheless, the older states generally supported the
liberal land-grant policy of the federal government, whereby the new
western states ultimately received nearly 200 million acres, including
grants to western railroads.[55] By the turn of the century, eastern states
tended not to argue as much that they deserved to share the common
benefit of the public lands, but they did assert their rights to determine
public land policy when the government began turning to the idea of re-
serving western forest land. With the massive forest withdrawals under
Theodore Roosevelt, the nature of the conflict between public land
states and the federal government, while echoing that of the past, took
on new shapes as westerners targeted the amount of discretionary power
handed over to the executive branch of the government.

   These new shapes emerged, first, from the power given to the president in the Forest Reserve Act of 1891, and, second, from the reversal
that this legislation marked from "the prevailing giveaway policy" in
American public land history.[56] From the perspective of many politicians in the East, the purpose of the public lands was now to ensure a
steady supply of natural resources that would benefit the entire nation.
Such an argument was made in explicitly national terms; it was no
longer an issue of what benefits eastern *states* would receive. On the
other side, however, westerners who aligned themselves against conservation continued to assert their claims to state sovereignty and autonomy, which meant getting the federal government out of the public land
business. [57]

   While they were hardly unanimous about federal involvement in the
West, states' rights advocates at the 1907 Public Land Convention and
other conventions protesting federal land reservations did formulate a
new discourse about the public lands—to a large degree in reaction to
the forest withdrawals. This discourse combined the older western language of state sovereignty with newer fears about "departmental government," and particularly about the degree of authority vested in individual federal officials, especially the secretary of agriculture. One of the
tougher-minded and more eloquent spokesmen for this view was
Wyoming Congressman Frank Mondell, whom we met earlier as a very

vocal supporter of the "bona fide" settler. At the 1907 convention, for instance, Mondell was asked to speak on "The Government as Landlord"—a provocative title to begin with. Although noting that the government was not at the moment the landlord of the public domain, because it did not exact any charges from the people who used it, Mondell was concerned over the prospect of the range coming under federal control.[58] Such a recommendation, he argued, "proposes the most tremendous and sweeping grant of arbitrary power and authority ever proposed to be granted in time of peace to an executive officer of the Government." It would in fact make the government a landlord and ultimately grant the nation sovereignty over the western states.[59] Once such a system was in place, the entire governmental and economic foundations of the states would have to be changed:

> Our people are not inclined to look with much greater favor on Government than on private landlordism. The western states were admitted into the Union with the understanding that their public lands were, by passing into private ownership, to become taxable. If the system of permanent Government ownership and control is to be established we must fundamentally readjust our fiscal policy so as to support our commonwealths from other sources than the taxation of lands. We must change our views relative to land ownership and depend for our growth in population and wealth not upon individual land owners, but on a system of tenantry, at the will of the agent of a federal landlord.[60]

Two things are evident in Mondell's observations. First, he drew parallels between private and public land ownership, noting that most people found tenancy distasteful, no matter who owned the lands. However, it was not simply the tenancy that was abhorrent (under "private" land ownership, plenty of ranchers certainly rented out or themselves rented lands); it was its institutionalization within the federal government, its subjection to "the will of the agent of a federal landlord." Mondell even admitted that he might support a bill that would allow ranchers to lease portions of the public domain, as leasing would give ranchers possession of the land and minimize government oversight. He was adamant, however, that he would never support the kind of permit system that the Forest Service proposed to use for federal range control.[61]

Western states' rights advocates never did gain much leverage in the debates about the public lands during the Progressive era, to a large degree because those debates revolved so much around the figure of the homesteader, and states' rightists never found much support within the livestock associations. By the mid 1920s, however, states' rights ideas were emerging in those associations in the context of a renewed interest nationally in states' rights with respect to issues such as prohibition, child labor legislation, and national education reform. A 1926 *New York Times* article noted, for instance, that "State rights have come back to a speaking part on the stage of American politics after many humble years of carrying a spear in the chorus." [62] Detailing the views from six senators in different regions of the country, the article showed the number of ways in which states' rights arguments were expressed. All the senators spoke of their fears of "centralization" and the continued development of a "remote" bureaucracy. But they differed over what kinds of dangers they saw in federal growth. Senator William King of Utah worried, not surprisingly, over the "mania for uniformity. The people want everybody to be orthodox in politics, in religion, in scientific thought, in culture and in every activity of life." King noted the federal government's "crushing" powers over the states and was especially concerned over proposals to take marriage and divorce laws away from the states. Such cultural concerns formed part of 1920s states' rights arguments, as Catholic groups and politicians fought against a national education act that would have standardized education guidelines across the country. But there was even evidently an older interstate resentment about federal involvement in public works. Senator William Cabell Bruce of Maryland opposed acts that required matching monies because, after collecting revenue from all the states, "in the case of many of the States," it gave "back to the State a mere pittance of what it has collected from it, and applies the balance to public objects in other states." [63]

Certainly, at the center of these expressions of states' rights claims was a concern for the political rights of individuals under an expanding, centralized government. As one historian has argued, "[T]he focus on bureaucracy . . . suggests that in the 1920s anti-statism served as a vehicle for expressing broader concerns about the fate of the individual and local autonomy in an increasingly bureaucratized and organized society." [64] But the relationship between the individual and states' rights, at least in the West, was somewhat more intricate than this: when westerners' discussed the rights of their states, such discussion was not "actually" about the individual. Instead, the individual and the state were positioned in strikingly similar ways in their relations to the federal government. More precisely still, the individual *gave meaning* to understanding states' rights in a federal system. States' rights did not simply express fears about the bureaucratic growth of the modern state either, but were also tied to very ambiguous understandings of what it meant for the government to own landed property.

Both of these qualities of states' rights ideology can be seen in the late 1920s struggle over federal range control. Since the turn of the century, the only consistent and fairly united voices speaking for states' rights regarding public grazing lands had been the livestock associations from Wyoming. The support Wyoming showed for ceding the public lands to the states only intensified in the 1920s. Wyoming Congressman Charles Winter, a former lawyer and judge from Casper, was the movement's most insistent advocate, even after losing his congressional seat in 1928. During the Hoover and Roosevelt administrations, Winter appeared regularly at congressional hearings to argue his case, and in 1932 he published *Four Hundred Million Acres: The Public Lands and Resources,* setting out his and others' opinions on the public land problem.[65] Containing his own writing, excerpts from court decisions, statutes, speeches, and a mass of statistics, Winter's book attempted to tackle the entire western public land struggle, but it paid particular attention to policies concerning the public domain. It merits a close look, not because it was widely read—there is no evidence that it was—but because it was the most developed articulation of the states' rights notions involved in public land debates.[66] That is, the very hodgepodge quality of the book signals a kind of canvassing of states' rights opinions, and it therefore reflected currently circulating notions about the political rights of the states.[67]

Perhaps Winter's most difficult task was balancing his states' rights views with his obvious patriotic pride in the development of the American nation-state. In fact, the opening chapters of his book read as an exaltation of Manifest Destiny: "Destiny determined that we must have entire dominion from ocean to ocean; that our physical base and material resources must be broad and wide and great and rich in order to be commensurate with, and to protect and advance, the great principles of free government which we had enunciated to the world. The United States has grown to be the mightiest nation of the earth."[68]

Winter was very careful to distinguish the states' rights claims of the antebellum South from his own. "Not only was it vital to the destiny of the Republic to acquire dominion from sea to sea," he argued, "but it was of even more importance to keep the area and the nation built upon it united." Westerners believed in "a strong central government . . . in a nation builded upon the constitution," he reiterated toward the end of his book, but it was a Constitution that "reserves certain rights in the States and the people."[69]

State sovereignty lay at the heart of Winter's critique. For him this meant that the state, not the federal government, was the final source of political authority in all matters relating to land disposal—which, in a broader sense, meant matters relating to the economy. Indeed, this argument was part of the longest-running states' rights argument in the West, which maintained that the federal ownership of lands held back the economic development of the states: settlers could not take up lands and establish substantial communities, and thus the states could not gain an ample tax base. But a political principle lay behind this question, for Winter declared that the United States, as a sovereign nation could not own land on which "private" economic activity occurred.[70] The Colton bill, for instance, which advocated federal range control, would "put the Government deeper and deeper into business operations, into absentee landlordism, into Federal exactions of fees, charges, tributes, levies and Government operations."[71] By using such words as "landlordism" and "tributes," Winter was flagging what he and other states' rights advocates saw as the feudal character of the U.S. government's control of public lands in the West—feudal because the government's rule was rooted in land ownership; indeed, that government landownership was rewriting the rules of American democratic sovereignty.

But the real crux of Winter's argument, echoed by others, was that the public land states could never achieve "equal terms" with the other states in the nation so long as the federal government owned so much land in the West. Winter emphasized that "political equality" in Congress did not produce true "equity." "Lines upon a map do not constitute a State," he wrote, "even though the State be given political equality."[72] Perry Jenkins made similar arguments. "The sovereignty of our State should extend to the boundaries of the State," he remarked, "and the jurisdiction should be to the boundaries of those States."[73] Like Winter, Jenkins objected to the notion that western states would have split authority over their lands if cession did not include handing over mineral rights to the western states. Westerners "can not tolerate, and you can not tolerate the existence of a dual government in the same piece of land."[74]

On the one hand, Jenkins's and Winter's concern with state sovereignty resurrected and reconstituted an older argument that had nearly disappeared in the early twentieth century. As R. Jeffrey Lustig has noted, the notion of what formed the basis of sovereignty was shifting dramatically during this period; not surprisingly, that shift, which was consonant with Progressive faith in expertise, was dislodging sovereignty from the people of the country.[75] And it certainly allowed little room for states as competing structures of American governance. "Higher and higher the locus of sovereignty had spiraled since the fractious people had locked themselves in civil war," Daniel Rodgers has noted in his analysis of professional political science in the early twentieth century.[76] The nationalism that partially underwrote this profession put "the state's own autonomous, indivisible sovereignty at the axiomatic, unchallengeable center of their science."[77] What Winter was attempting, like other states' rightists in the West, was to draw boundaries between the nation-state and the states to make room for more than one locus of sovereignty. A nationalist on the one hand, Winter also resented the "nationalization" of the West. "These States can not live and develop half State and half National as to their land areas," Winter argued. To do so compromised a venerable tradition of state autonomy in the country.[78]

But as with past conflicts in public land policy, this question of cession indicated how tightly bound up notions of sovereignty were with property ownership. Consider Jenkins's point, for instance. One could say that given American federalism, every piece of *private* land in the United States was under the rule of "a dual government": state and federal sovereignty fell over the entire nation. State and federal sovereignty defined national territoriality, and indeed some commentators at the time argued that state sovereignty itself had nothing to do with the amount of public land that existed within a state's borders—that sovereignty emerged from the political consent of the people, and that the western states had that consent with or without the public lands.[79] Just as clearly, however, states' rights proponents like Jenkins and Winter rejected that argument, claiming that public land ownership interfered with the states' political integrity. For them, state sovereignty was founded on property. "Without ownership of the soil," Winter argued, "there is not complete and equal sovereignty."[80] By "ownership," Winter meant two things: that Wyoming should in fact own its public lands and should be allowed to determine how to dispose of them; and that those public lands should be turned over to private ownership as soon as possible so that the state could tax them. Within states' rights ideology, these two meanings were often conflated, which masked a crucial problem: states' rightists never acknowledged that cession in and of itself did not resolve the government's presence in western lands, for it simply replaced federal ownership of land with state ownership. Why did they not see this? One answer is that they were confident that state-owned lands would be either sold or leased to individuals at very modest costs, and that state ownership would thus function only as a temporary holding pattern.[81] But the other answer is that states' rightists understood the states' ownership of land as so like that of an individual's property ownership that they could not see that cession would still leave government in the land business.

This likeness between the state and the individual was articulated, first, as a matter of political independence. It had been common to hear from westerners and easterners alike that federal land ownership made states dependent on the largesse of the government. But Winter stated the situation more baldly than others. To his mind, the federal government's relationship to the states was like that of a "guardian" to a "ward," and "the consequent doling out of appropriations for various purposes for which they must beg is not compatible with the dignity of the rights of sovereign States of the Union. They are not, and ought not to be, in a class of provinces or dependencies." [82] In a revealing remark that illuminates what "dependency" meant for Winter (and for other western politicians), he noted with regard to the state of Nevada, which was and is still over 80 percent federally owned, "The West says there is something in the Constitution to prevent such emasculation of a State of this Union." [83] Although Winter did not conceive of this dependency as analogous to the relationship between Native Americans and the government, the language of the guardian and the ward certainly brought that to mind, and it was an analogy that others had made. The western states were "humiliated" by their constant request for aid, Winter added, and only by giving them the public land could they achieve the kind of autonomy necessary to be fully part of the nation.[84] The picture he presented was loaded with highly racialized social values, for without cession of the public lands, the state could never achieve the dignity of the white male property owner. Secretary of the Interior Ray Lyman Wilbur made this connection explicit when he said that "[r]esponsibility makes for real statehood just as it makes for manhood. The Western states are man grown and capable of showing it." [85]

Underlying this fascinating homology between the state and the individual man [86] is what C. B. Macpherson termed "possessive individualism": the welter of political beliefs—central to American constitutional governance—about the connections between property and legitimate government. As Macpherson describes it, possessive individualism holds that a man's essential humanity stems from his independence from "the wills of others" and that what defines this freedom is the property he holds in his own person. Society then "becomes a lot of free equal individuals related to each other as proprietors of their own capacities and of what they have acquired by their exercise." [87] For Macpherson, possessive individualism has grounded the very structures of liberal democratic societies and has served as a pervasive justificatory theory in their governments. More specifically, for our purposes, possessive individualism is a theory that undergirded much of the public land question, serving as a ubiquitous framework in which ranchers, legislators, and bureaucrats interpreted public grazing policy. But Macpherson's interpretation also specifically clarifies the rhetoric of states' rights advocates like Winter who believed that the states could not achieve their "full equality" with eastern states because they had not been allowed to take control of their own property. This construction, it should be clear by now, involved and implicitly connected market relations and political rights: by not being allowed to own "their" property, the western states could not achieve either economic or political equality with other states in the nation.

That states' rightists described the western state as an individual property owner underscores how deeply their notions of political sovereignty were rooted in landownership. This was not a new connection. As we saw in chapter 2, the Supreme Court in the Progressive period understood the government's authority over public land as founded equally on its ownership of that land and on the constitutional right of Congress to make any rules it saw fit for the land. But of course in both the states' rights discourse, and in the arguments about the supreme authority of the federal government over these lands, a very particular notion of property shaped the link between political sovereignty and property ownership. That is, it was only complete ownership that constituted full sovereignty. This understanding was a highly idealized and unitary vision of property ownership, seeing that state or federal sovereignty could only be founded on having an unencumbered title to the land.[88] However, it helps explain Perry Jenkins's fear of a "dual government on the same piece of land," for without being granted a fee simple absolute, a western state like Wyoming would find its sovereignty violated by federal interference.

Former Congressman Frank Mondell made this point in a letter he wrote to James Garfield just after Garfield had been chosen to head the

Public Land Committee. Mondell noted that western opposition to Hoover's proposal stemmed only from a desire to have full title to the lands. "This opposition to a transfer of merely the surface of lands," he wrote, "is quite natural and is easily understood by anyone who is familiar with the history of land titles in America, and the experience of land owners." Dividing the title meant the prospect of a "multitude of annoying and vexatious questions"—a point that Perry Jenkins had also made in congressional hearings on the question of cession. But beyond the potential irritations of divided ownership, transferring only the surface rights to the land meant granting "an undesirable form of land title. Under such a title, the owner is not, in the generally accepted sense of the term, the proprietor, he is little more than an owner of the right to occupy." Mondell's emphasis on the importance of land title indicated how sure he was that, were cession to occur, the states would quickly dispose of the lands to individuals, but his vision of that title also defined the kind of property ownership that states' rightists like Winter and Jenkins saw as the foundation of state sovereignty:

> Land owners quite naturally desire to own their cellars as well as the surface on which their homes stand; they want an ownership that extends at least to the bottom of the family well; they wish to know that if they desire to use some of the stone or clay on or under their land for building or other purposes, they are free to do so without being compelled to take out a lease or pay a royalty. . . . [W]hy deny the fee simple title dear to the Anglo-Saxon soul in the transfer of such lands[?] [89]

That understanding of the property owner as the owner of a freehold estate had shaped public land policy since the early nineteenth century and affected a wide variety of arenas. It is ironic, however, that the livestock associations in particular began to latch onto it as a way to understand political sovereignty, because at least the ANLSA had been a leader in trying to move legislators away from the Jeffersonian model of landownership during the Progressive era, when it argued along with the Forest Service that ranchers could use public property in conjunction with their private property to help develop the region economically and socially. Moreover, during the grazing fee controversy, they had begun to articulate their dissatisfaction with the Forest Service as a matter of not having sufficient legal rights to grazing on the national forests. The livestock associations, in other words, had been moving to a position that emphasized the *use* of public land, and securing rights to that use, rather than its alienation into private hands, as the key to both good public land policy and the accumulation of wealth in the West. To borrow from a speech made by Utah Governor George Dern, the associations had argued that it was "not necessary to own a piece of land in order to get the benefit of it," and in fact many ranchers noted that only by *not* owning too much land could they make money in the business, given how heavy the burden of owning the large acreage required for ranching was.[90]

Indeed, I would emphasize again that it would be a mistake to think that the ANLSA and the NWGA fully embraced the idea of cession; rather, the activity of the Garfield Committee and the states' rights discourse then in political circulation drew enough supporters in the associations that, on the eve of the Taylor Grazing Act, the groups were deeply divided about what policy to pursue. Like most political observers in the West, leaders in the livestock associations were skeptical about the value of the government's transferring only the surface rights to the public domain. And yet that skepticism about Hoover's policy did not mean that they rejected the baggage of states' rights. If anything, the baggage stayed behind, even after the prospect of cession was fully off the table, as a discourse about property and sovereignty persisted for years in the debates about the public lands.

It is easier, however, to see the after-effects of states' rights arguments in the public grazing debates than to understand why livestock associations were drawn to them in the first place. The shift can be explained by a conjuncture of political events, particularly Hoover's initiative in taking up the option of transferring the surface rights to the states.[91] Hoover had been an ally of the livestock associations in their battle against the Forest Service over grazing fees, and his administration and their leadership were in basic agreement over the need to curb federal regulatory expansion over public grazing lands—witness, for instance, the Garfield Committee's recommendation that the boundaries of all the national forests be reviewed. But the grazing fee conflict did more than simply ally the associations with the president's position; it also deepened the associations' critique of federal land administration. From the institution of Forest Service management in 1905 to the mid 1920s, the livestock industry leaders who criticized the agency focused their discontent on the parameters of administrative power and the "petty regulations" that defined the relationship between national forest permittees and the Forest Service. During the grazing fee conflict, however, the ANLSA and the NWGA began to understand that political relationship in much more profound terms—that it involved the power of the federal government to determine the value of public grazing land, that it in-

volved the structures of property ownership in the West, and that it involved what they considered to be significant political rights. For some
in the livestock associations, then, the grazing fee conflict coalesced such
deep-seated problems in public property ownership that they saw cession as the only solution.

But even for those leaders in the association who were skeptical
about cession, the combination of the grazing fee conflict and Hoover's
proposal provoked a profound and sustained critique of federal land
management. On the one hand, the battles over the government's right
to establish the value on its own land took the form of a highly ab-
stracted debate, revolving around questions of market trends, tax assessments, and government rate setting. These debates took place within
other political discussions about the government's power to establish
rates and fees in other areas of the political economy, but in contrast to
these arenas, federal ownership of land in the West was also experienced
by many as entirely concrete, a geographical line drawn (at times literally) in the sand. That experienced concreteness was, of course, ultimately shaped by "abstractions" such as the economic value of the public lands: what made the geographical boundary important was that
land withdrawn by the government could not acquire what was considered legitimate value through exchange in the marketplace and could
not be incorporated into the state by taxation. We should therefore be
careful in positing the public lands as the most concrete form of the
state, as westerners like Charles Winter believed. But does this mean that
federal landownership was merely analogous to other forms of governmental regulation?

The legal scholar Joseph Sax made such an argument with regard to
the controversy in the late 1970s about privatizing the public lands, and
his analysis is a useful touchstone for examining the issue of public
landownership in the early twentieth century as well. Sax argues that
both those who want to retain federal control and those who seek to sell
or cede the lands to the states "overestimate the importance—*as such*—
of ownership. . . . [A] profound controversy over the legitimacy and the
importance of public values is often obscured by excessive focus on proprietorship."[92] Sax contends that the real controversy over the public
lands lies in the struggle over "the legitimacy of collective versus individual values"—with those advocating the disposal of the public lands
believing in the latter—and that this struggle is clearly not confined to
matters of ownership. That is, the government does not have to own

land to assert collective values in its policymaking: "[O]wnership and regulation are often used as alternative means of accomplishing the same end (one of which is to control external harm). Those who advocate the sale of public lands would not be any more content if the lands were sold into private ownership and immediately subjected to a wide range of regulatory controls, than they are with continuation of public proprietorship." [93]

Sax is correct in a couple of aspects. He is right to suspect that regulation of private lands would have been seen as just as burdensome to those who advocated cession as public ownership of those lands—perhaps more so, as one can imagine that people like Charles Winter would have howled about the government's interference in private affairs. And he is right that advocates of cession or public land sales do ground their positions in what he calls "individual values," although the preceding pages should indicate that that grounding was much more complicated than a simple assertion that the individual should be left alone. Rather, a very particular notion of private property ownership shaped the states' rightists' belief that both the individual rancher and the western state could only achieve their full political rights through possession of their land.

But Sax also misses key points. The states' rights discourse of the 1920s shows that adherents objected to *both* federal ownership and federal regulation: the federal government used the two not as alternatives but in combination, and it was that combination that seemed so potentially autocratic to states' rightists. Whereas conservationists saw the public land withdrawals as a break with the past—even a modern American invention of protecting natural resources through permanent public ownership and federal administration—states' rights advocates understood the withdrawals as both a break with and a reversion to the past: those withdrawals cut the nation loose from the policy of alienating land to individuals, but they also represented an older and oppressive structure of governance whereby the state exercised its regulatory authority through landed property.[94] Believing as they did that the federal government behaved as a landowner, states' rights proponents held that the government's authority was grounded in property ownership. This was not an irrational understanding of federal land management, as the government also understood that its power in public land policy derived from its proprietorship. And it was an understanding that ranchers had grasped during the grazing fee conflict, as they argued that the Forest Service's "commercialization" policy was part of a larger attempt by the service to exert the government's control more fully as the owner of the public lands.

The influence of state's rights ideas on the heels of the grazing fee conflict would have tremendous ramifications for public grazing policy in the next decade. The terminology is not insignificant here, as the issue of states' rights revolved around connections between property and political *rights*. Already during their battles with the Forest Service, ranchers and their allies in Congress had begun to articulate a more pronounced language of rights: that Forest Service permittees should have more protected rights in their permits, and that they should be secured more legal rights against the power of the Forest Service to make decisions over their property. The states' rights movement incorporated that language into a grander political drama about the rights of states to the property within their boundaries, and the language of rights and political sovereignty would shape both the Taylor Grazing Act and the debates thereafter.

CHAPTER 5

The Taylor Grazing Act and the "Vast National Estate"

I take it no one wishes to leave this land open for homesteading, or open for other bureaus of the Government to
reach in and give it further uses—and they never were so
hungry as they are now that they think all land is being withdrawn from their reach. People never want anything so badly
as when they think it is about to disappear.

—Farrington Carpenter

At any number of levels the passing of the Taylor Grazing Act in 1934
was one of the most significant pieces of legislation for the West in the
twentieth century, but historians and other scholars and observers have
largely focused on one reason in particular that made it so important:
the act effectively closed the era of homesteading, which was a symbolic
milestone for the nation and the region. In the words of one observer,
the act "represented official admission of the exhaustion of the values
which had made the public domain a dynamic force in the building of
the country."[1] It was also a kind of climactic piece of legislation, coming after decades of congressional attempts either to dispose of or control the public domain, and part of that climax was that the land ended
up in federal administration, as part of an expanding range of governmental activity in the New Deal. But important as this conclusion is, it
misses a singular point. The public domain represented something
greater than land, and the Taylor Grazing Act something more than the
"closing" of land. The public domain was a property (of the United
States); it had become deeply attached to ranchers' property interests;

and the Taylor Grazing Act would build on these histories of property, restructure them, and give them new meaning.

To shift our attention to how understandings of property were implicated in the act helps to shed new light on the *political* assessments that have typically been made of the act, which have largely divided into two camps. Most who have written on the subject have seen the act as the moment when the power of organized ranchers crystallized into a formidable force, as they were subsequently able to establish an "informal" system of governance that administers the range according to their interests. As it was most prominently articulated by Grant McConnell in his 1966 book, *Private Power and American Democracy,* the range livestock industry "captured" the federal administration of the range with the Taylor Grazing Act, which protected neither the public interest nor the land itself.[2] On the other hand, conservative and libertarian writers and scholars have argued that the act represents the moment when the state formally "locked" up the range. After the act, the administration of the range, like that of the national forests, was bound to an everexpanding amount of red tape and bureaucratization, quashing any initiative ranchers might have to improve the public land they used and fueling officials' need for personal power.[3] That the Taylor Grazing Act and the politics it produced have created such opposing arguments is certainly indicative of the volatility involved in western public land use, and as we shall see, there is truth in both sides. But that opposition has also obscured critical historical questions. For instance, in seeing federal land management as a kind of leviathan, conservative scholars cannot answer why organized ranchers have consistently supported federal control of the rangelands. Similarly, if organized ranchers so captured federal range administration after the Taylor Grazing Act, why did they (along with several western politicians) so enthusiastically try to dismantle that administration a mere ten years later?

This chapter will, I hope, provide answers to these questions, as we come to understand the Taylor Grazing Act as a political instrument to adjudicate existing property relations and rights. Other histories have focused on how the bill actually became law, and the legislative process per se does not illuminate the underlying assumptions about what property interests were at stake. Rather, this chapter explores a range of angles on the act, beginning with the view from Washington at the time the bill was under consideration. What is striking here is the contrast between Secretary of the Interior Harold Ickes's embrace of federal administrative power and the actual provisions of the act, which solidified the connection between ranchers' property and the public lands and gave substantial control to local stock growers. This contrast had a great deal to do with competing impulses in the New Deal and also contributed to the political conflicts around the act. From Washington, we then move our sights westward to look at how organized ranchers and the new grazing officials in the Department of the Interior understood the implications of the Taylor Grazing Act on ranchers' property interests. This focus will take us a long way from Ickes's language of national planning and shows just how deeply ranchers saw the public domain as encompassing a bundle of property rights to which they had some access. Finally, the chapter concludes by turning to the Forest Service to examine how the rearrangement of property relations sparked an administrative battle in Washington indicative of the powerful attachments that public land agencies had to public property.

When we think of the Great Depression, we tend to think of a seismic and catastrophic downturn in the nation's economy, and certainly it was for many Americans. But it was the fall of prices after World War I, not the Crash, that undermined ranchers' fortunes, and most livestock producers experienced the 1920s as an era of economic troubles. Although they had seen several good years near the end of the decade, the Depression that began in 1929 only made worse the conditions that they had grown used to. For instance, when the first director of grazing, Farrington R. Carpenter, spoke to cattle and sheep producers after the Taylor Grazing Act was passed, he did not detail the hard times of just the current Depression; he routinely spoke of ranchers' inability to make the cost of production over most of the previous *fourteen years.*

This is not to deny the profound hardship that many ranchers experienced in the 1930s, although as a rule those who engaged exclusively in livestock production fared slightly better than the dry farmers of the West. Both groups were faced with the drying up of credit and a severe drought, but that drought was especially devastating for plains farmers: the Dakotas were hit the worst, but the eastern parts of Montana and Colorado were filled with dry farmers desperate for relief.[4] Many of these were homesteaders who had entered on land after the 1916 Stock-Raising Homestead Act, and their failure was taken as confirmation by many ranchers and federal land managers of the inadequacies of that act. And in the 1930s, the evidence of that failure was everywhere to be seen—in the human suffering, in the environmental crisis, and in the increasingly vast amount of tax-default lands. But ranchers were not immune to the conditions of drought, and while many were able to hang on longer with cattle than the farmers who attempted to grow wheat, they walked a very precarious line. As Carpenter noted to western ranchers in 1934, the previous three years had made "whole areas" of the West into more arid country. "Communities usually getting fifteen inches of rainfall have been getting ten; those who have been getting ten have been getting six; and those formerly getting six are getting one and a half and two." [5] By all accounts, as Carpenter himself admitted, "[a] tremendous deterioration of the land has resulted, due to the overuse we have been making of it." [6]

The combination of the drought and the worsening economy re-shaped the political landscape around the question of public grazing policy. On the one hand, these crises lent the question a greater sense of urgency, which the new head of the Interior Department, Harold Ickes, encouraged. But equally important was how these critical conditions affected the terms of the debate about ceding lands to the states, because this option for a while ran neck-and-neck with the renewed congressional impulse to put the land under federal regulation. Indeed, hearings for both plans occurred at virtually the same time in 1932; the Department of Interior at that time was waffling between the two, despite the fact that its secretary, Ray Lyman Wilbur, had originally advocated cession; and the livestock associations were also deeply split over the two options. As we saw in chapter 4, at the heart of the question about cession was whether the public domain had any *value* if divested of mineral rights. With no end in sight to the economic fallout, what recognized value there was in public grazing land was rapidly seeping out; with hundreds of thousands of acres of private pasture land going into default because of the Depression, and with no one willing or able to purchase them, the public lands indeed seemed valueless. The cession of more lands that could not be alienated did appear very much to pose a burden on western states.

Yet while Congress began shifting its attention to federal control, the debates throughout the Hoover years over the role of the western states in managing the public domain had set up a kind of touchstone for the Taylor Grazing Act. Organized ranchers who testified against the bill routinely called up the Garfield Committee's report and argued for the primacy of state sovereignty over the public lands, while proponents of federal control explicitly framed their recommendations against the states' rights position. During the first set of hearings about establishing federal control over the range, Utah Senator Don Colton, who helped sponsor the initial bill, spoke against the Garfield Committee's report and advocated the need for a federal, "unified" organization to handle the problems of the public lands across all state boundaries.[7] Also, in contrast to the committee's report, he argued that the conservation of the public domain could only be effectively handled by the federal government, as grazing crossed state lines. This was a familiar argument made by conservationists and some ranchers during the Hoover years, but as we shall see, it would quickly take on different valences with the presidency of Franklin Roosevelt, when federal land managers spoke in national terms about the need for unified administrative authority over the public lands.

But there were other, familiar strains in the public land debates that could also be heard, as the language of homebuilding returned with the eponymous sponsor of the act, Edward T. Taylor, a senior congressman from Colorado.[8] Taylor had in fact also sponsored the Stock-Raising Homestead Act of 1916, and his reversal on the issue of federal range control was emblematic of Congress's own shift toward supporting that control. For up until the 1920s, Taylor was as staunch an advocate of homesteading the public domain lands as one could find, virulently opposing any proposal for grazing control. He began to change his mind, he said, as he saw "[o]n the western slope of Colorado and nearby States . . . waste, competition, overuse, and abuse of valuable range lands and watersheds eating into the very heart of western economy." [9] But Taylor also inserted the language of Progressive-era agrarianism into the debates. He argued that the bill "does protect the little man. I represent as many little people as anybody else, and I have been representing them as long as anybody else. . . . I am not appearing here in behalf of big cattle men, big sheep men, or anything of the kind. I am trying to protect the local man who pays taxes." [10]

A new twist was then put on old themes through the politics and personality of Roosevelt's secretary of the interior, Harold Ickes, who connected the public domain question to the larger landscape of the New Deal. Ickes recommended the passage of the act both because it would solve certain economic and national crises and because it would fit the goals of New Deal planning. In letters to the chair of the House Public Lands Committee, Rene DeRouen of Louisiana, before the start of hearings on the Taylor bill in 1933, he voiced his support for the legislation on both these grounds. First, he rued the previous lack of regulation on the public domain, noting that while the "Supreme Court has held that the public lands are a grazing common for the use of the public," Congress had given the Department of the Interior "but very limited authority to control their use," resulting in a greater harm to these lands.[11] The Taylor bill "would clothe this Department with the power to regulate the use of the remaining public lands" and "would be a great step forward in the interest of true conservation."[12] But Ickes urged passage of the bill in stronger terms than the need for regulation and conservation. He also noted that the immediate passage of the bill would bring the benefits of the Emergency Conservation Work Act, passed through Congress in March, which allowed for emergency work to prevent "flood and soil erosion . . . and such other work on the public domain, National and State, and Government reservations." But Ickes refused to implement any such program unless the land were securely under his department's control; with an implicit warning, he urged Congress to pass the bill to "meet the crisis that will doubtless be reached in the fall and winter when thousands of the emergency conservation workmen will be driven from their summer camps."[13]

Ickes's framing of the public domain question, before the hearings on Taylor's bill even began, had an immediate effect. De Rouen opened the hearings by noting that grazing control was "a controversial matter," but that "the emergency seems to be such at the present moment that the Secretary of the Interior would like to have control of this entire area in order to carry out the President's program of reforestation."[14] And Ickes showed no hesitation in playing the C.C.C. card. As the first witness to testify at the hearings, Ickes noted that "[t]he passage of the bill at this time is particularly desired because it would dovetail with present national policy" with regard to setting up emergency conservation camps. But he also stated emphatically that there had as yet been no authorization for conservation work on the public domain "because of the lack of control of these lands" and again warned about the potential amassing of young, unemployed men: "When inclement weather drives out the men now working in the higher altitudes of the forests and parks, a crisis will be at hand unless they can be supplied work on the public lands, which would be possible if the public domain is brought under control as provided in this bill."[15]

Ickes's rhetoric of crisis did not work in this case, although he would revert to other testimonies of crisis later, and Taylor's first bill never made it out of committee, because it contained a provision to allow states veto power over federal grazing regulations. A residue of the Hoover years, this provision was fiercely opposed by Ickes as "unprecedented so far as I am aware in legislation affecting the public lands of the

United States, and has the effect of impairing or defeating the control of the United States over its own lands." [16] Taylor then reintroduced the bill without this section, it went through the house committee easily, and both Ickes and Henry Wallace gave it their approval. The bill that reached Roosevelt's desk allowed the president to withdraw 173 million acres of the public domain, "pending final disposal"; the secretary of the interior would then designate 80 million acres of this land as grazing districts.[17] The secretary of the interior had the power to establish regulations over range use, authorized in broad terms "to perform such work as may be necessary amply to protect and rehabilitate" grazing lands. Most important, the Taylor bill gave preference "to those within or near a [grazing] district who are landowners engaged in the livestock business, bona-fide occupants or settlers, or owners of water or water rights, as may be necessary to permit the proper use of lands," and it stated that "nothing" in the bill could "be construed in any way to diminish, restrict, or impair any right which has been heretofore or may be hereafter initiated under existing law validly affecting the public lands." [18] But two provisions in particular were in so much tension that they nearly knocked each other out. On the one hand, section 3 of the act stated that "the creation of the grazing district or the issuance of a permit . . . shall not create any right, title, interest, or estate in or to the lands." On the other hand, the act gave the user a more solid foothold on the range than the grazing regulations in the national forests, as Nevada Senator Pat McCarran put through an amendment to the effect that "no permittee complying with the rules and regulations laid down by the Secretary of the Interior shall be denied the renewal of such permit, if such denial will impair the value of the grazing unit to the permittee, when such unit is pledged as security for any bona-fide loan." [19] The struggles over Forest Service grazing fees thus bore legislative fruit for western ranchers, who had consistently argued that access to public grazing lands formed an integral part of the valuation of their property. The Taylor Grazing Act essentially solidified that connection in policy.

Finally, the act gave western livestock owners and western states a greater role in making grazing policy than they had with the Forest Service. Like the Forest Service's grazing program, the Taylor legislation called for "cooperation with local associations of stockmen," but it expanded this commitment to include state officials.[20] The governing bureaucracy was thus highly decentralized into a true mélange of public and private interests. Clearly, the bill was partly inflected by the states' rights movement during the Hoover years. Again, Pat McCarran had been able to attach an amendment providing that "all laws heretofore enacted by the respective States or any thereof, or that hereafter be enacted as regards public health or public welfare, shall at all times be in full force and effect." Before the act left the Senate conference committee, it was able at least to "neutralize" these broad state powers by adding that the act could not "be construed as limiting or restricting the power and authority of the United States."[21] For critics of the bill, however, this section was at best contradictory and at worst an abdication of federal control.

Once the bill was passed by Congress, the Department of Agriculture and the Forest Service engaged in a full-fledged campaign against it. Writing to Henry Wallace—in a letter that Wallace would then send to Roosevelt—Chief Forester Ferdinand A. Silcox recommended that the president not sign the bill, arguing that it was not "a conservation measure as originally designed." By giving up strong federal control over the range, Silcox argued, the bill would be completely ineffective in halting the "cancerous-like growth and establishment of a great interior desert."[22] And that control was lacking because the bill presented such deeply divided authority that the solicitors for the USDA and the Department of Interior disagreed sharply over whether the government would have any real power at all over the grazing districts.[23] Silcox noted that while nominally "asserting Federal control," the act in fact "abdicates Federal control over these lands in favor of the States," which would result in numerous obstacles to conservation efforts. Equally distressing for Silcox, however, was that "[t]he bill grants permanent and inalienable rights to the present users of the range, conferring upon them substantial property rights which the Secretary of the Interior could neither diminish, restrict, nor impair, irrespective of public necessity." Silcox gravely warned the president that if he signed the bill into law, he could have no assurance that a court would not interpret the act as granting stockmen private property rights in the public rangeland, which then meant that the government could take that property "for public purposes" only under eminent domain law, requiring just compensation for stockmen's property loss.[24] With such legal constraints, the federal government would simply be unable to rehabilitate and conserve the land.

Roosevelt signed the bill in spite of Silcox's concerns, arguing that the secretary of interior's authority in the act was assured.[25] But the questions of divided governmental authority, property rights, and the dispute between the Departments of Agriculture and Interior were not resolved by the bill's passage, and certainly Ickes's brash public manner kept conflict alive.

Those who are familiar with Ickes's political activity during the New Deal know that he did not shrink from a political fight and had a reputation as being a bit of a pugilist. When he testified in support of the Taylor Grazing Act he exemplified all the qualities that have been ascribed to him: he was pugnacious, irritable, and arrogant, as well as principled, sharp, and direct. Most striking is that when he spoke of the public lands, he did so in the grandest of terms, by which I mean that he saw that conserving these lands reflected the moral strengths of the nation and the sovereignty of the federal government. The last of the public domain, he said, "constitutes a vast empire, over which there is at this time no adequate supervision or regulation," and he wasted no time in attempting to shift the terms of the debate: whereas the 1920s debates about the public domain revolved around whether the land had economic value, Ickes simply asserted that it had intrinsic value—not only because it was essential to livestock operations in the West, but because it represented a national resource. These lands were "one of the valuable natural assets of the Nation"; they needed immediate protection, and it was incumbent upon the nation to "assume the obligations inherent in its ownership of this land." In other words, Ickes established then and would continue to maintain that the regulation of the public domain was unalterably a national question that required national attention and national regulation.

But as his use of the term "empire" suggests, what was constitutive of the nation was also constitutive of the state, and solving the public domain problem was part and parcel of Ickes's desire to build up administrative authority in the Department of Interior. On the one hand, that desired authority could only come with "legislative sanction"—that is, the Taylor Grazing Act. On the other hand, Ickes implied that that authority rested on a simple fact: that the government already owned the land, and in that respect "[t]he Government is asking permission from Congress to exercise the same prudence and care in maintaining and protecting this great national asset that a private individual would use with respect to his own property." Such an assertion, fixing the analogy between the government and individual property owner, stood in stark contrast to his description at the start of his testimony of the legal relation between ranchers and the public range. Although several generations of range users had used the public domain, he noted, "no prescriptive right to such use has resulted." In other words, no rancher would be allowed to claim that he or she had generated a right to a certain range because of long-term adverse use.[26] The government owned the land outright and had all the rights; ranchers were not allowed legal possession of areas of the range they had used, and they had no *right* whatsoever to using the range.[27]

This was old news, of course. We saw in chapter 1 that the courts expressly argued in the late nineteenth century that the government allowed grazing on the range merely by sufferance, meaning that it could take away the privilege whenever it so chose. Ickes's divided stance on what constituted the government's authority over the Taylor lands also had resonances in the early twentieth-century Supreme Court decisions, which noted that that authority came both from constitutional directives *and* from the government's likeness to an individual property owner. Finally, Ickes's grand language about national duty had roots, of course, in early twentieth-century conservation. There were even fascinating administrative parallels between him and Gifford Pinchot, who set up the first public grazing administration in the national forests: both aggressively sought to build up their administrative authority; both couched their arguments for federal grazing control in national terms; both were engaged in an administrative rivalry—Pinchot with the Department of the Interior and Ickes with the Department of Agriculture; and both chose established ranchers to get their management programs up and running—Pinchot chose Albert Potter, and Ickes chose Farrington Carpenter.

Although both Ickes and Pinchot represented reform movements, the political context differed. In the American National Live Stock Association, Ickes faced much stronger opposition than Pinchot had. By the early 1930s, too, ranchers were not only nationally organized but more secure in their private holdings, because of longer customary use of the range. Reviled by some organized livestock owners as a dictator, and clearly wanting to expand his administrative power, Ickes in fact gave his stamp of approval to a highly localized bureaucracy.[28] In hearings on amending the act, he boasted to the House Committee on Public Lands, "You will appreciate that I have attempted to decentralize administration and to put the original jurisdiction in the stockmen themselves." Noting that the "ultimate jurisdiction" rested with him—and with the secretary's position generally—he reiterated that the administration would follow the desires of stockmen to govern themselves. He could swallow the political power of the western ranchers, it seemed, and he would give Farrington Carpenter a fairly wide berth to work out the early administration of the act with the help of western ranchers. But he drew the line on whether the western states could have any power in determining the parameters of federal land ownership. When Congress passed amendments to the act that included giving the states more of a say in exchanging their lands for lands in the public domain, Ickes wrote a stinging memorandum to Roosevelt, who then vetoed the amendment. The exchanges would not only take away needed power from the secretary of the interior, Ickes noted; they would mean that "[t]he federal government would have no option except to dispossess itself of its own land at the behest of the coveting state." Such a path would mean that the government could not effect the fundamental purpose of the Taylor Grazing Act, which was to administer "a well-considered land-use program." [29] Regulatory authority and clear property possession were, again, fused as inseparable forces in his mind.

The livestock associations had found a strange opponent in Harold Ickes, for while he vehemently stood for the public in the public lands, and while he vigorously defended the department's administrative rule, he also let them get in on the ground floor of administering the act. And one would think that, after the Taylor Grazing Act was passed, the ANSLA would have filled the pages of its journal with reports and opinions about it; but in fact the act received only a moderate article in the *American Cattle Producer* (and buried on page 14) with very little editorial response. Certainly, during the last major struggle over public domain policy—at the time of the Stock-Raising Homestead Act of 1916—the ANLSA had devoted great energy to discussing the issue. By the early 1930s, however, the organization remained in a continued argument with the Forest Service over fees and was involved with so many governmental issues that the public domain conflict consumed only a share of its efforts. At this time, a typical report in "What the Government Is Doing," a regular feature of the *Producer,* would include such issues as tariff legislation, marketing plans, and reports on the Federal Farm Board. And needless to say, as the New Deal expanded, the reports in this section multiplied.

In some sense, by the time of the Taylor Grazing Act, the steam had simply run out of the public domain contest in the ANSLA. Other economic issues swamped the public domain legislation: by 1933, the livestock associations were busy attempting to guide their members through the intricacies of the New Deal agricultural program, much of which they thought was deficient when it came to their own industries. In their 1934 convention, the National Wool Growers Association still left the option of federal regulation open to individual states, and the lack of a clear stand by the association on the issue was evident in the *National Wool Grower*'s first article on the passing of the Taylor Grazing Act in July. Significantly, the piece barely recounted the legislative battle to pass the bill and focused, as its title read, on the "administration of the Taylor Grazing Act." The matter-of-fact report of the article suggests a kind of resignation to the actual legislation, and a concomitant realization that many of the act's administrative parameters would be determined in the months that followed its passage, as Interior Department officials met with livestock owners. In particular, the article emphasized the importance of "home rule," which wool growers did not feel they had with the administration of the national forests; aside from a few "general supervisory actions," the piece noted, the Department of Interior should allow the "details of grazing . . . [to] be handled under a system of home rule by the holders of permits." [30] On the subject of grazing fees, about which the association was admittedly very sensitive, the article displayed the greatest caution. It noted that stock growers should look closely at the "broad grant of power" given to the secretary of the interior to set fees, while commenting that even western legislators in Congress seemed relatively indifferent to this matter that had taken on such importance to public land ranchers.[31] As it turned out, the stock growers would find their best ally yet in Congress when a new grazing fee controversy exploded in the 1940s. And the NWGA was prescient in understanding that, from ranchers' point of view, the beauty of the Taylor Grazing Act would lie in the details.

If the hurdle of passing the Taylor Grazing Act had been surmounted, establishing its administration was another thing entirely. However, Ickes's selection of the director of grazing allowed for at least a relatively smooth transition. Farrington Carpenter came into his position through the back door. An attorney from the western slope of Colorado, who had also been engaged in the cattle business since 1909, Carpenter initially involved himself in federal politics on other matters during the New Deal. With the enactment of the Agricultural Adjustment Act, livestock producers were concerned that beef would not be listed as a protected commodity, and Carpenter was chosen by cattle growers on the western slope to travel to Washington and lobby on their behalf. As one of Edward Taylor's constituents, Carpenter used Taylor's office as a "headquarters," and in the course of those operations, Taylor asked

Carpenter if he would testify for the bill. Carpenter's recounting of his reaction to the request varies, but to more than one group of ranchers he later told a story that emphasized his reluctance to support Taylor's bill:

> "No," I said, "I am not for any more of these Federal bureaus over me."
> . . . He says, "Have you ever read my bill?" I said, "No. I am just against
> bureaus and am not yet completely bureau-broke," and don't want to get
> bureau-broke." "Well," he says, "read the bill." I did. It seemed reasonable.
> I was glad to go and testify before the committee. I had spent my life in this
> region, and I had to plead guilty to a total lack of ignorance of what they were
> trying to do.[32]

This reluctance was the stance that he would take before western live-stock producers, emerging from a genuine belief in "self-governance" and in the ability of ranchers to adjudicate their own local ranges. If in the above instance he stretched the truth to say he had spent his life in the West—in fact, he had grown up in Evanston, Illinois, and received his undergraduate degree from Princeton and his law degree from Harvard—he nonetheless always maintained a western vocabulary for opposing the expansion of federal activity. But it was a somewhat fluid vocabulary, for his initial testimony in front of the House Committee on Public Lands would have been almost unrecognizable to the organized ranchers with whom he met later to develop the administration of the Taylor Grazing Act. Before the committee, he identified himself as both a homesteader and a cattle rancher (neglecting to mention that he had been district attorney from 1928 to 1932!) and as one who could speak for "the small men in our section of the country" who were "very strongly in favor of the bill."[33] It was pure Taylorism—that is, *Edward* Taylorism—as Carpenter argued that the social benefits of the bill would be to support the "little fellow" as against the "big interests" who, in monopolizing the range, had also "turned [it] into a dust pan."[34]

But even in this politically crafted testimony, Carpenter articulated a real concern that he and other ranchers, large and small, had about the public range. He wanted to bring "law and order" to the public domain, and this was impossible under the Stock-Raising Homestead Act, which in large parts of the West was being used by ranchers, as Carpenter noted to the committee, "to get a little strategic control over grazing areas."[35] While Colorado ranchers like others in western states had worked for state-level herd laws to bring greater order to the range, these laws could only go so far, and the range suffered from the vacuum of federal administrative authority. Although a self-declared Republican, Carpenter was apparently convinced by this point that only federal administration could enact a fair set of procedures for the range.

Carpenter's testimony and his connection to Taylor clearly had an effect; Ickes called Carpenter back to Washington for an interview several months after the Taylor Grazing Act was passed, and he was made director of the grazing on September 12, 1934. A mere five days later, he met with the livestock owners in his old stomping ground, the western slope, to begin drawing the lines for what would become Grazing District #1.

In the symbolic scheme of things, Farrington Carpenter perfectly embodied the Taylor Grazing Act, as he occupied the ambiguous position between having a deep association with politically active ranchers and a commitment to establishing proper grazing regulations. His meetings with ranchers showed that he could, on occasion, talk the New Deal talk, especially about the precarious state of agriculture. In a December meeting in Billings, Montana, for instance, he spoke of the act as "an experimental program . . . one of cooperative effort . . . And one, do not forget that will limit production." [36] While he only mentioned the "New Deal" by name once, and almost never mentioned Harold Ickes at all, he still grasped the overall problems faced by agricultural and land planners, which he boiled down to the "market" and "land." Repeatedly, he spoke well of governmental attempts to handle the enormous problems of providing rural relief, and as many experts were arguing in the Department of Agriculture, Carpenter noted that "[o]ur problem is to get our agricultural wheels meshed in such a way we will run along in an even way with the industrial world." To make this happen, however, would require "careful planning, thinking, and readjustment." [37]

But Carpenter never identified himself as a New Deal man in any way. His skepticism about government bureaucracy sometimes leaked out, as when he said to the California ranchers: "You have all heard of the T.V.A. Project in Tennessee. Something about it kind of made me mad. I hate to think about experimenting on people, and I feel like most westerners some way or other can handle things better than these bureaus can." [38] Carpenter was not strictly against federal activity; he believed that, given the dire state of both livestock production and the range that government experimentation was necessary. But he also wanted to fuse federal activity with practices of "self-governance," or what he called a "split control system." Such a system had little precedent, he argued. "Personally," he said, "I know of only one example of where that was successful," and to his mind it was the Draft Act in World War I, which involved "the meshing of Federal, state, and county governments in a common endeavor" and employed only "449 Federal men." Repeatedly, in these meetings, he referred to "the great national effort to mobilize this country for war" as a model for creating a small federal bureaucracy rooted in the work of local committees.[39]

Carpenter had an operating philosophy of government, in other words, and it would be a mistake simply to see him as a power broker in the organization of grazing politics. What is almost shocking in retrospect, however, is how far that philosophy was from that of Harold Ickes and other official conservationists in Washington. To begin with, Carpenter never used the word "conservation" after the first meeting in Grand Junction without a sharp comment. What follows is the most stark example from his meeting in Billings, Montana:

> It make me shudder every time I say that word. There is something about the word "conservation" western people don't like. They have the idea it belongs in the East somewhere. We are going to have to develop a word meaning just as much but which sounds better to us. I do not know what it will be, but it will mean we are not going to tramp our pastures into a dustpan. We are going to fix the carrying capacity of the range and then not go on and wreck it with any amount in excess of the number determined upon.[40]

In another setting Carpenter explained that "the word 'conservation' . . . is tinctured too much with the thought of locking things up and putting the 'don't touch' sign on them," reiterating that such a connotation did "not suit the people in the West. I think we have a better word. 'Land Use.' Proper land use includes conservation."[41] While Carpenter believed that halting overgrazing and bringing the forage on the public domain into a more productive state were important goals, he rejected any association with conservationists like Ickes. Part of this stemmed from ranchers' sense that conservation increasingly meant "non-use" of public lands, which was precisely the assumption that Carpenter tried to assail in his initial meetings with range livestock users. But it also had to do with the different registers of the discourse around conservation. Ickes and top officials in the Forest Service repeatedly emphasized the *national* or *public* interests in protecting public grazing lands; only once did Carpenter even mention "the public," when he stated at the Billings meeting that there had to be a governing machinery "which will be fair to everybody, first protecting the public from the standpoint of preserving the ranges, and then from the standpoint of stockmen between stockmen."[42] Carpenter's heart and his stated goals were with the ranchers, in setting up an administration that would reduce the uncertainty of their land tenure and bring back the productivity of the range.

It would be hard to overstate how gargantuan the task was that lay before Carpenter. As E. Louise Peffer noted, "The initial phase of the Taylor Grazing Act operations revealed it to be among the most ambitious public land undertakings ever embarked upon the United States."[43] The sheer area of land involved was enormous—ultimately over 140 million acres—but even more formidable was the land pattern of the public domain. For in many areas of the West, the remaining public domain lay only in small parcels, interspersed with private or state land, or land owned by the railroads. These areas would be impossible to place in a grazing district; they were lands "so scattered around in little patches that it would nearly drive you crazy to think about working out an administrative whole."[44] Those lands that could not be placed in a district would be taken care of some other way—either sold outright, exchanged with other lands, or leased to individual ranchers, and at least some of the heated politics would focus on what Carpenter and others called the "shot-gun" lands.

But when Carpenter began meeting with western livestock producers in 1934 and 1935, his primary concern was to form grazing districts, and the transcripts of these meetings represent unique sources to understand two things: first, the organization of range politics at the moment when the administration of the Taylor Grazing Act was launched; and, second, the exchange of ideas between Carpenter and ranchers about the new property relations involved in instituting federal management of the public domain. In Carpenter's lengthy introductory speeches at each meeting, and in the question-and-answer sessions following these, we see most prominently the gulf between Carpenter's and Ickes's understandings of the act, although Carpenter like Ickes clearly believed he was acting to halt the destruction of the range and provide for the "proper use of lands." Delving into these meetings will take us a long way into grasping what Carpenter had in mind when he was actually laying the groundwork for the grazing districts, into his ideas both about range governance and about the property relations between the government and ranchers.

When Carpenter stood before cattle and sheep growers in Grand Junction in September 1934, he seemed almost at sea about how to go about making a grazing district, as well as in awe of the magnitude of

what they were about to do.[45] And what they were about to do, he stated
with a boldness he would rarely reiterate thereafter, was to create "a political subdivision." That is, the grazing district and the advisory board
of ranchers attached to it would produce a new political structure in the
West.[46] Indeed, this was exactly the point that Grant McConnell made,
who argued that these boards created an informal locus of political
power that was responsible ostensibly for public policy. But this gets us
slightly ahead of our story, as ranchers had yet to elect advisory boards
when Carpenter met with them in 1934 and 1935. Elections were held
at these meetings, however, for committees to draw up the geographical
boundaries of the proposed districts, and the lack of formality involved
in this process was quite remarkable. Carpenter's meeting with ranchers
in Boise, Idaho, showed this process both most actively at work and at
its most contentious. After a long round of questions about the particu-
lars of the Taylor Grazing Act, Carpenter tried to move quickly toward
a hasty end to the meeting, noting that many members of the audience
had a long way to travel back home, and that he had to speak with the
committee about forming the proposed grazing districts. By this point,
a list of both cattlemen and sheepmen had been suggested as members
of the committee, and Carpenter asked a question he did at every meeting: "Is there anyone here who feels that they are not properly represented, or that the committee was improperly selected?" Typically, there
was little answer, but in Boise, one man began a complaint that would
be seconded by others. "Regarding the district [near Twin Falls]," he argued, "in the way the choice was made, and the noise, and the way they
were situated, there was only about ten people who had any voice in the
situation whatever. It was steamrollered through and these men were
chosen without any systematic voice whatever from the delegates." Carpenter responded by first stating that he did not have time to "debate"
the selection process for the committees, but he also allowed the man to
propose the name of someone to serve on the committee who would represent "the small group," which the man did.

There ensued several more complaints—by a cattle rancher that the
cattle interests were not well enough represented, and by an association
of sheep and cattle growers who also believed that more "small men"
needed to be placed on the committee. At this point Carpenter's audience began erupting with the names of prospective members, until Carpenter finally declared that both the sheep and cattle sections of the committee were filled:[47]

> *Carpenter:* This is a little like steamrollering, but
> we have to get through.
> *Voice:* There would have been objections if
> time had been given—
> *Carpenter:* They were not entered at a time—
> . . . *Mr. Nicholson [in the audience]:* Under this procedure of one man sug-
> gesting somebody and your adding
> him to the committee, do you con-
> sider that a proper procedure in elect-
> ing a committee?
> *Carpenter:* It is not proper, and I do not approve
> of it, but under the circumstances I
> have to do it to get this committee.[48]

Carpenter was, as McConnell put it "a clearheaded student of political reality," and two things are evident from these exchanges.[49] First, he
was not averse to "steamrollering"; in these initial meetings especially,
he simply wanted to map out the proposed grazing districts as quickly
as possible. The committees had no more power after that, although certainly many of their members would end up on the advisory boards of
their respective grazing districts. But whether through his pragmatism,
his belief in the importance of local control, or both, he also opened up
the membership in the Boise meeting in reaction to the lively protest that
emerged just under the wire. At the same time, it is clear that his openness to expanding the membership of the committees in Idaho came only
in reaction to ranchers' protests, and representation was a matter he left
wholly to the ranchers themselves, as he did not actively encourage fair
representation in other meetings.

But the meetings could also be steeped in other kinds of politics, not
just the question of local representation. When ranchers met with Carpenter in Bakersfield, California, the discussion quickly turned to highly
politicized issues about public grazing and federal power. Two politically active stockmen—W. P. Wing, a wool grower, and Victor Christensen, a cattle rancher—began pressing Carpenter about an apparent
plan in the Forest Service to buy 500,000 acres of private land surrounded by public domain in order to set up a wildlife refuge.[50] Their
concern was not only with the Forest Service's gaining additional land,
but also with what they believed to be its shifting priorities. "The Forest Service has taken the attitude that grazing is not perfectly and entirely essential," argued Christensen, who had held official positions in
the ANSLA. "I have been informed quite recently that the income from
the recreational and hunting activities equals the income from grazing

stock on the national forests." [51] While a Forest Service official was there to answer these charges (Carpenter had a number of its grazing experts on "loan" to him), the ranchers in the audience continued to complain to Carpenter about government land policy, switching their ire from the Forest Service to the Army, which had begun using a particular grazing area for bombing practice. Finally, Wing asked whether the group could pass a resolution against any government "land-grabbing," since "[t]his is a statewide meeting, conference, or gathering of graziers." To this Carpenter responded that such a resolution "would be out of order"— that, despite the frank talk he engaged in with them, "and while I would have no objection personally, and might favor any resolutions you passed, I wouldn't feel it would be in order for us to take up grievances with other bureaus."

Wing pressed him again, and Carpenter responded that if they wanted to call a meeting after he had adjourned the present one and left the room, and then "make such resolutions as you may wish in a stockman's meeting," they could do that. And then in a kind of political sleight-of-hand, Christensen proposed that they form a state grazing committee, of the type that was evolving in other western states, to meet and pass resolutions as soon as possible to handle statewide problems involved in setting up the districts. Carpenter encouraged this avenue, and the committee was formed and allowed to meet almost immediately, while Carpenter left the room. After Carpenter reentered, Wing then read the committee's resolution, which asked California senators and representatives not to allow either the Forest Service or the Army to acquire any land until the California grazing districts had been established. The ranchers in the room also passed a resolution of thanks to Carpenter. "[W]e all feel," Christensen said, "that there is not another man who could be named by the president to take your place and carry on the duties of your office as you have carried them on." [52]

This example from the California meeting bolsters the compelling point made by McConnell, that the governing bodies involved in administering the Taylor lands overlapped considerably with the already organized stockmen's associations—a feature, too, that has been long recognized in the administration of the Agricultural Adjustment Act. As McConnell argues, "The ranchers' associations completed the organization of power [in administering the Taylor Grazing Act]. These had, indeed existed previously, but with . . . the boards possessed of semi-official governing power, public authority was for practical purposes in the hands of organized ranchers." [53] The associational strength of the livestock organizations was also evident at a conference between Carpenter, the assistant solicitor of the Interior Department, Rufus Poole, and representative ranchers, who had all come together to discuss amendments to the Taylor Grazing Act. One sheep rancher noted, for instance, that he was a member of both the Wyoming Wool Growers Association and the National Wool Growers Association and that he was "representing them rather than Wyoming." Poole interrupted him to "make it clear in the record, you are voting as representative stockmen and not as representatives of organizations." [54] That the slipperiness between private and public associational boundaries can be seen at the very start of setting up districts, before advisory boards were chosen, provides even more evidence of the "capture" of public grazing administration. In fact, Poole was absolutely clear with the stockmen present at this conference that the leading members of the Senate Committee on Public Lands and Surveys had "told me that their attitude" about amendments to the act "would be governed largely on what took place here." [55]

But I would also argue that understanding the politics of grazing as "capture" presumes that there was something to be captured in the first place; that is, that there was an ideal of purely public administration that was undermined by the interest-group politics of the ranching lobby. The history of public grazing politics up to the Taylor Grazing Act should make us skeptical of such a notion. While it is true that the Forest Service developed an administration that garnered a good deal of authority, especially in the early years, when it instituted reductions in herd size, we have also seen how much influence organized ranchers had on Forest Service policy—witness the outcome of the grazing fee debate of the mid 1920s. Moreover, as I have argued in the preceding chapters, the structuring of property as instituted by the Forest Service meant that its permits were intricately tied to ranchers' private property, and this ultimately meant that the public policy debates routinely revolved around conflicts about property valuation. Finally, the Forest Service had been relatively unsuccessful in articulating to ranchers what public interests were at stake in protecting the grazing areas of the national forests. Again and again, their arguments for establishing more political autonomy from ranchers rested on what might be called *authority by ownership*—that is, that the power to regulate came from the government's owning the land. The murky technicality that all of the United States owned these lands, and the government was merely the agent, was repeatedly elided when it came down to the question of where the government's regulatory authority resided. The same problem was evident with Harold Ickes's public articulations: while he identified a national interest in protecting the range, he also underlined the fact of ownership as the legitimating force behind the regulations of the Taylor Grazing Act.

Such an emphasis by federal land managers, I would argue, both served to narrow the debate about what public policy the government should pursue and fueled the ranchers' argument that the government was merely acting as a "landlord." By the time of the Taylor Grazing Act, the conflicts around the public lands had the cast of property disputes, and because property relations lay so much at the heart of the debates about policy, that the public interest was not somehow better protected cannot be blamed solely on the political power of organized ranchers. Of course, the government was not the only body making a property claim to the public domain, although it was legally the only one that could have. Ranchers firmly believed that their property was implicated in the act, as the public rangelands were given administrative meaning only in relationship to ranchers' private property.

That relationship was understood as one that would both help restore the land and improve the economic conditions in ranching communities throughout the West. As for the latter goal, we have seen repeatedly that ranchers and federal land managers struggled to grasp the ramifications of the low economic value of rangeland; in the early 1900s, for instance, when the Homestead Act was clearly not working in the West, those who were interested in the public land question understood that the public domain represented a kind of market failure, that it had not been alienated into privately held parcels, which then could gain value from circulation in the marketplace. One might even say that the public domain represented something worse than a market failure, because the government was essentially giving away the land in 160-acre homesteads, and still no one came up to the counter. What happened in the 1930s, however, was a true market failure; homesteaders and ranchers who had entered on 640-acre parcels could not carry the costs—that is, the lands could not produce enough to cover the taxes on them—and they could not sell the lands either, as no buyers could carry the costs, either. In his typically vivid language, Carpenter described the route these lands took: "Their title has been taken from Uncle Sam, has gone through the conduit of homesteading and the tax title, and is emerging like a blossom between the crevices as publicly owned, county land." It was, he said, the "new public domain." [56]

Carpenter's overriding interest was in a very specific construal of the act's goal to provide for the "proper use of lands," and that was to sta-bilize the relationship between ranchers' private operations—and, spe-cifically, their private lands—and the public range. By "stabilizing," Carpenter imagined several things. First, he simply wanted to put an end to the competition for the unregulated range; it had not only produced the deteriorated conditions facing ranchers, but also made the business of ranching difficult, as livestock producers could not depend on range use while the land was open for homesteading. But more important, Carpenter understood that there was little value in private ranch land without the public rangeland. "The whole object of the entire Taylor Act," he said, "is to try to help the private lands which are useless with-out range rights, and if it fails to do it, it had better be taken off the books." [57] He therefore believed that ranchers' assured access to range would secure and increase the land values in the rural West, and he wanted to tie ranchers' private lands to, as we see in the quote above, *range rights*. Speaking of when Franklin Roosevelt signed the Taylor Grazing Act, Carpenter said to Montana ranchers, "It seems to me res-urrection of land values started on that day. When range rights are tied to the land it becomes valuable. You realize the leasehold value of all this land is going to go up, and when that goes up the sale value goes up accordingly." [58]

It was a theme that he would repeat again and again with the range livestock users and one that we need to explore in more depth. Our en-tryway for such an exploration is Carpenter's discussion of the rule of "commensurability." Focusing on one rule in the administration of the Taylor Grazing Act may seem to distract us from the overall picture of grazing politics at this crucial time, and yet I would argue that it was not only central to those politics but also embodies the deep political prob-lems of public grazing. As with ranchers' use of the national forests, ranchers' use of the Taylor lands rested on certain preconditions. Ranch-ers would be evaluated according to their dependency on the range, to how long they had used the range (known as "priority"), and to whether they owned "commensurate" property; of the three, the latter took up most of Carpenter's discussion in his meetings with livestock producers. Because the notion of commensurate property was not new, since the Forest Service had also used it, ranchers largely accepted its basic tenet: that they had to provide enough forage or water to care for their animals during the months that those animals were not on their allotments. [59] And Carpenter truly saw it as the building block for the "proper use" of all lands in the West, as it represented the critical link between private and public lands, between conservation and good business, between public policy and range rights.

First, the commensurate property rule would eliminate the so-called "tramp sheepmen" who simply ranged their animals on the public domain without having a base property from which to operate. This had been seen as an increasing problem in the West, particularly as ranchers had a more difficult time carrying the costs of owning property during the Depression, and it was a practice primarily associated with the Basques. While there is still little historical information on what happened to these sheep producers, it is clear that the act was intended to shut down their businesses, and it has long been seen as successful in doing so. Carpenter had no compunction about this consequence, and he understood that he was regarded as being "anti-sheep" generally; his main concern, as he articulated it to ranchers in his meetings, was that the market for sheep did not become glutted by putting a large number of sheep ranchers out of business all at once.[60] Second, "commensurability" knitted the rural West into an "economic whole," and by that Carpenter meant that the public and private land of the rural West would *together* provide a secure foundation for the livestock industry.[61] And finally, the rule was an administrative avenue for solving the problem that had dogged those parts of the West with large amounts of public domain land: that land simply did not produce enough to be owned. As he argued repeatedly to ranchers, if these lands did not enter the market, because no one was willing to buy them, then they had to come under some control that would link them to private property. He saw federal ownership as the only fair way to do this.

While Carpenter put great stock in commensurability to stabilize the livestock industry, he also had a good grasp of how varied the conditions of it would be in the West, noting that it would be measured differently in different areas. In the northern part of the intermountain West, from Colorado on up, the Division of Grazing would evaluate it according to how much owned or leased forage land a rancher had to provide for his or her animals. But in the Southwest and Nevada, where ranchers tended to put animals on the public range year-round, the critical index of commensurability would be how much water a rancher owned or had legal access to. In Idaho, Carpenter anticipated that the problem was too much commensurability: because there was so much irrigated land in the state, and farmers and ranchers put up an enormous amount of hay, there would be many more applicants with commensurate property than the public range could handle.[62] In contrast, Nevada had "low" commensurability. Ranchers there had built their businesses almost entirely on public lands (Carpenter noted that less than 1.5 percent of the state was cultivated land), and while Carpenter was loath to give up the administration's emphasis on commensurate property for adjudicating range privileges, he also agreed that "priority rule" would have to govern who received permits in areas where ranchers had little commensurability.[63]

But in discussing the great variety of potential scenarios, Carpenter returned repeatedly to the same argument: that linking private operations with public range through the commensurability rule would raise land values and "stabilize" the "real estate foundation" of local areas.[64] What is remarkable, however, is Carpenter's language in describing this process:

> An owner with adjunctive range rights will find he has a salable piece of property with a value to it. He finds he has a setup on which he can run livestock for six months of the year and can obtain public range rights for the other six months. These range rights are as much a part of the land as the gravel in the soil. *They are sold, transferred, foreclosed, and inherited with the land and are a covenant which runs with the land.* They are part and parcel of the land.[65]

Had Harold Ickes been present when Carpenter said this, he would surely have intervened to remind his audience that they would be requesting grazing *privileges,* not grazing rights. The Forest Service, for example, always painstakingly made it clear that users of the national forest range had no legal rights to such land, and this was certainly how Ickes understood the Taylor Grazing Act.[66] We must therefore pause a moment over Carpenter's statement, not simply because his declaration of rights was technically wrong, and not only because he made similar statements at other meetings—conveying to his audience that grazing permits involved grazing rights—but also because it so folded federal land into ranchers' private property.

Why, first, was Carpenter technically wrong? Ranchers could not have a right in their permit because that would set up the expectation that they could use that public rangeland in perpetuity, with possible other powers associated with that right—for instance, the power to decide how many animals they could put on their allotments. In the Taylor Grazing Act, as in the rules on the national forests, the government as owner of the land had a keen interest in keeping such powers to itself, particularly the right to reduce herd sizes and, if necessary, deny grazing privileges altogether. But if this was the technical truth, that the property rights rested with the government as the owner of the land, the act *and* the understandings of the act reduced that bundle of rights. Carpenter's emphasis on commensurability, for instance, was reflected in the critical section of the Taylor Grazing Act that stated that the government could not deny the renewal of a permit "if such denial will impair the value of the grazing unit to the permittee, when such unit is pledged as security for any bona-fide loan." As bankers had long used Forest Service permits as a basis for loans, and would likely do so with permits on the Taylor lands, this provision sealed the economic relationship between public and private lands. Clearly, denying a permit to a rancher would "impair the value of the grazing unit," and it would therefore be very difficult for the government to do so.[67] To understand the burden this section represented to the government, we might imagine a private transaction where a landowner leasing a pasture to a rancher would not be allowed to refuse to renew that lease, because doing so would "impair" the value of the rancher's overall operations if his or her property stood security for any loans. The analogy breaks down, of course, because whereas government grazing land was not subject to competitive bidding, a private landowner might very well get a higher rental fee for a pasture than a rancher was willing to pay. At least theoretically, public rangeland could thus become much more firmly attached to individual holdings.

However, as Carpenter often pointed out, the grazing "rights" to government range were not connected to the individual; they were connected to particular land itself. And the way he understood this in the early stages of administration was utterly concrete, which is to say that the range "rights" had to be attached to some form of land tenure. The question came up, for instance, whether a rancher could simply ship in oil cake or other concentrates to feed his or her livestock over the months the animals were not on the range. In theory, such a practice would accomplish the goals of the Taylor Grazing Act, which required ranchers to take care of their animals when not using government land. But if all a livestock owner had to do was ship in feed, it would potentially create too many ranchers with commensurability. More important, from Carpenter's point of view, commensurability had to be "a product of the soil"; it had to be based on a lease and not only a contract. "If the contract gives [the potential permittee] tenure in the land," he argued, "it goes over from what we call purely personal property, for historical reasons, and becomes a leasehold and real estate recognizable by the Taylor Act." [68]

The grazing "right" to the range could only inhere in real property, in other words: to the consternation of some ranchers, it was not something that they could transfer from individual to individual, like their property rights to their own land and livestock. But the attachment of the permit to real estate meant that, as a lawyer, Carpenter could still turn to the wealth of other property relationships to describe the property interests that the Taylor Grazing Act was establishing, and it is illuminating that he spoke of the "rights" as a "covenant that runs with the land." Technically speaking, the permit gave a rancher merely a *license* to use the range, meaning that the rancher's use of the range was a privilege conferred by the government for a finite period. Grazing permits were granted for ten years and were typically renewable, but they could also be revoked. In speaking of a covenant, however, Carpenter articulated a relationship that was much more like an *easement*—that is, a right to use the public range that could pass with the title of the privately owned land. Such an articulation ran right up against the explicit statement in the act itself, that "the creation of the grazing district or the issuance of a permit pursuant to the provisions of this act shall not create any right, title, interest, or estate in or to the lands." [69]

The ambiguities of the act were therefore enormous—and the stakes of the ambiguities even greater. That the act seemed both to grant ranchers property interests in the range and to deny that it was doing so would reverberate politically to our present day.[70] That the government was both asserting its status as property owner and letting go some of its rights to that property would cause constant conflict among federal land managers. Indeed, it did so immediately.

The jurisdictional rivalry between the Department of Agriculture and the Department of Interior, which had flared up in the Progressive period and then again in the early 1920s, never fully subsided. In the hearings for the Colton and Taylor bills, for instance, the Department of Agriculture only barely countenanced having the public domain lands given to the Department of the Interior, and certain congressmen in these hearings clearly favored Forest Service control and questioned witnesses accordingly. The rivalry exploded specifically in the aftermath of the Taylor Grazing Act over two interrelated issues. In 1936, the Forest Service attempted to gain control of the public domain lands, and

throughout his presidency, Roosevelt proposed that the Department of
the Interior be renamed the "Department of Conservation" and should
therefore house the Forest Service.

Both of these moves failed. However, this political struggle left behind a remarkable 600-page Forest Service report on the public grazing
lands, entitled *The Western Range,* whose clear intent was that the public domain be under the jurisdiction of the Forest Service and the Department of Agriculture. Produced in response to a Senate resolution,
introduced by Senator George Norris of South Dakota, to collect all
available information on the country's range resources, this report was
"not a modest document."[71] In an introductory letter of transmittal,
Secretary of Agriculture Henry Wallace stated up front that "[s]ince the
administration of the range resource and its use is agriculture . . . the
grazing districts and the public domain should be transferred to the Department of Agriculture."[72] The length and bulk of this report is thus
taken up with proving these two assertions. It has been read both as the
most thorough appraisal of the range *and* as a political tool for the Forest Service. But as a political tool, it was more than simply a crass statement of the Forest Service's desire to have the property of the Interior
Department. It argued instead that the consolidation of the public
rangelands in the Agriculture Department was necessary in order to consolidate the technical and managerial functions of the federal government in overseeing those lands. "The national forests and grazing districts are not merely so much range land which the Government has to
protect and rent to the public," the Forest Service maintained, "as a
landlord holds a farm or range which he is willing to let to some qualified user."[73] Rather, the public grazing lands "are an inseparable part of
western agriculture" and therefore "are inseparable from other lands in
developing a national agricultural program."[74] While agriculture had
been a part of a national program and a part of federal growth since the
late nineteenth century, it was at the center of the New Deal, whose
architects—in *The Western Range* and elsewhere—emphasized the
need for "adjustment," particularly of farmers.[75] To develop "a sound
program," it stated, the USDA "must deal with adjustments in land
for farming, grazing, forestry, and wildlife. It will involve public land as
well as privately owned farm, forest, or range land. In the West especially, public lands, in a large measure, are the very key to the needed
adjustments."[76]

Public ownership without sound regulation was not enough to conserve the rangelands, the agency argued; nor could regulation alone do

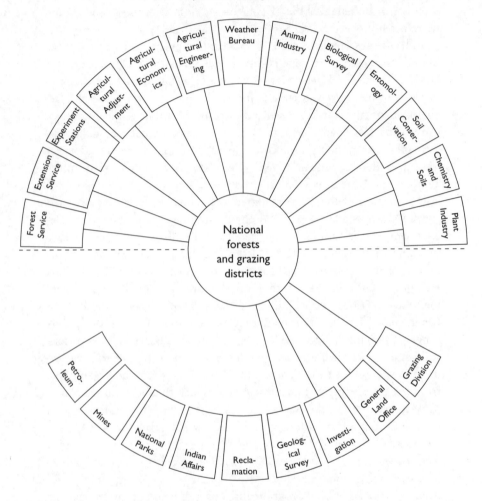

Department of Agriculture

Department of the Interior

Figure 3. The Forest Service's conception of administrative functions related to the public grazing lands. The original caption read, "Many bureaus of the Department of Agriculture are vitally and directly concerned with the biological problems confronting forest and range conservation. On the other hand, but few agencies of the Department of the Interior are so concerned." Source: U.S. Congress, Senate, *The Western Range: . . . A Report on the Western Range—A Great but Neglected Resource,* 74th Cong., 2d sess., doc. 199 (Washington, D.C.: GPO, 1936), 473.

the work of restoring the land. Only when strong federal management was combined with expansive public ownership could the public interest be truly protected. With government authority over the public domain now institutionalized, the Forest Service's arguments for gaining administration of the land revolved around its contentions that the range was a critical part of the entire agricultural program, for both the West and the nation, and that good government required that those lands be placed with the USDA. "A basic principle of good organization in government," it argued, "is the grouping of related activities into combinations that will provide the most efficient, systematic, and coordinated application of the available effort to the duties to be performed."[77] But as we saw in chapter 3, the critical administrative question was how in fact to categorize "the grouping of related activities," how to establish what the "objectives in administration" were.[78] Because the move was on to change the Department of the Interior to the Department of Conservation, the Forest Service had to argue that it was dedicated to conservation of the range—this was the essential watchword in federal grazing control—but a conservation that, from the agency's point of view, had to be carried out from an agricultural point of view.

At the broadest level, the Forest Service argued that "[t]he best division between the two departments is on the basis of organic and inorganic resources."[79] Because the grazing districts and the national forests had to deal with plants, soil, and animals, this division in and of itself logically put both soundly within the USDA (see figure 3). More specifically, the agency argued that "the functions" of the bureaus within the Department of the Interior, "although essential in the handling of the public lands, are only remotely if at all involved in the conservation and management of the resources of the soil in relation to the general agricultural problems of the Nation."[80] One should note here, again, the influence of New Deal ideals about agricultural planning: whereas the Forest Service and the USDA had always maintained that the public domain concerned matters of agriculture or "crop production," not just "land administration," the range was now a part of national agricultural *problems* that had to be solved by the government. But the Forest Service's arguments also went beyond categorizing the nature of the public domain; indeed, these arguments were completely tied to arguments about the legitimacy and integrity of the Forest Service's, and the Department of Agriculture's, authority.

First, the Forest Service maintained that the USDA was "the only con-

stituted and authorized agency of the Government to deal with the agriculturalists." [81] Secondly, that contact with the "agriculturalist" was
based on decades of experience in "specialized agricultural technique,"
and that technique was possible because all the agencies of the department "work[ed] in close cooperation with the State agricultural colleges,
agricultural experiment stations, and State extension services in range
and forestry, as well as in all other phases of agriculture." Finally, these
arguments about the legitimacy of Forest Service authority were bound
to its arguments about concentrating the public rangelands under its
agency; that is, a "concentration of jurisdiction" was necessary for "the
Federal Government to redeem its full responsibility in the restoration
and care of this much neglected resource." [82] Contradicting the bulk of
the document, the agency even argued at one point that the Taylor lands
and public domain should be transferred simply for the sake of "territorial" integrity and not kept in the Interior Department merely because
it had established a grazing administration.[83] Moreover, it clearly and
repeatedly argued that the Taylor Grazing Act had effectively given away
rights to the range that the Forest Service would never have countenanced. As Henry Wallace argued in a letter to Harold Ickes, after the
publication of The Western Range, the Department of Agriculture had
profound concerns about the extent to which the act would "permit establishment of vested or prescriptive rights under which public interests
in a vast empire legally will be subordinated to interests of a comparatively small number of livestock growers and owners of range lands." [84]

Ickes always denied that the legislation sanctioned such rights, and at
the same time he matched the desires of the Forest Service and the USDA
to "concentrate" all activities related to land conservation in one department. Ickes tirelessly supported the proposed reorganization plan,
which would have reestablished the Department of Interior as the Department of Conservation and involved a transfer of the national forests,
something Henry Wallace and the entire USDA fiercely opposed. It was
a battle that took a toll on the two secretaries themselves; as Ickes's bi-
ographer T. H. Watkins has remarked, "[T]he controversy over the
transfers would grow so virulent as to effectively poison an already
troubled relationship, with neither man giving an inch." [85] Gifford Pinchot joined in the fight, too, and although he was a former friend of
Ickes's, his pummeling of the proposed transfer suggested he still har-
bored deep animosity against the Interior Department.[86] As for Ickes, he
clearly became obsessed with effecting the transfer, at one point admitting in his diary that his "nerves were raw" when he met with Roosevelt

to discuss the proposal. Realizing that Roosevelt was now backing away from supporting it, due to substantial opposition, Ickes added that the "result was that I became emotional." [87]

Emotion was evident on both sides, of course, but the Interior Department produced nothing like *The Western Range* to support Ickes's determined belief that the forests should be transferred to a new Conservation Department, which he would lead. Instead, Ickes iterated and reiterated that proper administration would naturally put the forests in the department that dealt with the conservation of natural resources: the transfer would simply add forest management, as well as additional grazing management, to the other land-related activities located in the department, such as reclamation and mining. For Ickes, the crucial distinction was not between organic and inorganic resources, as the Agriculture Department maintained, but between the conservation of natural resources on the public lands and the problems of farming.[88] In the words of his 1936 annual report, "The work of the Department of the Interior is concerned predominately with the custodianship of a vast national estate," [89] and like Wallace and the Forest Service, Ickes believed that proper governmental custodianship involved *consolidating* federal land activity, although he believed that that consolidation should be given to his department.

Ickes's political goals were closely tied to his personal ambitions both to garner greater respect for the Interior Department, which had traditionally been viewed as a repository of corruption and fraud, and to amass greater political capital to shape Congress's policymaking. Throughout his effort to establish a Department of Conservation, for instance, Ickes was involved in the planning and construction of a new building to house the Interior Department that would embody the grand hopes he had for it. Not surprisingly, Ickes gave advice on every aspect of the building, including the choice of subjects for the murals and the rather lavishly decorated office for himself. That the building held great symbolic weight was not lost on Franklin Roosevelt when he dedicated it in the spring of 1936 by saying that he "like[d] to think of it as symbolical of the Nation's vast resources that we are sworn to protect." [90]

Yet Ickes's political ambitions did not alone drive his plans, for when he spoke of the department's "custodianship of a vast national estate," he also signaled an important shift in the relationship of the West to the federal government and to the rest of the country. That estate lay in the West, of course, where almost all of the public lands were located, and like Henry Wallace, Ickes articulated that these public lands now con-

stituted a permanent national property.[91] Historically, the public domain had always been land for the nation, as it was distributed to homesteaders and whoever else could get their hands on it. But its "national-
ness" then was connected to its future privatization. With the Taylor
Grazing Act, however, the public domain was no longer free for private
property ownership, or land held in escrow for potential private property owners. It was now subject to federal management, like the national
forests. The act closed the book on homesteading, just as it also completed the picture of government land withdrawals in the West; the public domain and the national forests together comprised a very substantial property removed from the market. And that act of taking the land
off the market involved a striking shift in how the Department of the Interior saw the land. One indication of this can be found in a story that
Farrington Carpenter loved to tell, which recounts his first visit to the
General Land Office after having been made the director of grazing. He
asked for a map of the public domain, and the official responded that the
office had no so such thing.

> I said, "You have been running [things] here for over 100 years and don't
> know where your land is?"
> "How could we?" he said. "We have 17 land offices scattered throughout
> the West and the status of the land is in township plats. During every 24
> hours some fellow is going in there and filing on a homestead, taking timber
> and stone entries, filing on desert entries, Carey land withdrawals, the Indi-
> ans get in on it, the Forest Service gets it. It is kaleidoscopic. It is changing all
> the time. We don't know where the land is. . . ."
> I said, "Well , how do you expect me to set up a district if I don't know
> where it is?"[92]

This apocryphal story can serve up different conclusions. For Carpenter, it proved the incompetence of government bureaucrats and the
necessity of ranchers' involvement in the administration of public grazing lands: he clearly relished the punch line of the story, which was that
public land ranchers had no trouble identifying what land was owned
by the government and themselves drew the boundaries of what would
become the Taylor grazing districts. But while Carpenter's conclusion
pivots on governmental ineptitude, his account also underlines how
porous the boundaries between public and private land had been under
the government's policy of land disposal. And Carpenter was right to
point out that, without clear property boundaries—what was public,
what was private—it was impossible to create a legitimate official graz-

ing administration. The government could only begin to regulate when its property lines were defined.

However, the administrative rivalry during the 1930s indicates that, while Ickes and Wallace viewed the public lands as national property, the institutional identities of their respective departments were themselves tied up with the public lands. That is, they did not see the public lands as simply so much land that the United States owned, but also as land that inevitably fell into certain institutional domains. The two agencies were therefore not simply fighting for control over an abstract regulatory apparatus; they were fighting for property. This is not to say that the departments were merely proprietary in their goals. Ickes and Wallace both genuinely believed that these lands had to be protected for the sake of the nation, and each man thought his department could do that better than the other's. But each also understood that his department would be fundamentally diminished if its authority over the land in question were abrogated (i.e., in the case of the Department of Agriculture, if the forests were transferred to Ickes's domain, and in the case of the Department of the Interior, if the grazing districts were transferred to the USDA), and, conversely, that the acquisition of the other department's lands would add to the institutional stature of his own administration.

Real property was thus at the center of the two departments' desires to consolidate their administrative control, just as it had been at the center of states' rightists desire to consolidate western states' political authority. And in fighting for their department's share of national property, Wallace and Ickes engaged in an unseemly conflict. But if the two men appear like adjacent landowners squabbling over their property lines, their dispute also suggests that control over property formed an integral part of their understanding of administrative strength. That is, the act of administering the public lands involved issues of control and power that inhered in property ownership, and it is no wonder, then, that both public grazing agencies had deeply proprietary attitudes about the lands they managed—and desired to manage.[93] This fusion between the powers of regulation and the powers of ownership was well captured by Gifford Pinchot, as quoted in chapter 2, in his description of what happened when the Forest Bureau was given administrative control over the national forests: "Before the transfer, we were limited to peaceful penetration. . . . After the transfer the situation was radically changed. While we could still saying nothing but 'Please' to private forest owners, on the

national Forest Reserves we could say, and we did say, 'Do this,' and
'Don't do that.' " [94] It is a description strikingly close to popular understandings of property, which privilege the powers of absolute ownership
in which all the rights are consolidated in the property owner's hands.
But such an understanding ignores the multitude of forms property can
take. And as public land officials argued over which agency would have
the public grazing lands, public land ranchers and their political allies
were again shifting the discourse in a different direction—away from
what the property as a whole meant politically to the specific rights they
believed they had won from the Taylor Grazing Act.

CHAPTER 6

Property Rights
and Political Meaning

The landlord and tenant relationship between the Government and the ranchmen is a matter of grave concern to the inhabitants of this region where range livestock is the dominant agricultural industry. . . . The Federal Agencies now engaged in administering grazing are, like all government bureaus, composed in the main of reasonable and considerate persons, but history has taught no truer lesson than that the governed should not have to rely entirely upon the good graces of governmental officials.

—The Stockmen's Grazing Committee

In October 1935, a little over a year after he hired Farrington Carpenter to head up the Grazing Division, Harold Ickes sent him an eleven-page letter of stinging criticism. Ickes threw no punches. "I have been disturbed about the administration of the grazing program," he wrote, before launching into his charges. The first of these was Carpenter's apparent unwillingness to build a sufficient administrative organization. In Ickes's opinion, Carpenter never fully used the agencies within the Department of the Interior that could have helped him set up the program—indeed, Ickes complained, "[y]ou have never accepted this principle of organization"—which meant that "instead of setting up an adequate organization of your own you have relied upon a skeleton staff, plus the advisory committees, for such administrative work as has been accomplished." [1] The result was that "after almost fourteen months the grazing program has not only never been completely organized but you have not developed sufficient personnel even to protect the

Government's interests let alone develop an adequate range conservation program."

Carpenter's seeming reluctance to build an administration was, in
Ickes's view, matched only by his inability or unwillingness to engage
in truly administrative work. The policies articulated by the Grazing Division seemed subject to constant change, Ickes noted, and "[t]hese
changes have frequently been made without consulting other responsible officials in the Department, including myself, and ill-considered an-
nouncements have been made by you personally in public meetings."
Carpenter also had a tendency to proclaim certain decisions that he later
was forced to retract, and his overall lack of consistency was bringing
"our administration into ill-repute to the extent that our good faith has
been seriously impugned." More important, Ickes observed, Carpenter
refused to sit still in Washington and do his job:

> At the beginning of your administration I had no objection to your appear-
> ance before grazing bodies and groups that you called together for the pur-
> pose of explaining the grazing program in an effort to secure their support.
> But after fourteen months of these meetings arranged by you in one series af-
> ter another I have come to the conclusion that you have never progressed be-
> yond the promotional stage, not realizing, as others have done, that your
> message has lost its tang by repetition and your promises their virtue by non-
> fulfillment.

From these general charges Ickes then presented a series of specific complaints—examples of insubordination, indiscretion, and chronic misun-
derstandings. "I am not presenting this letter to you by way of formal
charges against your record," he concluded, "but I believe in fairness to
you I should state in writing some of the faults that have been found
with your administration. . . . You may not wish this reflection against
your record to go unanswered."[2]

Indeed, Carpenter did not, and he wrote a 42-page reply. Things only
went downhill from there. Ickes and Carpenter had never liked each
other; upon first meeting Carpenter, Ickes thought he "look[ed] like
a typical cow man," despite his Harvard law degree, and Carpenter
thought Ickes was mostly intent on self-aggrandizement.[3] But their animosity was rooted in more than personal dislike; from the moment that
Carpenter stepped in as director of the Grazing Division, it was clear
that their philosophies of governance were very different. And immediately after the elections of 1938, Ickes asked for Carpenter's resignation,
which he received only after an almost parodic song and dance between

the two of them, because Carpenter refused to resign without Ickes's writing a letter "of commendation on both my work and character."[4]

Carpenter did not publicly attack Ickes after his resignation, but he did not retire from the stage of grazing politics either. Instead, like other politically organized stock growers in the West, he ratcheted up his criticism of the federal government throughout the end of the 1930s and into the 1940s.

Carpenter's increasingly anti-federal stance was indicative of much larger changes in grazing politics, which culminated in the dismantling of the Grazing Service in 1946. Although the agency would be reconstituted as part of the Bureau of Land Management, the battles surrounding its dissolution showed the national livestock associations turning more and more to the right—so much so that, even after the Bureau of Land Management was formed, the leadership in the associations began actively lobbying to sell the public domain off to individual ranchers. This call did not go unnoticed by the public, and in the backlash against ranchers' apparent "land grab" the seeds of modern environmental politics were sown. Of course, the Forest Service had long pointed out the dangers of overgrazing, and in the 1930s, organized hunters had joined in condemning public land ranchers for their political influence in shaping public grazing policy in the national forests. But in the late 1940s, the criticisms came from many directions—from foresters and hunters, as before, but also from civic groups and wilderness advocates, and perhaps most famously, from the writer Bernard DeVoto, who used his high-profile column in *Harper's* to excoriate western stockmen. In addition to the wider range of critical voices, an important change in the tenor of the criticism could also be heard. Whereas previous battles had found land managers and conservationists speaking of the government's duty to protect the public interest, and whereas the most prominent land officials in Washington often identified the public grazing lands as belonging to the government, DeVoto got across more successfully than anyone had done before that these lands were public property and belonged to all the American people. Although the conflict would die down in the early 1950s, the foundation had clearly been laid for a polarized politics around public grazing between organized ranchers and the various groups and leaders in the conservation movement, which would produce the profound controversies of the 1960s and 1970s.

Other histories of the public lands have told of what happened in the 1940s; it is a compelling story, because tempers flared white-hot, especially among ranchers and their political allies, for such a long time. The government hearings devoted to the public grazing controversies ran virtually continuously from 1941 to 1948, filling thousands upon thousands of pages and involving the testimonies of hundreds of people, prominent and otherwise. What sustained industry leaders in their anger against the federal government? What lay at the heart of their criticisms of federal control of the range? Historians and other scholars who have examined this period have largely left these questions unanswered, focusing instead on the *effects* of stock growers' political power. It is certainly true that groups such as the American National Live Stock Association and the National Wool Growers Association, and politicians such as Senator Pat McCarran (D-Nev.) and Congressman Frank Barrett (R-Wyo.), appeared at times to be bullying those who opposed them. But we still have little understanding of what went into the conflagrations of the 1940s—what, in other words, was exactly at stake for both the government and organized ranchers. It is difficult not to concede McCarrran in particular a great deal of influence in the grazing politics of the 1940s, as has typically been done in histories of this episode. E. Louise Peffer writes, for instance, that "Senator McCarran initiated what was to become the lengthiest, most concerted, and, in some respects, the most successful attempt made in the twentieth century by one person to force a reinterpretation of land policy more in accordance with the wishes of the using interests."[5] Such hyperbole may accord with McCarrran's high visibility during the conflict, but I would argue that this view ignores the degree to which the Taylor Grazing Act forced a renegotiation both of the balance of political power between the government and organized ranchers and of the meanings that the two sides had formed of the public grazing property. While McCarran did much to fan the flames, in other words, he was not alone responsible for the contentiousness of the 1940s dispute.

On the one hand, ranchers were very much on the defensive. In the early 1940s, the House Appropriations Committee demanded a fee increase from the Grazing Service, sparking the first and most momentous political battle of the decade, which was remarkably similar to the grazing fee controversy in the 1920s. Moreover, on the heels of this conflict, just after the end of World War II, the Forest Service called for herd reductions in the national forests. Thus, very specific issues—what appeared as threats to the industry from ranchers' point of view—set the debates in motion. On the other hand, the political landscape at large contributed to shaping the battles; the late 1930s and 1940s saw a growing skepticism about the activist federal government, particularly within the business community, which allowed anti-federal sentiment to flourish within the arena of public land decision making. But equally important was the effect of the Taylor Grazing Act itself: by institutionalizing a property regime parallel to the market, the act and its administration made ranchers and federal land managers see the public domain differently than they had before. Politically, legally, economically—in every way, the public domain now meant something distinctly different. After the passage of the act, the public domain land was so structurally attached to ranchers' private properties that ranchers' political goals shifted sharply to fighting for more recognition of their property rights. It was a goal that was presumably antithetical to the spirit of the Taylor Grazing Act, at the same time that it was given shape by the act. How that irony came about can be traced back to the tensions written into the act and the competing interpretations of its early administration.

Ever the lawyer, Farrington Carpenter constantly sought legal advice on the Taylor Grazing Act from the lawyers in both the Interior Department and other departments. After receiving the critical letter from Ickes, he sought advice for himself and was counseled to draft a response. In his lengthy reply to his superior, Carpenter addressed each of Ickes's charges, noting that he had "been so engrossed in getting grazing districts organized" that he "may have neglected what is considered in Governmental activities almost as important as accomplishing one's mission, that is, keeping the Department fully advised at all times as to details of the development of policies and practices." Already in such a comment, the distance between Carpenter and Ickes—between Carpenter and bureaucratic culture—is apparent. Although it suggests an admission of guilt, Carpenter also blamed the department itself, arguing that outside of the Solicitor's Office in the General Land Office, "there was no one on your present staff with a complete understanding of the program and work," and his brief visits to Washington thus included little conferring with either Ickes or the officials close to him. But Carpenter's response also indicates how wide the gulf was between his and Ickes's understandings of the act. He was explicit, for instance, that he sought to create a grazing program "without the building up of a large new Federal bureau," and he emphasized further that "the success of the program depended," not just on the help of bureaus within the Department of the Interior, but also "upon the cooperation of the stockmen affected. That was why I conditioned my acceptance of the position of Director of Grazing upon the right to develop local autonomy as an integral part of the proposed administrative organization." Moreover, that cooperation was so necessary because the Department requested such a small appropriation in its first year. From Carpenter's perspective, of course, the small budget was a good thing, "and this opportunity to demonstrate that a proper balance between local control and Federal supervision was possible, and that it could produce efficiency of conservation with unprecedented economy, became at once the most attractive and challenging feature of the program." [6]

Carpenter ably dismissed the charge that he was engaging in purely promotional work, as Ickes had claimed, noting that after an initial period of pitching the program, his sojourns in the West had involved the administrative task of setting up grazing districts. Of all of Ickes's charges, in fact, this was the most unfair, just as it was also the most sweeping: Carpenter *had* established the ligaments of a grazing administration, although because the conditions of ranching were different in almost every area, he was faced with a mind-boggling job of establishing regulations. And because he relied so much on stockmen's advisory committees for figuring out these rules, his trips to the West may have looked very much like "promotional" ventures from Ickes's perspective. But Carpenter also tried to defend his program against Ickes's attack that it encouraged only big livestock producers:

> I appreciate the backing you have given me against several attacks on minor aspects of the policies of the Division and I have been impressed by your repeated warning "to look out for the little man." Every item of the policy I have pursued has been under the belief that I was forwarding a plan of which you approved, and I still firmly believe that the *only* way to protect the little man is to give him an *opportunity* to protect himself. . . . The result is the most democratic organization of range livestockmen this country has ever seen and the most extensive. This is not in my opinion a Frankenstein but is only a demonstration of the manner in which local self-government *can* be integrated in a sensible way with a Federal bureau.[7]

The question of whether the administration of the Taylor Grazing Act was protecting the "little man" would ultimately be the wedge that drove Carpenter out. In the spring of 1938, just six months before Carpenter's forced resignation, Ickes sent a memo to the director of investigations within the Interior Department and asked that a "complete investigation" of the Grazing Division be accomplished "with a view to determining. . . . [w]hether a fair deal is being given the small stockman." [8] Ickes's doubts about Carpenter's administrative competence and fears that he was selling out the grazing program to the large western ranchers and embarrassing the department were certainly enough to get Carpenter fired. But Ickes also thought the cowman's politicking was dangerous to the department. In the spring of 1937, for instance, Ickes lambasted Carpenter for a letter of support he was apparently planning to send to western members of Congress whose state legislatures had passed laws that allowed money from the grazing program to go directly to the advisory boards instead of to the states' treasuries, as originally envisioned by the Taylor Grazing Act. "I cannot understand how anyone would think of sending out such a letter as this without referring it to me personally," Ickes complained. *"Here again is a move on your part which might have the effect of dispossessing the Department of the Interior and the United States Government so far as the public lands are concerned."* Whether Ickes imagined that dispossession as real or symbolic is difficult to discern. Although the department in no way approved of such state legislation, he noted, "it would be quite a different thing if the States decided to forego their share of the fees and leave [administration of the Taylor Grazing Act] to the Department of the Interior." [9] In other words, the fees represented the government's ownership of the land, and the federal government should therefore be in charge of deciding how the money was to be spent. To allow the advisory boards to do so would divest the government of its authority as legitimate owner of the lands.

Whatever the specific shape of Ickes's concerns, the question that remains is whether Carpenter effectively "dispossessed" the government of its land. In the most literal sense, of course, he did not. The Bureau of Land Management continues to manage the Taylor lands and remains the target of precisely the same kind of criticism from ranchers that it was subjected to in the 1940s, and that the Forest Service has endured since its creation—that the government is a heavy-handed landlord, subjecting public land ranchers to reams of needless red tape and inhibiting their business. It is significant that Carpenter also remained a supporter of both the Bureau of Land Management and the principle of government ownership of the public lands. As we saw in chapter 5, he believed that most of these lands were not productive enough to cover the taxes on them. Moreover, he maintained later that the governance structure he established, relying so heavily on advisory committees, was "a democratic way of administering lands which have a joint federal and local interest" and should be followed "in reorganizing the administrative agencies governing those immense empires of federal lands which we call the national forests." [10] In other words, Carpenter did not object to federal ownership per se, although he was wary of its expansion over the lands of the West; he objected to the federal management of public lands that did not weave the actual users of them into the structures of administration and adjudication.

However, although common wisdom holds that possession is nine-tenths of the law, it was a slippery category when it came to ranchers' use of the public lands. Ickes's concern that the government was being "dispossessed" of the public domain was not far off the mark. Carpenter saw the government's land ownership as a relatively limited "bundle of rights." The government had the power to charge "reasonable" fees, to dispossess ranchers who were deliberately violating department rules, and to support or oppose the recommendations of local and state advisory committees. In Carpenter's view, however, the Taylor Grazing Act also not only gave livestock producers substantial power to shape the regulations governing use of the land but attached range "rights" to ranchers' private property. Granted, if pressed, Carpenter likely would have acknowledged that ranchers did not have a right to use the public rangelands, but in his meetings with western stock growers he never clarified the distinction between rights and privileges and indeed did much to give the impression that their permits were, for all intents and purposes, irrevocable.

That lack of clarity became evident in other areas. In 1938, for instance, the U.S. Court of Appeals acknowledged "[m]ore than a color of legal value of Taylor Grazing licenses." In the case of *Red Canyon Sheep Co. v. Ickes,* the court walked a delicate line. Although it did not go so far as to grant users a vested right in their permits, it did state that ranchers who had used the public rangelands, who had acquired a pre-ferred status to use the Taylor lands as against other applicants, and whose businesses now relied on those lands had established an expecta-tion of continued use that could be protected by the court. What that ex-pectation was in precise terms flummoxed the court: "We recognize that the rights under the Taylor Grazing Act do not fall within the conven-tional category of vested rights in property. Yet, whether they be called rights, privileges, or by whatever name, while they exist they are some-thing of real value to the possessors and something which have their source in an enactment of Congress." [11] But even the court's grasping for the correct term did not block it from slipping into the language of rights and explaining in its decision that the Taylor Grazing Act was meant "to define [stock growers'] grazing rights and to protect those rights by regulation against interference." [12] Such slippage, I would emphasize, was not simply a random mistake: it was emblematic of the murky legal nature of ranchers' use of the range and of the legal parameters of their grazing licenses or permits. Indeed, one may rightly be astonished at both articulations in the same opinion—in the first case, that the court was so lackadaisical about determining precisely what interests were involved, and, in the second, that despite its uncertainty, it went ahead and called those interests "rights." [13]

If the Taylor Grazing Act and its early administration created confusion about the extent of ranchers' rights, it was also never clear about the administrative powers granted to the Department of the Interior. On the day that Carpenter became director of grazing, for instance, he wrote Nathan Margold, the solicitor for the Interior Department, to ask whether he had the authority to issue revocable, one-year grazing licenses, but without a fee, for the Taylor lands. The reason for doing so was fairly obvious: there was simply no way that the department could get an administration of those lands up and running until lengthy work had been done, and it would therefore be unwise to issue ten-year permits, as stipulated under the Taylor Act. Carpenter's primary concern was that the act made even temporary licenses difficult to revoke, because McCarran's amendment, under section 3, stated that permits could not be denied if that denial would impair the value of a permittees' property, if that property "were pledged for security for any bona fide loan." This requirement in and of itself bothered Carpenter, because it would "in a practical way defeat many of the benefits which the Act meant to confer to the permittees on grazing districts." But it also suggested to him that perhaps even "a one-year permit . . . would become as irrevocable and ultimately as unjust to the other users of the range as a ten year permit." [14] Margold's response is surprising in light not only of Carpenter's concerns but also of how scholars and observers have judged the act—namely, that it conferred very weak powers on the secretary of the interior. In fact, Margold replied, "The general regulatory powers given to the Secretary of the Interior under the Taylor Act are much broader than those given the Secretary of Agriculture under the National Forests acts, and they are for the express purpose of regulating grazing. The Secretary of the Interior can *a fortiori* regulate grazing under [section 2] by any system he deems advisable." The problem, however, was to "reconcile" section 2—which set out what the secretary was empowered to do—with section 3, which included the McCarran amendment and laid out the terms of establishing a permit system. Margold believed that the two could be reconciled and suggested that the department was on safe legal ground in issuing temporary licenses if this made possible the administration of the statute.[15]

Margold's optimism was both well and ill founded, for a group of Nevada ranchers contested the secretary's authority to issue temporary licenses when the department decided to do so again in 1936 *and* charge fees. While the lower courts ruled against the department, the Supreme Court did, in fact, support Margold's presumption that the Taylor Grazing Act conferred "broad powers" on the secretary and that, since Congress had known about the licenses and had not seen fit to contest them, their issuance was legal under the statute.[16] But that decision did not resolve the dilemma that, although the act did give the secretary of the interior expansive regulatory authority to establish a public grazing administration, it also very much constrained that authority—by reason of the McCarran amendment in particular—in the way it connected property requirements to the administration of the act. Since the act explicitly stated that access to the public domain was linked to ranchers' owning "dependent, base properties," it was fundamentally pulled in two directions—between articulating broad regulatory powers and affirming a structure of private property relations—even before Farrington Carpenter gave advisory committees a powerful role in shaping the administration. This split inherent *in the act itself* was the launchpad for the politics of public land grazing in the 1940s; that is, while McCarran and other western politicians encouraged the conflict, the act contained profound contradictions that the subsequent battles merely brought to light.

Although historians of this subject have generally thought the controversies of the 1940s were sparked by the question of grazing fees, which first emerged in 1941, stock growers' dissatisfaction with the federal government had, in fact, been brewing since 1939. For a start, the ANLSA and the NWGA expressed trepidation about Carpenter's "resignation," knowing that it was unlikely that he would be replaced by someone as close to their views as he was.[17] In that they were right, for the directors who immediately followed were much more attached to the department's point of view than the more freewheeling Carpenter had been. But what they lost in Carpenter's advocacy was made up for when Senator McCarran reappeared in the political limelight on public grazing issues. Although he was a Democrat who entered Congress the same year Roosevelt assumed the presidency, as Peffer has noted, he was never what one might call a New Deal Democrat. Although he was not averse to calling on the government when he saw fit, McCarran opposed expanding the federal bureaucracy,[18] and as the most visible figure representing the stock growers' associations, he had already begun attacking the grazing program in the late 1930s, focusing on the two issues that had split the coherence of the Taylor Grazing Act—the extent of federal administrative authority and the status of ranchers' property rights to use the federal ranges. In February 1939, for instance, McCarran gave a long and stirring speech to the American National Live Stock Association on problems ranging from the importation of livestock to proposed national animal theft legislation. But he saved his strongest rhetoric for the subject of public grazing. "The right of commons, as that incorporeal hereditament was known," he noted, "has by recent legislation been curtailed if not entirely eliminated from human affairs." McCarran did not mention the legislation by name, which was likely less important to him than the message he was sending to organized ranchers: by using the phrase "incorporeal hereditament," which dated back to medieval law and by this time was a term mostly associated with easements, McCarran gave the impression that the western stock growers had a longstanding right to use the public lands—an impression he would give again and again.[19] And while he criticized the Forest Service, he was more intent on discussing the Taylor Grazing Act, remarking that with the act, "high percentages of the territory comprising that of the several grazing states came under the absolute sovereignty of the federal government." McCarran neglected to say that, technically, the public domain had always been under the "absolute sovereignty of the federal government" and was never the territory of the states. But he was right in this respect: that until the Taylor Grazing Act, the western states were allowed to enact certain laws concerning the public domain, as long as they were not in conflict with those of the federal government. Although the act did now wipe those laws off the books, McCarran added that the existence of the advisory boards "would go far toward effecting an accord between the sovereignty of the state and that of the federal government," and he had introduced a bill in the Senate which would give those boards legal status, meaning that the secretary of the interior would not be able to eliminate them for any reason.[20] The bill would also give advisory boards greater powers to adjudicate conflicts over the government's allocation of range.

It was a law that Congress ultimately passed, although not without the loud objections of Harold Ickes. In the same ANLSA meeting at which McCarran spoke, Ickes presented his side of the matter, declaring several times that the advisory boards should not be allowed "to perform executive functions," that is, to make any decisions that were administrative in character. "The advisory boards are bodies set up voluntarily by the Secretary of the Interior and their function is implicit in the word 'advisory,'" he argued. Not only was the boards' existence dependent on the secretary, but their functions were also "at all times subordinate to officials of the Department who are required to exercise impartial and independent judgment in all cases." This stance on Ickes's part is unsurprising. Unlike Carpenter and McCarran, he doubted whether the system of advisory committees could either protect range use for the "little fellow" or limit it in the name of conservation. He knew he had a tough audience in front of him, however, and resorted to other arguments to try to convince the assembled stock growers of the validity of his position. The most striking is the one we have seen before, for he turned again to the figure of the individual proprietor to make his point:

> To be sure, [the Taylor lands] are used for grazing purposes and stockmen have an interest in them. However, no owner of land, and this would apply to you stockmen as well as to anyone else, would tolerate the thought of permitting his property to be administered by someone else. . . . [A]dministration by advisory boards would mean control by beneficiaries whose interests, as the past has shown, in essence are or may be, antagonistic to those of the owner.

Ickes made other arguments that likely played better to the ranchers in his audience, including the fact that empowering the boards might not serve their interests well: they might find, for instance, that their grazing privileges were being administered by their local rivals. But he kept returning to the necessary primacy of federal authority. The secretary of the interior had to retain all the mandated powers to administer the act: that authority had to be firmly established in statute, but it was required because the government owned the lands.[21]

However, throughout the 1940s, organized ranchers and the politicians who supported them made competing property claims to the public lands, in combination with increasingly attacking the bureaucratic expansion of public land administration. Again, it should be stressed that this resistance to the government's proprietorship began before the crisis over grazing fees. In meetings with Carpenter in 1934 and 1935, for example, Elmer Brock, a Wyoming cattle rancher who had been a prominent states' rightist in the late 1920s and was a longtime critic of federal management of the range, had raised considerable objections to the Taylor Grazing Act.[22] Brock, who "had a fiery disposition," in the words of the official ANLSA historian, became president of the American National Live Stock Association in 1940.[23] The ANLSA legislative committee met shortly thereafter with the chair of the Senate Committee on Public Lands in order to explain the association's objections to the federal grazing program. The chair met in turn with the Public Lands Committee, and the result was Senator McCarran's proposal that an investigation "of the entire public domain question, not only as to administration, but also as to the law's effects on the tax structures of state and local governments" be launched. The ANLSA committee then gave McCarran a list of grievances that became, in a paraphrased way, a part of the official Senate Resolution 241.[24]

These grievances revolved primarily around complaints about federal administrative power—simply put, that under FDR's administration, the public land agencies had enlarged too far. Of course, within Congress a coalition of conservatives among both Republicans and Democrats had been protesting the centralization of administrative powers within the executive branch, and by the late 1930s, their presence was expanding and proving quite formidable. The "zenith" of that coalition, as James T. Patterson termed it, came in 1939 when the conservative legislators were particularly successful in attacking Roosevelt's labor, housing, and relief policies following the 1938 recession.[25] Like other business groups, the livestock trade associations joined the chorus of anti–New Deal voices. The ANLSA complained about the expansion of federal land purchases; about the government's "abuse of emergency powers"; about its avoidance or misuse of the courts; and about alleged "coercive tactics" by officials in the Department of the Interior against public land users. Both sets of grievances—the ANLSA's and McCarran's—ended with the sweeping if ineptly phrased charge that "there has been interference with the established principles relating to supervision of the livestock industry which have long been applied by governmental bureaus and agencies charged with administering public lands."[26] In what was a classic case of poor political timing, the Grazing Service then launched a survey to decide whether grazing fees should be raised from the rates set after the Taylor Grazing Act—5 cents per "animal unit month," or a.u.m., for cattle and 1 cent per a.u.m. for sheep.[27] The survey concluded that the value of the federal range forage warranted a sizable increase in most districts, and the service presented its findings to both the state advisory boards and the newly formed National Advisory Board Council, which was made up of representatives of the state boards. Not surprisingly, the state and national boards all voted against the proposed increases. Shortly after the United States entered the war, Harold Ickes promised range users that fees would not be increased "for the present," and that "the entire fee question should receive serious and comprehensive consideration." [28]

The fee question was given serious attention in the journals of the livestock associations, but as was also the case during the controversy over Forest Service fees in the 1920s, whether to raise grazing fees or not was a question that never stood alone; it was connected to a wealth of other unresolved issues having to do with public range use. As in the 1920s, ranchers and federal officials battled over how the government should even go about determining the value of private and public grazing lands, and what relationship the latter should have to the former, given that the value of public lands could not be determined by the market. This question inevitably brought up conflicts over how much authority the federal government had to increase the fees in the first place and over what kind of security ranchers would receive in exchange for those fees. [29] These issues would become enormously important during the full-blown grazing fee crisis of the mid 1940s, and Pat McCarran did much with such concerns in running his hearings.

It is important to note a few things about McCarran's political views before examining the crisis itself. First, one cannot overstate the importance of his representing Nevada in the Senate. As Farrington Carpenter noted in his lengthy letter of rebuttal to Harold Ickes, "Grazing in Nevada is of such transcending importance that whenever any grazing meetings are held in that State by the Division of Grazing, the legislature if in session adjourns to attend the grazing meeting, together with the Governor of the State." [30] The reason for grazing's importance was that over 85 percent of Nevada's land was federally owned—at the time of the Taylor Grazing Act, the state contained one-third of the public domain left in the continental United States—and most of that fell under the Department of the Interior. Before this land came under the Taylor Grazing Act, it had been subject to the most extensive *state* lawmaking in the West. Under what were known as the "stock-watering acts," stock growers who made "beneficial uses" of water on the public range could continue to control not only that water but the surrounding range. In the words of Nevada's other senator, Key Pittman, in testimony during hearings on the Taylor Grazing Act, these acts were intended "to vest a right in a range on the public domain through control of water rights." [31]

When Carpenter stepped before Nevada ranchers in 1935 to begin creating grazing districts in the state, this history of state-recognized range rights emerged in the general discussion of the Taylor Grazing Act. In one case, a large cattleman noted to Carpenter that while he only owned 40 acres of land, he controlled the range, through recognized water rights, for approximately "fifteen or twenty miles in every direction." [32] Indeed, the stock-watering acts, combined with the low productivity of the land, made Nevada home to larger ranch operations than in any other state in the West. [33] While many Nevada ranchers supported the Taylor Grazing Act, because they knew they could not afford to acquire the public lands, they also were deeply concerned that the act would wipe away the rights they had acquired under state legislation.

This structure of laws had an unmistakable effect on McCarran's political discourse. Perhaps the clearest articulation of his worldview came in another speech to the ANLSA in 1942, shortly after hearings on S. Res. 241 had begun. This speech sheds light on the oddity of his using a notion such as "incorporeal hereditament" as a political rallying point, for it is a lengthy, if also strange, rumination on the history of rights of the commons. Common lands, he told his audience, "have been by historians noted as existing in all countries, even prior to the birth of the Savior." In "more recent history," he went on, "the right to use the open public domain as an appurtenant sprang from customs, practices, rules, and mandates . . . emanating from the Germanic tribes" that settled Europe. In England, legal commentators had long recognized "the right to the individual to pasture his commonable [sic] animals on the wastes of the manor." And in the United States, the federal government had "used the open public domain" as a way to draw people to the unsettled areas of the West: those who took up the challenge to come West, McCarran remarked, "regarded the use of the open public domain surrounding their homestead or settlement as an inalienable right, an appurtenant hereditament in the nature of property which, dealt with as an economic unit, could be enjoyed, defended, given as pledge of security, and disposed of." While western states tried both "to crystallize rights on the open public domain" and to protect that land from overgrazing, the stock grower himself "knew that his greatest asset for the success of his endeavor was the right which he enjoyed to graze his livestock on the open country. He regarded that right as sacred. He regarded it as something that would sustain him and his dependents and that he, in turn, would hand down to his descendants to carry on." McCarran noted that he had grown up in a ranching community, and that he "had learned from my very infancy what I believed to be sacred rights of the use of the open public domain for grazing purposes." It was only when the Forest Service came along that "the federal government . . . departed from the principles of the old common law which, as I have said, recognized the incorporeal hereditament known as the right of commons." [34]

McCarran's history, at least once he took up the United States, was patently wrong, and at one level he would have known it. The case history at every turn declared that the government had never recognized ranchers' property rights to the public domain, and despite his relentless deployment of old legal phrases, the government had never recognized that users of the public domain had anything like easements to the public lands attached to their private property. Moreover, McCarran was likely inaccurate even in describing how ranchers, as a group across the West, viewed their own use of the public domain. If there really had been some recognized system of rights on the range, one would have liked to have asked him, why were ranchers so embattled with one another in the late nineteenth century, and why did many of them push so hard for government control of the range?

Such profound inaccuracies must be attributed, first, to his political style. McCarran was a master of incendiary rhetoric, and in the 1940s, he was not only the chosen advocate on the national stage for western stock growers but also at the center of a firestorm that he had helped create. That power seemed to prod him into making outrageous statements, as opposed to tempering his language; that he was up against one of the most outspoken members of the New Deal, Harold Ickes, only exacerbated that tendency. McCarran was also clearly fighting a more limited battle, and that was for the legitimization of Nevada's range legislation, even after the Taylor Grazing Act, as futile as that was from a legal standpoint. But if we look at the speech not as a historical account of the law but as a political expression of opposition to federal growth, its misstatements indicate a general shift in the debate over grazing on the public lands: concern over individual "rights" of property in the public domain now marked the discourse from the stock growers' side, and while neither the NWGA nor the ANLSA articulated the revisionist history so "sacred" to McCarran, they also turned to a platform that emphasized the privatization of the public domain.

McCarran and the stock growers who backed him politically never used the word "privatization," which was so much the creation of the late 1970s and 1980s, but I use it here because the term captures a range of political positions that aimed to transfer some or all of the "bundle of rights" that the government had in its lands to the users. As we shall see, some stock growers sought to purchase public domain lands from the government—that is, to gain possession of the title in fee simple—which was as much of the "bundle" as they could have. Some still clung to the hope of transferring the public domain to the states, where stock growers could control land policies more closely. Others, and this group included McCarran, sought to keep the lands in federal ownership, but under the disciplining power of the stock growers, who would be recognized as having certain political authority over administration and certain rights to the use of the Taylor lands and the national forests. The goals of privatization, it should be emphasized, thus fell along a spectrum, but what connected them all was a common understanding that since the passage of the Taylor Grazing Act, the balance of powers between the government and range users was fully up for negotiation. Stock growers and western politicians articulated this understanding in two ways throughout the McCarran hearings: one way concerned what constituted proper administration of the public domain lands, and the other concerned the parameters of rights in ranchers' use of the federal lands. Ultimately, these two concerns overlapped, merged, and implicated each other, and it is therefore somewhat artificial to discuss them separately. But teasing the two apart will allow us to see that the stock growers' attack involved both the regulatory and propertied arms of the state.

As soon as McCarran's hearings got off the ground in 1941, there was considerable criticism of the expanding bureaucracy of the Grazing Service. McCarran was fond of reciting the numbers that indicated the growth of the service—from having 45 employees and being appropriated $250,000 in 1936 to having 234 employees and garnering $750,000 from Congress in 1941.[35] Such expansion on its own would have made McCarran suspicious, but he was all the more critical because of the service's recent, if weak, attempt to broach the question of raising fees. With Ickes's consent not to raise fees during the "emergency" of the war, the issue lay dormant until 1944. In that year, the new director of the Grazing Service, the former Forest Service official Clarence Forsling, announced that grazing fees should be increased by as much as 200 percent, which produced waves of indignation among range users and their political representatives. At nearly the same time, the House Appropriations Committee began pressuring the Grazing Service to increase the fees, threatening to cut back on the agency's appropriations.[36] The Grazing Service was then put in a political squeeze:

McCarran and the leaders of the livestock industry refused to countenance a fee, while the Appropriations Committee seemed intent on chiseling away at the fledgling administration.[37]

Most historians who have examined this squeeze are, quite understandably, puzzled by the refusal among the stock growers' leadership to accept the increase: while 200 percent was a sizable relative increase, the suggested fee of 15 cents per a.u.m. was still vastly lower than what ranchers paid on private lands, and much lower than what they paid in the national forests. Spokesmen for the industry were hard put to argue that the current fee of 5 cents per a.u.m. represented the true value of the forage, and their tendency to, in E. Louise Peffer's words, "shout 'bureaucracy'" has often seemed like a red herring, used to distract Congress from their desire to get the cheapest possible grass.[38] No doubt this was true for some of the men who protested the increase. But I would also argue that there were critical issues at stake, which we have already looked at in connection with the struggle over fees in the 1920s. Unlike C. E. Rachford, Forsling did not argue for a "commercial" fee, but his arguments for a "reasonable" one bore a resemblance to Rachford's justifications. He reasoned that the livestock industry, and especially the cattle industry, was doing quite well, because prices for beef had gone up since the Depression, and that the Grazing Service was now able to offer more benefits to the users than it had in its formative stages—for instance, drilling for wells and building much-needed fences and stock driveways. Equally important, he argued, in much the same vein as the Forest Service had in the 1920s, users of the Taylor Grazing lands "were paying approximately 2 to 12 times as much for the rental of railroad-owned or other privately owned range land as for the use of similar Federal range."[39] It was only fair that the Grazing Service fees should better reflect the market value of the land, and the tool used to achieve this would be the market price for beef.

In the McCarran hearings, which showcased protests against the fees, many ranchers did note that they were pleased with the relationship they had established with the Grazing Service, but they also contested almost every point the service used to support its proposal. For instance, they quickly noted a fundamental problem in Forsling's resorting to beef prices—that is, his turn to the market—to determine the price of public grazing forage. Although beef prices had indeed risen, so had production costs, which in some areas had increased over 100 percent. The most critical area was, of course, the cost of labor because of the war.

Most witnesses testified convincingly to this fact, although McCarran's remarks on this point had the most rhetorical flavor: "A cowboy we could hire 5 years ago for $65 . . . a month we now pay $150 a month . . . and the sustenance that was called ordinary food in the old days is today perhaps the most expensive food there is. We used to board them on sowbelly and beans, but you cannot do that any more; that is a luxury—both of them. You cannot even get it at the Senate Restaurant." [40] More strikingly, it was the ranchers who testified before the committee who commented that beef prices were an inappropriate benchmark from which to determine the value of the public range. For one thing, because of the danger of wartime inflation, the Office of Price Administration had put a ceiling on how high the price of beef could go, at the same time that costs were doubling in certain areas of production—not only labor, but also winter feed. But ranchers also objected to the very notion that the market for beef could determine the value of grazing land. Beef prices were notoriously volatile, and, as the president of the New Mexico Wool Growers Association put it, "The market always falls faster than it goes up." [41] A sliding scale fee struck most witnesses as a bad idea, even though (or because) the Forest Service had instituted it in the wake of the grazing fee controversy of the 1920s: it could not be adjusted fast enough, and ranchers could not estimate the cost of public grazing in advance.[42] But at least a few ranchers betrayed uneasiness about what information the beef market could give the government. As one rancher argued, the proposed fee increase "is based not on the net costs or net return for production, it is based on the market, and it is the market in Chicago or Kansas City, some central market, [for] the finished product. It is not based on the price of the animal on the range." [43]

Forsling was in fact using two "private" benchmarks to determine the grazing fee on Taylor grazing lands: the cost of leases on private lands and the price of beef. The market rates for private lands indicated to him that Taylor grazing fees were set much too low—and thus that the fees on the public range did not come close to reflecting the land's market value—and the market rates for beef indicated that cattlemen were earning enough of a return to justify higher fees. But, as when the Forest Service attempted the same strategy, this turning to the market was fraught with difficulties. Given that one of the explicit missives of the Grazing Service was to "stabilize" the industry, basing grazing fees on the market price for beef during or at the close of a war did inject a degree of uncertainty into the ranching industry. Forsling nonetheless turned to the market, which he constructed as outside the governmental arena, because it appeared to contain the real truth about the value of land, an assumption that the Forest Service also made in the 1920s. And yet at least at the point when Forsling made his proposal, the price of beef was itself partially determined by public authority, that is, by the Office of Price Administration. Similarly, Forsling turned to the leases on private lands as an authoritative source of information about value, and ranchers responded much as they had in the 1920s—to remind government officials that the uses, and therefore the values, of private and public lands were so intertwined as to be quite impossible to separate.

But other reactions against the fee increase had roots in the recent history of ranchers' conflict with federal land managers. As in the case of the Forest Service's recommendations twenty years before, ranchers also expressed a sense of betrayal, this time on two fronts. First, many leaders who came before McCarran's subcommittee argued that they took Ickes's promise in 1941 to mean that the Grazing Service would not raise fees until the livestock industry was on a firm footing after the war was over, as they very much feared the prospect of a postwar depression. Given their experience of the economic slump after World War I, this was not an unreasonable concern. Their second sense of betrayal revolved around what many of them saw as the initial intent of the Taylor Grazing Act itself, and in this case the Department of the Interior had itself partially to blame. In order to secure the passing of the act in 1934, Ickes had argued that the public domain could be administered for only $150,000—a figure that was laughable to the Forest Service, whose officials argued that it would cost a couple million dollars. Now this estimate came back to haunt Forsling. McCarran, other members of the committee and the National Advisory Board, and witnesses all argued that the Taylor Grazing Act would not have gotten the support of ranchers if this "promise" had not been made. Such a retort was partially about grazing fees, as they argued that they did not want to pay higher fees to bankroll a more costly administration. But it was also about the anticipated authority of the Grazing Service itself. As the president of the New Mexico Cattle Growers put it:

> When the Grazing Service was created by Congress, the law was passed . . . with the assurance . . . that the Grazing Service would be maintained as a skeleton land controlling organization to promote proper use of the Government range, and to establish stability on public lands. We now find that the Grazing Service has taken it upon themselves to branch out into a major de-

partment of the Government with a vast postwar spending plan of . . . redeveloping our desert ranges on a scale never before seen in history.[44]

"Skeleton land controlling organization" was certainly a mouthful, but it is striking because ranchers and their political leaders relied on this precise description—that the Grazing Service was meant to be a kind of "skeleton" of governmental administration, entailing the barest possible governmental oversight of range use. The significance of this description lay in the relationship between the "skeleton" land management and fees, and the hearings saw stock growers developing two positions: first, that fees should only cover the cost of administering the grazing lands, and, second, that determining what constituted proper administration should be left to the stock growers. This was understood by one sheep grower to mean that Taylor lands ranchers should "take full authority on the allotments made to us, ask nothing of the government officials, treat the land very much on the basis that we were to have permanent control thereof. . . . This whole theory is opposed to the proposition that we need government agents at our elbow to tell us to do this and not to do that at all times."[45]

There was no doubt that Ickes and other department officials had stated that the Grazing Division would only require $150,000 in appropriations in its first year, a figure that was increased to $250,000 after the Interior Department agreed to provide members of the advisory boards with a small compensation for their work. Even that increase was contested in congressional hearings in 1935, indicating that conservative opposition to the Grazing Division's expansion was already in place at the time the administration was just getting off the ground.[46] But it is also true that Ickes did not publicly say that grazing fees should cover only the cost of administering the lands; indeed, he had simply not given much thought to the question until the crisis blew up. By the time the McCarran hearings were in full swing against the increase, Ickes had developed his position more carefully, noting in a 1945 letter to Senator Carl Hatch (D-N.M.), chair of the Committee on Public Lands and Surveys, that a "reasonable fee is considered to be one that represents a fair value of the forage obtained by the user," and that the Taylor Grazing Act granted the Interior Department the power to determine that value. "Nowhere in the Act is there an expression," Ickes continued, "or even an implication, that the cost to the government in carrying out the provisions of the Act and the fees to be charged should necessarily bear any relationship to each other."[47] That refusal to connect the two sparked protests that, again, echoed the grazing fee controversy of the 1920s: the Grazing Service was intent simply on producing "revenue" and ultimately on seeking to charge "all [that] the traffic will bear"—in other words, using competitive bidding for grazing permits.[48]

The stock growers took their arguments even further, however, stating that "the Grazing Service is not selling feed to the livestock operators but is merely rendering an administrative service, as the permittees established the right to the feed on the range through use and by building up dependent ranch properties."[49] The service (and probably many ranchers) would surely have been surprised to hear that ranchers were not *buying* feed on the public range, but this argument reflected how the Taylor Grazing Act had produced a new understanding of the property relations between public land ranchers and federal grazing managers. It had done this in two ways. The first was by instituting a system of licensing that allowed preferred ranchers to graze their animals on federal lands administered by the Interior Department. Such permission created a legal interest for ranchers and a legal relation between them and the federal government, although to this day, the two sides argue over whether that interest is a privilege or a right.[50] Of course, the same could be said for the effects of managed grazing in the national forests, except that permittees there always argued that they were on much less secure footing, as the forest acts of the 1890s never specifically mentioned grazing as a recognized use of the national forests. In contrast, the Taylor Grazing Act was a statute designed to manage grazing on the public range, and the combination of that statutory legitimacy and the legal mechanism of licensing use quickly opened the way for ranchers to see that use as a right.

Moreover, the act did not simply create new legal relations between ranchers and the federal government through the act of the license; it also did so by precisely defining ranchers' reliance on the public range. Ranchers simply could not have the chance to become permittees on the Taylor lands if they did not have dependent base properties and commensurable forage. To put it more starkly, they could not become permittees if they did not have to be permittees. This stipulation inscribed ranchers' economic vulnerability into their political and legal relationship with the federal government, and ranchers saw correctly that in their dependence on the public range, they were exposed to the powers of the federal government as a property owner.[51]

The refusal by organized stock growers' to allow a fee increase was thus more than simple greed and more than a frontier reaction to the forces of the regulatory state. It marked a transformation in the legal relations between the federal government as the owner of the public domain and the ranchers who used it under the Taylor Grazing Act. And only by trying to grasp this transformation in their thinking can we understand why the leaders of the livestock associations, with McCarran as their political spokesperson, seemed so ready to shoot themselves politically in the foot. For the result of the impasse over fees was that the Senate Committee in charge of overseeing the administration of the public lands ended up supporting the House Appropriations Committee's desire to slash the Grazing Service's budget, which it did by half. Simply in terms of personnel, the number of employees in the Grazing Service dropped from 250 to 86, and Forsling was effectively exiled to the field. The cut in appropriations was then followed even more dramatically by a reorganization in the department, whereby the General Land Office and the Grazing Service were merged to become the Bureau of Land Management.[52]

McCarran saw this reorganization as a victory for western stock growers, believing it would check the growth of federal grazing management, and in its August 1946 issue, the *National Wool Grower* noted in the tone of an obituary that the "Grazing Service passed out of existence as a separate government bureau." Naming the new officials and excerpting a large portion of President Truman's reorganization plan establishing the BLM, the article in its tone of detachment stood in sharp contrast to the article on the following page, "The Grazing Land Problem: What's the Solution?" There, Norman Winder, the president of the NWGA, and Dan Hughes, a Colorado sheepman, gave their personal answers, which, although not officially representing any association's views, indicated that the battle over the federal grazing lands had not reached its climax. While some western politicians still supported transferring public lands to the states, Winder noted, this did not go "far enough toward getting the land into private ownership, nor does it safeguard sufficiently the rights of the present users after the land is granted to the states. . . . [S]ome people recognize," he went on, that "it is an appropriate time to get the government lands into private ownership."[53] Thus, just when McCarran's political putsch had succeeded and the Grazing Service had been dismantled, so that one might have assumed that the controversy would die down, a group of organized stock growers launched an even grander political program, which brought them more public attention than any other episode since the demise of the "cattle kingdom" in the late 1880s.

"So we come to the business which created to the West's most powerful illusion about itself and . . . has done more damage to the West than any other: The cattle business." These words from Bernard DeVoto opened the condemnation of the ranching industry in his oft-cited article "The West against Itself," which came out in January 1947.[54] DeVoto slammed the industry on a number of issues, but he hit hardest at ranchers' political aims to control the public lands. After first insulting the early cattle ranchers—"[t]hey were always arrogant and always deluded"—DeVoto went on to say: "[T]he Cattle Kingdom never did own more than a minute fraction of one per cent of the range it grazed: it was national domain, it belonged to the people of the United States. They do not own the range now: mostly it belongs to you and me. . . . [T]hey always acted as if they owned the public range and act so now . . . and they are trying to take title to it." Not only was such political behavior an affront to the American public, DeVoto argued, but underlying it was a much graver problem—that, in using the public range for so many decades, ranchers' livestock had utterly devastated the land. That overgrazing would profoundly affect the streams and rivers of the West, which were now burdened with the silt that was ultimately the product of overstocked ranges. DeVoto was never at a loss for words to describe the environmental deterioration of the West or to evoke his moral shock at this process: "For when you watch the Missouri [River] sliding greasily past Kansas City you are watching those gallant horsemen out of Owen Wister shovel Wyoming into the Gulf of Mexico. It is even more important that their heirs hope to shovel most of the remaining West into its rivers."[55]

Although DeVoto also directed his fire at other groups in the West, including the mining and timber industries, he focused on the struggle over public grazing in Congress, where Pat McCarran and other western politicians, such as Congressman Frank Barrett and Senator Edward Robertson of Wyoming, led the stock growers' supporters. In recent sessions of Congress, McCarran, Barrett, and Robertson had all introduced bills that in one form or another attempted to take a portion of the public lands out of federal ownership. De Voto accurately charged that public land ranchers were attempting to convert their grazing privileges into vested rights and that they wanted the land turned over to the states, ultimately for individual purchase. "This is your land we are talking about," DeVoto reminded his readers. "Their immediate objectives make this attempt one of the biggest land grabs in American history."[56]

Such incitement was a relatively new thing in the national press. Of course, other observers and players in the public grazing conflicts had gone public and branded the stock growers as land-grabbers; DeVoto's article is reminiscent, for instance, of the piece that William Greeley, the head of the Forest Service, wrote for the *Saturday Evening Post* in 1925, which made very similar criticisms. But what distinguished DeVoto's essay from Greeley's was, first, the depth of the outrage—or, at least, De-Voto's unabashed and articulate ways of expressing it—and second, his continual reassertion that the public lands did not belong to the cattle and sheep ranchers but to "us." That this property belonged to "us," the American public, meant that it had to be safeguarded from its users.[57]

DeVoto's article, which he followed with other essays and editorials about the state of the West, created yet more animosity among organized ranchers against easterners and against the federal government, and it produced several responses in the pages of the stock growers' journals. And the piece was yet another sign of the growing gulf between many ranchers' understanding of the public grazing problem and that of interested parties outside the ranching industry. From the conservationist side, as Peffer has written, the "big, bad cattle baron again rode the literary horizon, trying to rob the people of the land."[58] From the stock growers' side, the conservationists (whom they identified as mostly from the East) were intent on "locking up" resources as they had always wanted to do. That the two sides relied on old political stereotypes obviously did not further the cause of reconciliation. But while DeVoto's portrait in particular captured none of the political divisions among stock growers, he did correctly discern that, at least in the leadership of the livestock associations, the political discourse embraced the eventual privatization of the public range; and in doing so the leaders of the livestock associations were leaving themselves wide open to the storm of criticism they received.

Nonetheless, in portraying the ranchers' goal as a simple land grab, DeVoto missed the opportunity of asking why this shift to privatization had occurred and what it meant. Like many other critics of public land ranching, DeVoto assumed that most ranchers sought such a land grab —that, in fact, it was in the nature of ranchers always to want to own the public lands. Of course, that had not been the case, and ranchers had a multitude of reasons for wanting to keep public lands in federal ownership. More fundamentally, the experience of the Depression suggested to many stock growers, including Farrington Carpenter, that much of the public land was not worth owning. And yet it was also true that ranchers who had established themselves as users of public grazing land, whether in the national forests or on the Taylor lands, wanted more security of tenure.

Both these goals—the individual purchase of public domain lands and federal recognition of more secure rights to the use of those lands—had been targeted by public land ranchers throughout the 1940s; one might even say that they had been targeted for decades. Since the debates about what to do with the public domain had begun in full force around the turn of the century, there had been ranchers who advocated selling off the public range or creating a homestead act much more amenable to ranchers. But their voices could hardly be heard in the din of voices supporting the "small fellow," or the "homebuilder," who was the focus of government policy until the 1920s. By the end of that decade, as we have also seen, influenced by a conjunction of forces, the national livestock associations shifted from supporting federal management of the public domain to ambivalently encouraging the transfer of those lands to the states; up to the very moment of the Taylor Grazing Act, cession remained a live possibility, at least in the opinions of many leaders in the associations and some politicians as well. And while the Taylor Grazing Act was a "stockmen's bill" if ever there were one—it certainly received a great deal of grassroots support—it also produced the expectation among some ranchers that it would generate real property rights in the public range, and when it did not, the livestock organizations leaned further toward a political agenda of privatization.

In fact, there were early signs of the shift toward supporting public land sales even before the controversies over grazing fees and reductions on the national forests. In 1941, for instance—around the time of the Grazing Service's initial proposal to raise fees—the ANLSA published a pamphlet titled *Control and Value of Western Grazing Lands,* which contained the testimony of University of Wyoming economist A. F. Vass before McCarran's hearings in Casper, Wyoming. The president of the ANLSA at this time was the outspoken Elmer Brock of Wyoming, and the introduction to Vass's testimony noted that the "Wyoming witnesses [in the hearings] stressed the fact that the Taylor Grazing Act . . . was not designed to build up a permanent bureau to reach out into rangeland like an octopus," a position certainly in line with Brock's. In the association's view, Vass was "an exceedingly practical man," and despite over four hours of testimony by government experts on the need to increase grazing fees, Vass's arguments against the increase "check[ed] with the experience of our stockmen." [59]

Vass was a serious agricultural economist who had made specific economic studies of livestock production on federal lands. While he made a detailed argument about instituting a very different benchmark for federal grazing fees, based on an animal's consumption and the amount of land it grazed, more important for our purposes are the questions he posed directly to the committee. "Why should not the livestock rancher be given the same consideration as the farmer in owning and managing his property?" he asked. "Why is it necessary or even desirable for [the] Federal Government to own and control one-half of the ranch property used in production of agricultural products, and not apply the same reasoning to the Middle Western farmer?" The problem was not simply one between ranchers and midwestern farmers, he noted; federal ownership of the range produced a "maladjusted land control pattern," as well as "inequalities between ranchers," specifically between those who used the low-cost public range and those who did not and were saddled with high investment costs for their private lands. Indeed, this latter point indicates that Vass was no simple lackey of the stock growers. He fully acknowledged that the low grazing fee was a "subsidy" to western ranchers, saying, "[i]f the federal grazing fees are less than the interest and taxes on similar privately owned lands in the area, it indicates that there is an attempt to secure the stockmen's approval of this federal control through the use of subsidies in the form of low fees, a practice not in keeping with the tradition of this country." Moreover, despite the low fees on the public range, Vass argued, ranchers still would rather overinvest in land in order to gain title to it. That the rancher "owns and continues to buy land on which the taxes alone may be double the grazing fee charged by the federal agency . . . shows that he places a rather high premium on the security and freedom that private ownership afford him." Vass himself placed a "high premium" on land ownership, believing that it would produce better land management and adjust the economic problems of land valuation in the state, and encouraged the government to pursue a policy that would allow stock growers "an opportunity to own the land." [60]

In the same year that Vass's pamphlet was published, Brock went on record as president of the ANLSA as favoring the sale of "the public lands at a price commensurate with their value. . . . They should be sold to those to whom they are now allotted. This is important in order not to disrupt the stability of the livestock industry or impair the value of owned lands." [61] While the issue remained a live one throughout the grazing fee crisis, the associations did not mobilize politically around the proposal until late summer of 1946, when the leaders of the ANLSA and the NWGA met to form the Joint Livestock Committee on Public Lands. "The purpose of the committee is to work for the ultimate goal of private ownership of public lands," its initial announcement stated, and the committee would work for legislation to effect this, specifically so "that the present users of the public domain should have first preference for the acquisition of lands upon which they hold a license, lease or permit." Made up of prominent anti-federal spokesmen, the committee formed objectives based on its obvious belief that private ownership created the "greatest good for the greatest number" and that the grazing program represented an unnecessary government service, one that stock growers could perform themselves if given the opportunity to own the public lands. But the committee also voiced other principles and goals that were sure to incite conflict. The most striking concerned the Taylor Grazing Act, which, in the committee's opinion, "secures us in the possession of this land and any interpretation should be made upon this basis; that if this is not correct, there should be an immediate amendment to the act which will give to the user such security." And yet, the members of the committee concluded, "ultimately this security can only be obtained through private ownership." [62] They believed not only that they had a right to use their allotted range but also that they already had legal possession of it. Perhaps knowing that asserting these rights did not make them true in the eyes of federal land agencies, they fell back on the argument that only by divesting the government of its lands could stock growers really gain secure possession of them.

No single event can be said to have caused the creation of the committee, and on the one hand, the timing is puzzling, given that the Grazing Service had just been eliminated and reconstituted in the Bureau of Land Management, which "struggled in its first two years to simply survive." [63] The stock growers were not facing the "mushroom growth" of a government agency, in other words. But as if the relationship between the federal government and organized ranchers *required* constant friction, conflicts over the use of national forest lands had also reemerged with a vengeance. In what might be regarded as a case of fatefully poor timing, the ten-year permits granted to ranchers in 1935 had come up for renewal, and it was clear that the Forest Service was countenancing deep reductions in certain regions. Moreover, the agency was also intent on tightening its administrative control over its public grazing lands. As

William Rowley has written, the Forest Service's renewed "forthrightness (even aggressiveness) made it appear to be walking into the lion's
den." [64] Primed and empowered from their fight with the Grazing Service, leaders of the livestock associations lashed out at Forest Service
policy, and their hostility toward the service helped to fuel the property
rights discourse that the Joint Livestock Committee on Public Lands engaged in.

The *National Wool Grower* covered the committee's first meeting in
detail, excerpting some of the speeches and clearly trying to persuade
the members of the association to support the committee's plans. What
is striking about the meeting is the relative extremity of the committee's
views; in fact, it was largely this meeting, in conjunction with the Mc-
Carran hearings, that sparked DeVoto's blasting of the western stock
growers. For one thing, it was evident that even the option of ceding the
public domain to the states was off the table. As its chairman, Dan
Hughes, a Colorado sheepman, argued, the committee needed a clear
legislative plan, because it did not want to find itself supporting "private
ownership and then have a law passed which will permit state ownership." (In fact, Hughes was correct, in that western leaders of Congress
did not propose bills to allow for individual land purchases, but continued to fight for cession to the states.) Norman Winder of the NWGA
also noted that ceding the lands to the states was not enough anymore,
and the goal of land sales even shaped more pragmatic approaches to
the politics of the issue. As vice-chairman of the committee, Elmer Brock
declared that until livestock leaders attained their ultimate goal of transferring the public lands to private ownership, "we don't want to give up
any of the advantages we have under the Taylor Grazing Act." Of particular importance was holding the line on fees, which Brock saw as a
potent symbol of the politics of public grazing. If ranchers agreed "to
any increase in fees," it would mean "an admission on our part that we
feel rather weakly toward getting private ownership of the lands, and it
will intensify the opposition of passing these lands to private ownership." Fees also represented the finger in the dike of federal expansion,
in Brock's view: "[I]f we ever concede the fact that the government is in
the business of selling grass, or the commercial disposal of the range, we
are sunk. They will never receive enough to satisfy themselves. Federal
administration is something that increases, and they develop their own
expansions." [65]

Although the committee projected a formidable sense of its own
power, many ranchers in fact opposed the privatization plan from the

very beginning of its existence. The *Wool Grower's* first article about the committee noted briefly that opposition to the plan came from some stockmen in the states of Utah, Oregon, Idaho, and Nevada, who were concerned that many stock growers would not be protected by such a change in policy. This opposition would never go away, as it turned out, although the *Wool Grower* tried hard in this article and others to explain that "all present users of the public domain, both small and large" would benefit from the sale of the public lands.[66] As it became increasingly clear that private ownership was not universally desired by public land ranchers, the leadership shifted to a position of supporting voluntary purchase—much as it had in the early 1930s when the associations suggested that western states should be given the option to have public lands transferred to them.[67] Even Pat McCarran cautioned the committee against attempting to dispose of the public domain, because in his mind he and his Senate committee had worked hard to reshape a grazing administration that met the approval of stock growers.[68] And the committee soon stopped insisting on the issue of private ownership and focused on more specific issues related to public grazing on the Taylor lands and in the national forests. While this political denouement did not mean the end of conflict during the decade, it did ultimately ease the tension between organized ranchers and the federal government. And yet even in that denouement, the stock growers' associations continued their emphasis on securing rights to graze their animals on the public range. In the 1949 NWGA platform, for instance, it is clear that the Joint Livestock Committee on Public Lands had given up its zeal for the idea of land sales, as the platform made no mention of it. However, the association did argue that "[t]he aim of this committee should be, insofar as possible, to see that laws as enacted by Congress recognize grazing as one of the essential uses of public lands, and that the rights to graze be governed by statute and not by opinions of Federal administrative officials."[69] The associations had long sought to restrain the discretionary power of administrators, but now they also argued for statutory recognition of their grazing rights.

The privatization scheme was a short-lived phenomenon, although it thrust grazing politics into the limelight and created bad publicity for organized stock growers. But while the goal faded rapidly because of internal opposition, it also remains an important signal of the transformation in the political meaning of the public grazing lands. Why did the leaders of the association pursue such an extreme position? It is true that a particular set of leaders, both within and outside the industry, helped to push this cause, and their vocal support for privatization was an important influence in moving ranchers to the right. Moreover, organized ranchers by this point had become seasoned veterans in attacking federal land management. But a third reason lies in the Taylor Grazing Act itself, for by structuring property relations the way that it did, the act provided an opening for politically minded ranchers to argue that it was only a short step to allowing users full ownership of the public rangeland.

The leaders in the movement to sell off the lands understood the connection between the Taylor Grazing Act and their position. In 1946, for instance, Norman Winder wrote that the act was a critical stepping stone to private ownership:

> The administration of federal lands under the Taylor Act was a necessary step in the process of final disposition of these lands. Before the passage of the Taylor Act we had vast areas of unregulated lands and before any final disposition of the lands could be made it was necessary to bring them under control and to work out a pattern of coordinated land use. Now that the pattern has been laid out, I think the livestock industry is ready for the next step toward final disposition, which is private ownership not state ownership." [70]

The Joint Committee's chairman, Dan Hughes, also tried to articulate this link. In testimony before the McCarran committee in 1942, Hughes disagreed with the notion that "the public domain belongs to the United States to do with as they see fit. That could not, in my opinion, be said of the public domain up to the present in the Taylor Grazing Act." The reason, he argued, was that the act had created vested rights for users— so much so that he believed that the grazing rights recognized on the public domain lands should also be recognized in the national forests. [71]

If Hughes had been alone in his inaccurate rendering of ranchers' legal status, we could easily dismiss him as a misguided leader of the livestock industry, but other leaders also asserted that ranchers had rights to the public range, and those assertions were echoed even by ranchers who did not make up the inner circles of either the ANLSA or the NWGA—men who were the heads of smaller local associations. [72] Surely, for the Forest Service and Grazing Service officials who sat through the hearings and were grilled by the committee, these assertions, which ranchers repeated endlessly, must have been galling; they certainly were for Bernard DeVoto, whose animus against the stock growers was driven by their rights-based language. At times during the hearings, the gulf between ranchers and public land officials on this issue was noticeable only as an unarticulated abrasion in the general contentiousness of the exercise; at other times, federal officials simply noted the tendency among ranchers to presume falsely that they either had attained rights to the range or deserved to.[73] And at still other times the issue came into the center of open conflict.

As the McCarran committee set its sights on the Forest Service in 1945, for instance, it pressed hard against the service's chief of range management, Walt Dutton. Dutton distinguished himself by being able to hold his own much more confidently against the committee than, say, Clarence Forsling, and when faced with a series of angry Wyoming witnesses in Casper, he never hesitated to speak from the administration's point of view and to reiterate its rights in the range. He especially singled out the common practice among stock growers of paying extra for livestock or property that had attached grazing preferences, explaining that the service didn't "believe that any individual has a right to traffic in grazing preferences, or make a profit in the transfer of a preference, when it is not his but belongs to the Government." This declaration raised the hackles of the committee members—who, at that moment consisted only of the two Wyoming senators, Joseph O'Mahoney (D-Wyo.) and Edward Robertson (R-Wyo.), and the clerk of the committee—as well as of the Wyoming stock growers in the room. While Dutton remained firm that the Forest Service *assigned preferences* to ranchers, they believed that the permit was a right owned by the rancher, as indicated by the following exchange between Dutton and Edwin Magagna, secretary of the Bridger-Washakie Forest Association of permittees. As in all the hearings, the witnesses were able to question other witnesses, and Magagna interrupted the proceedings to have Dutton explain why he did not approve of ranchers paying a bonus for property with permits to forest grazing. Dutton said again that he did not believe that a person should make money from "a national-forest grazing preference which is not his in his own legal right."

> *Magagna:* In other words, your objection is that he is selling something he does not have, and that you can cancel at any time, and therefore you don't want him to sell it? . . . [Y]ou feel he should not be entitled to sell it because it is not a right but a privilege you can cancel at any time?
>
> *Dutton:* That's pretty well stated, sir. . . .
>
> *Magagna:* It brings back the point . . . [that] the livestock grower feels he should be given a right, so he's got something, instead of a privilege you feel not only can be canceled, but that he should not even be able to sell.

Magagna even tried the old argument that the right should be given to the pioneers of the industry because they had established their use of the forests when they "took up commensurate property" decades before. Dutton would have none of it. The question of whether the permit was a right or a privilege was, as he said, a "basic disagreement right now." Magagna concurred. "[T]hat is the difference, that you people are on one side and we're on the other; that's the reason I interrupted; *I wanted to bring out that's where we're at odds all the time."* [74]

What did such a simple statement capture about the politics of public grazing at midcentury? It captured the fact that there was a gulf between public land ranchers and federal managers that they could not bridge, that while they could iron out the minutest details of policy and even tailor grazing policy to specific areas and even to specific ranchers, on the question of property rights, a chasm opened up between the two groups. Land managers believed that they had to hold the line in assigning grazing permits as privileges and not as rights, because to give in on this issue would be to dispossess the government of its land and undercut its regulatory authority. However, many ranchers continued to demand recognized rights, because their private property's value, even its existence as a productive piece of land, was dependent on the public range, and they believed that the permit itself had become property: it certainly had a value in the market, as attached to land or livestock, and within a limited framework, it could be transferred to other people.

This disagreement concerned the land itself: who would have control over it and how it would be used. But the conflict also involved a much less tangible problem. As any property theorist would point out, property is not a thing, although it revolves around a thing; it is a right. "It is," in the words of Charles Reich, "an enforceable claim to some use or benefit of something (and sometimes, but not always, to its disposal)." [75] The government and ranchers were now locked into a debate that would run to the present day about who held the rights to the property of the public lands, a debate that stemmed directly from the passing of the Taylor Grazing Act, which opened up the question of rights in a more profound way than anything that had come before. By putting the last of the public domain into essentially permanent federal management, it boosted the government's confidence in its property rights. This was now no longer land that could potentially be disposed of; it was the federal government's, and under Harold Ickes's tenure as secretary of the interior, that department had a keen sense of its possessing the land.

Thus, when the government asserted its rights as the owner of the public lands, that assertion served as a reminder to ranchers that the government's real property was not simply land that it owned, but that the property entailed a relationship: the government held the ultimate power to exclude, as any property owner would have. This was not only a legal right, of course. It concerned political rights, because the government backed its regulatory powers over the public lands by asserting its property rights as owner of the lands. It could set up regulations as it saw fit because it was like an individual property owner. While the government also argued that its regulatory authority came from having to protect the public interest, which was the reigning explanation for why the federal government should intervene in property relations, that argument always coexisted uneasily with what was considered the basic premise of public land law: the government owned the land and had the right to do with it whatever it chose.

On the ranchers' side, the Taylor Grazing Act helped to create a belief that they had established property interests in the public lands. It did this by structuring property relations according to much local customary use, thus appearing to recognize long-standing, if often informal, range "codes." More important, the act attached permits to privately owned property, and the early administration of the act by Carpenter interpreted that attachment as a right. That sense, that grazing permits entailed a right to use property, also involved another articulation of rights, because by the late 1940s, organized stock growers were asserting their rights as citizens against what they saw as the oppressive governmental regimentation of public grazing administration. Ranchers were not the only people discussing rights in the 1940s. Rights talk had seeped into American political discourse. During the reign of the Office of Price Administration, for instance, Franklin Roosevelt declared that consumers should have an economic bill of rights, which he wove into a more general declaration of the rights that Americans might reasonably expect, including the rights of social and moral security.[76] Conservative legislators in Congress forged a "new bill of rights" for labor, passed as the Taft-Hartley Act in 1947, which sought to curb the activities of labor unions; opponents of the bill likewise framed their response in a language of rights—that is, the rights now given to employers to block fair bargaining.[77] To public land ranchers who derided federal red tape and accused the government of replacing due process of law with discretionary administrative power, their political and property rights appeared to be the victims of an overreaching state.

Hot tempers among leading ranchers and their political allies and frustrated policymakers among public land officials contributed to the profound impasse in grazing politics in the 1940s. Here, too, the Taylor Grazing Act had created the very structures that made the ranchers' attack possible. But on an even larger scale, the nature of the public lands as property created a tremendous obstacle to political resolution, because the conflict tended alternately to bypass and to focus on the question with which this study began: Who owns the public lands? The conflict ignored this question to the degree that, by the mid 1940s, few people challenged the working parlance of the grazing debates, which either implicitly or explicitly described the public lands as owned by the federal government. For this reason, DeVoto's incitement of the American public to claim the lands as their own was a refreshing challenge to the oversimplified understanding of who represented the property's owner. But when ranchers did begin to make property claims on the public grazing lands, as they did in the 1940s, federal officials responded by asserting that that the government's authority over the lands was like that of an individual property owner and that it held all the rights to those lands. This seeking to consolidate all the property rights in the government's hands resembles what the property theorist Joseph Singer argues has been the reigning model within property law at large; that is, "the presumption is that the legal rules identify a single owner of all valued resources and that that owner has the legal power to control those resources to the exclusion of others."[78] But, as Singer notes, another model has been available to the courts, which contains a multitude of legal rules that force "a sharing or shifting of property interests from the 'owner' to the 'non-owner' to protect the more vulnerable party to the relationship." By looking at these rules—such as adverse possession and prescriptive easements, to name just two—Singer emphasizes that the important question is not "Who owns the property?" but "What relationships have been established?" This is a shift that moves us "from focusing on the relation between the owner and the resources owned to the relation between the owner and non-owners who have benefited from the resources."[79]

It is a shift that organized ranchers themselves have attempted to make at times, and they continue to do so today; even in Pat McCarran's bumbling legal rhetoric, we see the outlines of a more relational model of property than the one that the federal government, and particularly the Forest Service, subscribed to. But stock growers could just as easily embrace the unitary model of property ownership: in their interest in states' rights during the late 1920s, for instance, they deployed just such a model, and the formation of the Joint Livestock Committee on Public Lands was an attempt to privatize all of the rights of ownership in the hands of individual ranchers. And so while ranchers have periodically raised serious challenges to the government's desire to concentrate property rights on its side, they too have often argued that only outright private ownership will solve the political crises on the range.

The crises of the 1940s eventually passed—in fact, through much the same machinations as during the 1920s. The grazing fee controversy was solved by the appointment of a California cattle rancher, Rex Nicholson, to make a study of fees and present a new set of proposals, just as Dan Casement had done in the late 1920s. Not surprisingly, like Casement, Nicholson's recommended fees were lower than those originally proposed and were accepted by the Department of the Interior; thereafter, relative peace reigned throughout the decade between the Bureau of Land Management and ranchers on the Taylor lands. And while stock growers and the Forest Service remained in conflict during the last years of the decade, by the early 1950s, with the change in presidential administrations, officials also paid more attention to bettering the service's relations with stock growers. But the decade's quietude would stand in sharp contrast to those that followed, when ranchers' claims to the public lands ran up explosively against the growing environmental movement.

Epilogue

Shortly after the election of Ronald Reagan to the presidency, a group of mostly conservative scholars, activists, and politicians held a conference in Washington to discuss the future of public land policy. Included in this group was Senator Steven Symms of Idaho, who had been elected to office in 1980 on the wave of the most nationally visible sagebrush rebellion of the century. While in his speech Symms did not support the immediate privatization of public lands (except, he noted, "in certain circumstances"), he did want to see the public lands transferred to the western states at less than market value. He criticized the government's lack of economic efficiency, he criticized the elitism of federal land officials, and he condemned the government's continued land acquisition program. "By the way," he remarked to his audience, "they are government lands, not public lands. They are owned and operated by the federal government, and access is permitted by the government, not the public. Allocation of the resources found on the lands is governed by a federal land manager, not by the marketplace or an unknown 'public good.'"[1]

The sagebrush rebellion of the late 1970s and early 1980s, of which Symms was a part, had strong ideological connections to the rebellions of the 1920s and 1940s, and Symms spoke a language that had roots in this longer history of confrontation between the federal government and public land users. Public land ranchers of an earlier day would likely have agreed with Symms's characterization of what the public rangeland meant: that whatever the technical, legal meaning of "public lands," the government was the owner, and "public good" meant little. Beyond Symms's specific comment, they might have been amazed, as any historian would be, at the regularity of the conflict and the repetition of criticisms and demands.

But Symms's reaction, like those of others at the conference, also marked a departure from the early twentieth-century political history of the public lands, because it came as a direct reaction to very specific changes in federal land policy that had been building for years in response to the environmental movement. Of course, that movement had a monumental impact on the West generally during the 1960s and 1970s, and in the case of grazing lands specifically, it succeeded in doing several things. At the level of policy, public grazing law went through dramatic changes. With the implementation of the National Environmental Policy Act in 1970, federal agencies engaged in "actions significantly affecting the quality of the human environment" had to provide a "detailed statement" about the environmental impact of such activity. These environmental impact statements, or EISs, then became the source of legal conflict, as conservationists began to file suit against the Bureau of Land Management in particular, contesting the BLM's assessment of the impact of livestock grazing on public rangeland. By the early 1970s, environmental pressure on the BLM and successful litigation forced the agency to prepare 144 EISs. The process not only required time and money, but it also indicated that public grazing policy was undergoing a tremendous transformation. As one group of legal commentators has noted, "Future historians may date the beginning of modern rangeland management from December 1974 when a federal district court ordered the BLM to comply with the NEPA." [2]

These steps were just the beginning, however. Two more legislative acts had profound effects on public grazing. The Federal Land Policy and Management Act (or FLPMA) of 1976 was a culmination of environmentalist efforts to widen the expressed purposes of the public grazing lands under the Bureau of Land Management. FLPMA both specifically authorized the participation of recreational and wildlife interests in making range policy and declared—seemingly beyond a shadow of a doubt—that the public lands would remain "in federal ownership." [3] Privatization under any form, whether sales to individuals or a transfer to the states, appeared to be forever off the table. And only two years later, Congress passed the Public Rangeland Improvement Act (PRIA), which, while keeping grazing fees still below market levels, put the health of public grazing lands front and center in public grazing policy. The combination of FLPMA and PRIA was then powerful legislative sanction for the Carter administration's attempt to reduce the numbers of livestock on the range—an attempt that was first slowed down by Congress and then by the sagebrush rebellion, which both reacted against the Carter administration and helped elect a president whose interior secretary, James Watt, actively supported relinquishing some public lands by the federal government.[4] The rebellion's political goals most closely resembled those of the Joint Livestock Committee on Public Lands in the 1940s, calling for privatization of the public lands either through direct sales to ranchers or through ceding the lands to the states, which would then likely convey them at very low cost to ranchers. But the legislative bills that sought to authorize these actions went nowhere, and by the 1980s, organized ranchers and their allies in Congress focused instead on lobbying the Interior Department to ratchet down the amount of federal oversight of ranchers using BLM lands, which was largely successful until the change in the political party occupying the White House—that is, until Bill Clinton's election.[5]

If the rebellion was déjà vu all over again, the rebels also found themselves up against a very different political discourse and legal context than the struggles of the 1920s and 1940s, as the environmental movement had blown open notions of property at their seams. Like Bernard DeVoto in the 1940s, environmentalists pressed hard to convince the American people that they were the owners of the public lands and should therefore have a role in deciding how the government should manage them. As two of the most vocal critics of public lands ranching put it in the wake of the sagebrush rebellion, "Public lands belong to *all* Americans. Ownership establishes responsibility for management." [6] This argument challenged both the right of ranchers to control public land policy and the government's claim that it was acting in the public's interest, which environmentalists disputed. If the BLM and the Forest Service were acting in the public's interest on the public lands, why was so much of the land deemed overgrazed by the government itself?

Environmental oversight, in other words, explicitly tried to take the public grazing lands out of the prevailing property arrangements that the federal government had established between itself and public land ranchers. Not only did environmentalists assert the "unorganized public" to be the owner of these lands, but they also pushed to have other values recognized on the lands—values that directly challenged the prevailing view of these lands as property. As biologists and ecologists (many of them former employees of such federal agencies as the Forest Service and the BLM) fought to protect the flora and fauna on the public rangelands, they understood the lands through ecological models that transcended property lines, that explicitly rejected the "imaginative lens" of property. Instead, environmentalists have emphasized the need to build, in Aldo Leopold's words, "an ethical underpinning for land economics," which seeks to safeguard the ecological health of the land as a whole.[7] For many environmentalists this has meant removing livestock from the rangelands altogether. And even more significantly, over the past decade, some have argued that the government will have to reserve even larger bodies of rangeland to attempt to restore its health. In a book that caused a fierce backlash among Wyoming stock growers, Debra Donahue has maintained not only that all livestock must be "evicted," but also that assuring biodiversity on the BLM's lands will require thinking "at the landscape level." Although "[e]cology in its early years focused on individual ecosystems," Donahue writes, "ecosystems are not, and should not be viewed as, discrete entities." Managing public lands under the "landscape paradigm" would thus mean shifting environmentalists' focus from preserving single ecosystems to understanding and protecting the relationships between different plant and animal communities spread out over a large area.[8]

By thinking "outside the box" of property, ecologists and environmentalists have helped the public in the West and in the nation generally to understand that livestock grazing may not be a desirable use of the public lands—ecologically, politically, or economically. But environmentalists have also found themselves sometimes caught in the box of property in asserting a political program to battle both the power of the livestock industry and the ingrained policies of federal land agencies. For instance, the political legitimacy of environmental legislation on the public lands has often rested on the timeworn analogy between the government's property rights as an owner and those of an individual proprietor. Critical legal decisions have continued to support and reinscribe this comparison. In the 1976 case of *Kleppe v. New Mexico*—which involved the authority of the federal government to manage wild animals within the state—the Supreme Court "finally and firmly shut the door" on the question of Congress's legal powers to make policy for the public lands. In the words of the Court, "Congress exercises the powers both of a proprietor and of a legislator over the public domain."[9] Although this argument about the government's proprietorship is a powerful legal and political tool for protecting the public lands, it runs the

risks that have been explored in this book. First, it helps to calcify the
political divide between ranchers and the federal government by reducing the government's role to simply that of a property owner. Of course,
one effect of that calcification has been some environmental successes,
as the government has been able to implement policy changes, such as
FLPMA, that have helped reduce the place of livestock in public land
management. But the hardness of the property divide between ranchers
and the federal government has also made it difficult to forge new management techniques that could stand outside this model. Environmentalists have recognized this, and for those who do not advocate removing all livestock from the public lands, there is hope that true democratic
participation at the local level—including ranchers, environmentalists,
recreationists, and business people—will produce effective and ecologically worthy administration of the public grazing lands.[10]

The sagebrush rebellion dissipated in the 1980s, as Congress refused to
consider any kind of privatization, but the end of the decade saw yet another round of anti-federal activism emerge in the guise of the wise use
movement. While the movement was and continues to be part of a larger
discourse and politics about protecting private property rights, it also
has been directed very much against the policies of public land ownership and has been widely embraced by western ranchers, who rose up
again in protest following the Clinton administration's proposal to increase grazing fees on public lands.[11] This latest resistance drew understandable expressions of exasperation from liberal journalists and environmentalists, as public land ranchers seemed once more to be so
recalcitrant to change. Even one scholar critical of "big government,"
Karl Hess, Jr., has thrown up his hands at the West's ranchers who continue to ask for federal assistance, whether in the form of low grazing
fees or emergency loans, while mouthing the wise use agenda: "Stockmen of all stripes, on private and public lands alike, belie their wise-use
cause . . . by making mockery of deeply held principles. They speak
glowingly of free markets and free enterprise, but when push comes to
shove they opt for protectionism and less-than-free enterprise." [12]

   Hess clearly understands the link between ranchers' relationship with
the federal government and their property rights language; indeed, he
argues, "The wise-use West that now chomps at the federal bit is the
West that welcomed federal assistance for over a hundred years with
nary a discouraging word." [13] Nevertheless, he too has not quite captured the substance of that link. Organized ranchers, and particularly

public land ranchers, are not reacting simply against their own dependence on federal largesse. Nor is their espoused anti-statism an ideology
that has somehow been transmitted to them through the generations
and that stands outside and against the federal government. Rather,
their reactions have been fully produced by the acts that established the
national forests and the BLM lands. Their language of individual or
states' rights to the range was given shape by the structures of property
on the public lands. Their understanding of their rights to the range was
forged in conversation with federal land officials whose very job was to
assert that the government was the sole owner of the rights to that land.

That conversation was not always a civil one, but it signaled how
closely the two sides were politically intertwined. Indeed, environmentalists have long argued that it is this closeness—and, in particular, the
government's ultimate willingness to cooperate with ranchers—that has
produced the ecological and political problems on the range today.
Those problems are very real and seemingly intractable under the current policies regarding public grazing lands, and yet they must be seen
as arising from something other than the early capture of public agencies by private interest groups.[14] There was no capture, because the public grazing lands from the very beginning were infused with meaning
from the world of private property. Ranchers and government officials
were thus trapped in a struggle from which they could not break free:
unable to agree on that meaning, they were nonetheless bound together
in a relationship of politics and property, with each side laying claim to
the lands that stood between them.

Notes

PREFACE

1. Sally Fairfax has argued that "public-lands management issues are likely to continue to be less and less important as topics of national attention, and that state officials and evolving local groups will play a larger and more decisive role in decision making." She may be right, but as the population of the West continues to increase, and national leaders pay more attention to western concerns, these issues may reemerge powerfully in the national consciousness. See Sally K. Fairfax, "The Lands, Natural Resources, and Economy of the West," in *A Society to Match the Scenery: Personal Visions of the Future of the American West,* ed. Gary Holthaus et al. (Niwot, Colo.: University Press of Colorado, 1991), 198.

2. Patricia Nelson Limerick's article may be found in her collection of essays, *Something in the Soil: Legacies and Reckonings in the New West* (New York: Norton, 2000), 103, 97.

3. Katherine Van Wezel Stone, "The Post-War Paradigm in American Labor Law," *Yale Law Journal* 90 (June 1981): 1512. While Stone sees the establishment of the National Labor Relations Board as an important federal intervention, in practice, she argues, the NLRB has chosen private arbitration and has kept itself largely out of the adjudication of workers' rights.

4. Grant McConnell, *Private Power and American Democracy* (New York: Vintage Books, 1966), 201.

5. Clearly, there have been other important periods when the country has taken up the question of how far to extend government power—during Reconstruction, for instance, and during the 1960s. But what is so striking about the

period from 1900 to 1945 is that we see two distinct periods of great activity at
the federal level: the Progressive period and the New Deal. And, of course, lib-
erals in the 1960s saw their reforms as an extension of the New Deal.

6. Richard White, "Contested Terrain: The Business of Land in the American West," in *Land in the American West: Private Claims and the Common
Good,* ed. William G. Robbins and James C. Foster (Seattle: University of Washington Press, 2000), 190.

INTRODUCTION

1. George Stevens's film *Shane,* based on Jack Schaefer's 1949 novel, came
out in 1953.

2. The historical literature on public grazing in the American West is very
large. I found the two most helpful general works to be E. Louise Peffer, *The
Closing of the Public Domain: Disposal and Reservation Policies, 1900–1950*
(Stanford, Calif.: Stanford University Press, 1951), and Paul Wallace Gates, *The
History of Public Land Law Development* (Washington, D.C.: Zenger Publish-
ing Co., 1968), esp. 495–529, 607–34. But see also Benjamin Horace Hibbard,
A History of the Public Land Policies (1924; repr., Madison: University of Wis-
consin Press, 1965), esp. 476–87, 560–70; Phillip O. Foss, *Politics and Grass:
The Administration of Grazing on the Public Domain* (Seattle: University of
Washington Press, 1960); William D. Rowley, *U.S. Forest Service Grazing and
Rangelands: A History* (College Station: Texas A&M University Press, 1985);
Wesley Calef, *Private Grazing and Public Lands: Studies of the Local Manage-
ment of the Taylor Grazing Act* (Chicago: University of Chicago Press, 1961);
William L. Graf, *Wilderness Preservation and the Sagebrush Rebellions* (Savage,
Md.: Rowman & Littlefield, 1990); William J. Voigt, *Public Grazing Lands*
(New Brunswick, N.J.: Rutgers University Press, 1976).

3. See, e.g., Edward Abbey, "Something about Mac, Cows, Poker, Ranchers,
Cowboys, Sex, and Power . . . and Almost Nothing about American Lit," in
Northern Lights: A Selection of New Writing from the American West, ed. Deb-
orah Clow and Donald Snow (New York: Vintage Books, 1994), 137–58; Denzel and Nancy Ferguson, *Sacred Cows at the Public Trough* (Bend, Ore.: Maverick Publications, 1983); Lynn Jacobs, *Waste of the West: Public Lands
Ranching* (self-published, 1991). A more moderate and reflective work in this
vein is Sharman Apt Russell, *Kill the Cowboy: A Battle of Mythology in the
New West* (Reading, Mass.: Addison-Wesley, 1993). For a recent account of a
fierce battle over public grazing, see Stephen Stuebner, "Jon Marvel vs. the Marl-
boro Man," *High Country News,* August 2, 1999, 1, 8–10.

4. The latest scholarly version of this is Debra Donahue, *The Western Range
Revisited: Removing Livestock from Public Lands to Conserve Native Biodiversity* (Norman: University of Oklahoma Press, 2000).

5. See Donald Worster, *Under Western Skies: Nature and History in the
American West* (New York: Oxford University Press, 1982), 34–52; Charles F.
Wilkinson, *Crossing the Next Meridian: Land, Water, and the Future of the
West* (Washington, D.C.: Island Press, 1992). See also the five-part series of ar-
ticles that George Cameron Coggins published in 1982 and 1983 in *Environ-*

mental Law, all beginning with the title, "The Law of Public Rangeland Management." The most relevant of these to this work are "The Extent and Distribution of Federal Power," *Environmental Law* 12 (1982): 535–621 (co-authored with Parthenia Blessing Evans and Margaret Lindberg-Johnson) and "The Commons and the Taylor Act," *Environmental Law* 13 (1982): 1–101 (co-authored with Margaret Lindberg-Johnson).

6. Gary D. Libecap, *Locking up the Range: Federal Land Controls and Grazing* (Cambridge, Mass.: Ballinger., 1981); Karl Hess, Jr., *Visions upon the Land: Man and Nature on the Western Range* (Washington, D.C.: Island Press, 1992).

7. Paul Starrs has also sought to provide answers for why ranchers and the federal government have been so embattled, but as a geographer, he has explored this question in a very different way than I have. Moreover, his interest lies more in detailing how ranchers have understood their use of the land than in interpreting their understandings of what he calls "the ineffable term *property.*" In contrast, my book argues that we can only make sense of the conflicted political relationship between ranchers and land managers by tracing their competing visions of property on the public lands. See *Let the Cowboy Ride: Cattle Ranching in the American West* (Baltimore: Johns Hopkins University Press, 1998), xvi.

8. See Carol M. Rose's work on "the comedy of the commons" in *Property and Persuasion: Essays on the History, Theory, and Rhetoric of Ownership* (Boulder, Colo.: Westview Press, 1994), 105–62. Of course, Rose's essay is a play on Garrett Hardin's oft-cited essay "The Tragedy of the Commons," *Science* 162 (1968): 1243–48.

9. Scholars of the state routinely define "the state," in part, as a political entity that controls territory; or in the words of Gianfranco Poggi, "The state does not *have* a territory, it *is* a territory" (*The State: Its Nature, Development and Prospects* [Stanford, Calif.: Stanford University Press, 1990], 22). But social scientists and historians who have sought to "bring the state back in" have not considered the role that the administration of public property in the West played in state growth and strength. My work here argues that in fact the claims to property ownership formed a fundamental part of land agencies' sense of their administrative capacities and integrity. On the question of the state's involvement in the western United States, see Karen R. Merrill, "In Search of the 'Federal Presence' in the American West," *Western Historical Quarterly* 30 (Winter 1999): 449–73. The most influential books on the state in American political history have remained *Bringing the State Back In,* ed. Peter B. Evans, Dietrich Rueschemeyer, and Theda Skocpol (Cambridge: Cambridge University Press, 1985), and Stephen Skowronek, *Building a New American State: The Expansion of National Administrative Capacities, 1877–1920* (Cambridge: Cambridge University Press, 1982). The phrase "uneasy state" comes from Barry D. Karl, *The Uneasy State: the United States from 1915 to 1945* (Chicago: University of Chicago Press, 1983). For an exploration of the meanings of "territorial" and "jurisdictional" sovereignty in early modern state formation, see Peter Sahlins, *Boundaries: The Making of France and Spain in the Pyrenees* (Berkeley and Los Angeles: University of California Press, 1989).

CHAPTER 1. POLICING AND POLICYMAKING
ON THE RANGE

Epigraph: Theodore Roosevelt, *Ranch Life and the Hunting-Trail* (1888; Lincoln: University of Nebraska Press, 1983), 24.

1. Quoted in Agnes W. Spring, "A 'Genius for Handling Cattle': John W. Iliff," in *When Grass Was King: Contributions to the Western Range Cattle Industry Study,* ed. Maurice Frink et al. (Boulder: University of Colorado Press, 1956), 389.

2. For an especially good and concise discussion of the late nineteenth-century cattle industry, see Richard White, "Animals and Enterprise," in *The Oxford History of the American West,* ed. Clyde A. Milner II, Carol A. O'Connor, and Martha A. Sandweiss (New York: Oxford University Press, 1994), 252–67.

3. Walter Prescott Webb quoted in *The Cowboy Reader,* ed. Lon Tinkle and Allen Maxwell (New York: Longmans, 1959), 293.

4. Terry G. Jordan, *North American Cattle-Ranching Frontiers* (Albuquerque: University of New Mexico Press, 1993), 308. Here is Jordan's own characterization of the voluminous amount of work on the Anglo-Texan system of cattle raising: "The number of publications on this overemphasized, absurdly mythologized subject is simply mind-numbing." In fact, I would simply point the reader to Jordan's book as the best place to begin understanding this topic.

5. Ibid., 208.

6. Edward Everett Dale, *The Range Cattle Industry: Ranching on the Great Plains from 1865 to 1925* (1930; repr., Norman: University of Oklahoma Press, 1960), 4.

7. Texas cattle fever broke out among the Texas longhorns, which were used in the early days of the cattle industry because of their ability to endure the drives to market. Missouri had issued a quarantine before the Civil War. In 1867, Kansas closed its eastern farming section to Texas cattle, fearing widespread decimation. See Ernest Staples Osgood, *The Day of the Cattleman* (1929; repr., Chicago: University of Chicago Press, 1968), 36.

8. Dale, *Range Cattle Industry,* 38–44. See also Lewis Atherton, *The Cattle Kings* (Bloomington: Indiana University Press, 1961); Robert G. Athearn, *High Country Empire: The High Plains and Rockies* (Lincoln: University of Nebraska Press, 1960); and White, "Animals and Enterprise," 253.

9. On the decimation of the northern plains bison, see Andrew C. Isenberg, *The Destruction of the Bison* (Cambridge: Cambridge University Press, 2000), 140–43. See also Osgood, *Day of the Cattlemen,* ch. 3; Dale, *Range Cattle Industry,* 45–46; and Richard White, *"It's Your Misfortune and None of My Own": A History of the American West* (Norman: University of Oklahoma Press, 1991), 218.

10. Dale, *Range Cattle Industry,* 76.

11. "Between 1882 and 1886, as many capitalists as cowboys seemed to be chasing cattle in the West. Much of the total British cattle investment of forty-five million dollars entered the West during these years, and Eastern investors outspent the British" (White, "Animals and Enterprise," 261).

12. Gene Gressley, *Bankers and Cattlemen* (New York: Knopf, 1966), 67.

13. Osgood, *Day of the Cattleman*, 97–98; *When Grass Was King*, ed. Frink et al., 24.

14. Quoted in Osgood, *Day of the Cattleman*, 101. For a close look at the British and Scottish element in western—especially Wyoming—ranching, see Laurence M. Woods, *British Gentlemen in the Wild West: The Era of the Intensely English Cowboy* (New York: Free Press, 1989).

15. Review of *Report in Regard to the Range and Ranch Cattle Business in the United States*, by Joseph Nimmo, Jr., *The Nation*, July 2, 1885, 17.

16. In 1887, Congress passed the Alien Land Law, which made it illegal for foreign corporations and foreigners not intent on becoming citizens to own land in the western territories. But as Richard White has noted, "The law . . . proved largely a statement of pious intentions. Ten years later there had apparently not been a single forfeiture of land under its provisions" (White, "*It's Your Misfortune*," 262). Lewis Atherton appropriately emphasizes the diversity of ranch owners' economic and social backgrounds (Atherton, *Cattle Kings* 2–3).

17. As we shall see in greater depth in chapter 2, many Americans maligned ranching's place in the nation's political economy because in the late nineteenth century, the family was not the ranch's productive unit, as it was on most farms in America. Throughout the early twentieth century, family ranching became more common, but the occupation was still stigmatized as being run by "cattle kings."

18. In the political and cultural terms of the late nineteenth century, the term "improvements" meant roughly what it had meant since the settlement of the colonies, but without religious overtones. As William Cronon notes in *Changes in the Land: Indians, Colonists, and the Ecology of New England* (New York: Hill & Wang, 1983), the "imperative" to "improve" the land "was not just the biblical injunction to 'fill the earth and subdue it.' Colonists were moved to transform the soil by a property system that taught them to treat land as capital" (77). One example "was the fence, which to colonists represented perhaps the most visible symbol of an 'improved' landscape" (130). In the case of western ranchers who tried to fence the public range, the fence was really a representation of a fence; that is, it could not function as an improvement, because the rancher did not own the land. By fencing land he used but did not own, the rancher attempted to appropriate customary grazing as a legal (and thus commercial) right.

19. Quoted in David Emmons, *Garden in the Grasslands: Boomer Literature of the Central Plains* (Lincoln: University of Nebraska Press), 191.

20. Theodore Roosevelt, *Ranch Life and the Hunting-Trail*, 2. Of the cowboy, whom he carefully distinguished from the ranch owner, Roosevelt wrote: "Brave, hospitable, hardy, and adventurous, he is the grim pioneer of our race; he prepares the way for the civilization from before whose face he must himself disappear" (100).

21. Ibid., 6. This curious Middle Eastern metaphor took on biblical proportions when Roosevelt described the Lincoln County war in New Mexico: "It had origination in a quarrel between two great ranches over their respective water rights and range rights—a quarrel of a kind rife among pastoral peoples

since the days when the herdsmen of Lot and Abraham strove together for the grazing lands round the mouth of Jordan" (88).

22. Roosevelt drew this connection out further by claiming that most of the ranchers and cowboys of the "Northwest" (that is, in Dakota and Montana territory) came from the South and the East. "The rough-rider of the plains, the hero of rope and revolver, is first cousin to the backwoodsman of the southern Alleghanies, the man of the ax and rifle; he is only a unique offshoot of the frontier stock of the Southwest" (ibid., 15). Thus, in a sense, ranchers derived genetically, not from the industrializing East, but from the southern backcountry, a region of complex connotations. Like Owen Wister's Virginian, Roosevelt's transplanted southerners combined the virtues of frontier strength with a respect for hierarchical social order and an almost aristocratic nobility.

23. Ibid.

24. Ibid., 97.

25. Women were important symbolically to farming because they were so critical to the production on family farms. See, for instance, Mary Neth, *Preserving the Family Farm: Women, Community, and the Foundations of Agribusiness in the Midwest, 1900–1940* (Baltimore: Johns Hopkins University Press, 1995), esp. 214–43.

26. Roosevelt, *Ranch Life and the Hunting-Trail*, 24.

27. Osgood, *Day of the Cattleman*, 116.

28. Ibid., 126–27.

29. Ibid., 121; T. A. Larson, *History of Wyoming* (Lincoln: University of Nebraska Press, 1965), 172.

30. Dale, *Range Cattle Industry*, 86.

31. Osgood, *Day of the Cattleman*, 131–34, and Larson, *History of Wyoming*, ch. 7. The most far-reaching and controversial law was the Maverick Law of 1884. The legal problem of mavericks—or unbranded cattle—had dogged the range industry for some time and was particularly acute at the spring roundup when thousands of calves were born on the range. Any calf seen following a female was assumed to be hers and would then be a part of that herd. But there were also many orphaned calves, and with the influx of cattle ranchers and the overstocking of the range, it was not always evident to which herd orphaned calves belonged. The law of 1884 put that decision entirely in the hands of the WSGA. It became illegal for anyone to brand cattle between February 15 and the legal date set for the spring roundup. All mavericks rounded up were sold at auction to the highest bidder, with the proceeds going to the WSGA. See Osgood, 135–36, and Larson, 182–86.

32. Osgood, *Day of the Cattleman*, 135.

33. Hon. William N. Byers, "The Humane Treatment of Livestock," *Proceedings of the National Stock Growers' Convention* (Denver: New Job Printing Co., 1898), 63. Hereafter cited as *Proceedings*, with year (e.g., *Proceedings, 1898*).

34. *When Grass Was King*, ed. Frink et al., 260.

35. White, "Animals and Enterprise," 266.

36. Terry Jordan's work provides the most detail about ranching practices and in particular about why midwestern grazing practices, which provided win-

ter feed, triumphed after the winter of 1886–87. See *North American Cattle-Ranching Frontiers,* esp. 236–40, 267–307.

37. Alexander Campbell McGregor, *Counting Sheep: From Open Range to Agribusiness* (Seattle: University of Washington Press, 1982), 25–26.

38. For accounts of the Johnson County war, see Helena Huntington Smith, *The War on Powder River: The History of an Insurrection* (Lincoln: University of Nebraska Press, 1966), and T. A. Larson, *History of Wyoming,* 2d rev. ed. (Lincoln: University of Nebraska Press, 1978), 268–84.

39. Elwood Mead, "How Best to Prevent Clashing between Sheep and Cattle Men on Ranges," *Proceedings, 1898,* 94–97.

40. *Buford v. Houtz,* 133 U.S. 326 (1890).

41. Ibid., 328.

42. Osgood, *Day of the Cattleman,* 191–93. See also Osgood's discussion of the creative ways in which ranchers used legal fences on land they had purchased or leased from the railroads to enclose government tracts. Osgood wryly notes that "[i]f, by this process of fencing his outside [purchased] sections, the alternate sections of government land were enclosed, it appeared to the cattleman as a fortunate arrangement, incident on the Government's policy of granting alternate sections to the railroads" (212–13). See also Charles F. Wilkinson, *Crossing the Next Meridian: Land, Water, and the Future of the West* (Washington, D.C.: Island Press, 1992), 87.

43. Paul W. Gates, *The History of Public Land Law Development* (Washington, D.C.: Zenger Publishing Co., 1968), 435–62; Lawrence M. Friedman, *A History of American Law,* 2d ed. (New York: Simon & Schuster, 1985), 416–21.

44. "If we think of the American land system as a warehouse containing the nation's resources, then it was coming by the 1860s to be a warehouse that consisted almost entirely of doors. If the Homestead Act had been the only doorway to the public domain, then it probably would have distributed far more land than it did. But the Homestead Act was not the only doorway, and when farmers filed through it and reached the public domain, they found much of the land already gone. Those who took it had entered through other doors." White, "*It's Your Misfortune,*" 143.

45. Ibid., 140. For a discussion of the political debates about the public lands in the early 1800s, see Daniel Feller, *The Public Lands in Jacksonian Politics* (Madison: University of Wisconsin Press, 1984).

46. For an account of these two acts, see Peter S. Onuf, *Statehood and Union: A History of the Northwest Ordinance* (Bloomington: University of Indiana Press, 1987), esp. chs. 2 and 3.

47. The government also designated section 16 in each township (and after 1848, also section 36) as "school land," the proceeds of which after sale would support the state's public schools.

48. Gates, *History of Public Land Law Development,* 219–46.

49. Ibid., 393–99.

50. Settlers could buy their entries at the minimum price, which was generally $1.25 an acre (Gates, ibid., 393–98). When Theodore Roosevelt's Public Lands Commission studied the problem of commutation, it found that "[i]n the timber belt of Minnesota 89 percent of the commuted entries were transferred

to other parties, 36 percent in the agricultural belt, and 96 percent in the mineral belt, the transfers mostly being made either by the day of payment of shortly thereafter" (ibid., 490).

51. The Timber Culture Act of 1873 allowed a prospective settler 160 acres, provided he or she planted 40 acres of trees. Politicians hoped that the act would cover the plains with trees, not recognizing, of course, that there was not enough water. The Timber and Stone Culture Act of 1878 was intended to help settle nonagricultural lands. Settlers could purchase 160 acres, promising to use the timber and stone on that land for their personal use, but not for sale. Needless to say, lumbermen, miners, and ranchers all took advantage of this act. Finally, the Desert Land Act of 1877 made available 640-acre "homesteads," so long as the settler agreed to irrigate that land within three years. This was perhaps the most ludicrous of the settlement acts, because no individual or family could possibly irrigate that much land. Speculators, ranchers, and others who used this act to gain land fraudulently could purchase the land after three years with relatively minimal indications that they were irrigating the land. See White, "It's Your Misfortune," 150–52.

52. Not surprisingly, too, western politicians had a different view of these fraudulent entries than did officials in Washington. Governors of the intermountain states thought such acts as the Desert Land Act were very beneficial, "making possible economic units of land, if not for irrigation farming." The governor of Wyoming in 1883 even advertised how much land a man could get under these acts. Gates, History of Public Land Law Development, 640–41.

53. E. Louise Peffer, The Closing of the Public Domain: Disposal and Reservation Policies, 1900–1950 (Stanford, Calif.: Stanford University Press, 1951), 12. For the commission's report, see Report of the Public Lands Commission, Created by the Act of March 3, 1879, Relating to Public Lands in the Western Portion of the United States and to the Operation of Existing Land Laws (Washington, D.C.: GPO, 1880). Thomas Donaldson's The Public Domain: Its History, with Statistics . . . (Washington, D.C.: GPO, 1884) is one of the most important compendia of information on the public domain. And see also John Wesley Powell, Report on the Lands of the Arid Region of the United States, with a More Detailed Account of the Lands of Utah (Washington, D.C.: GPO, 1878).

54. For a fascinating reassessment of Powell, see Donald Worster, "The Legacy of John Wesley Powell," in Reopening the American West, ed. Hal K. Rothman (Tucson: University of Arizona Press, 1998), 77–89.

55. Samuel Hays, Conservation and the Gospel of Efficiency: The Progressive Conservation Movement (1959; repr., New York: Atheneum, 1980), 51–52. This is a point that Paul Starrs also makes in Let the Cowboy Ride: Cattle Ranching in the American West (Baltimore: Johns Hopkins University Press, 1998), 43.

56. Gates, History of Public Land Law, 580.

57. Quoted in Hays, Conservation and the Gospel of Efficiency, 57, n. 22.

58. See Daniel Rodgers, Atlantic Crossings: Social Politics in a Progressive Age (Cambridge, Mass.: Harvard University Press, 1998), 52–111.

59. Gifford Pinchot, *Breaking New Ground* (New York: Harcourt, Brace, 1947), 147.

60. Ibid., 152.

61. Ibid., 31.

62. Ibid., 28.

63. Ibid., 145.

64. Ibid., 179. His own physical prowess and "practical" knowledge of the forests distinguished him in his own mind from men like Charles Sargent, foresters in Pinchot's father's generation. "Sargent doesn't fish or hunt or know anything about the mountains," he noted at the time he served on the National Forest Commission in the mid 1890s (101). In contrast, he respected Roosevelt as "an outdoor man—more a wilderness hunter. He knew open country, East and West, the forests and the mountains, from much personal experience" (189).

65. Ibid., 148.

66. Ibid., 21.

67. Ibid., 120.

68. Ibid., 79 (emphases added.)

69. Paul Gates, "The Federal Lands—Why We Retained Them," in *Rethinking the Federal Lands,* ed. Sterling Brubaker (Washington, D.C.: Resources for the Future, 1984), 50.

70. "Out in the Great Open Spaces where Men were Men the domination of concentrated wealth over mere human beings was something to make you shudder" (Pinchot, *Breaking New Ground, 79*).

71. The first attempt at forming a permanent national organization of cattle producers was the National Cattle Growers' Association of America, which met initially in 1883. Tension between eastern and western producers would follow this organization, however, and it went through different associational forms, ending up as the Consolidated Cattle Growers' Association, which did not survive the break up of the industry after the winter of 1886–87. A short-lived western group calling itself the International Range Association lasted only a few years at the end of the 1880s, and some cattlemen joined eastern financiers in forming the American Cattle Trust, also in the 1880s. Although the trust "included ranches in Texas, New Mexico, Colorado and Wyoming encompassing 218,934 head of cattle," as well as feedlots and a packing plant, it did not survive financially. Charles Ball, *Building the Beef Industry: A Century of Commitment* (Denver: National Cattlemen's Foundation, 1998), 6–7, 8–16.

72. Ibid., 20.

73. Hon. Alva Adams, "Address of Welcome on Behalf of the State of Colorado," *Proceedings, 1898, 16.*

74. For an incisive look at some of Mead's ideas, along with other reclamation leaders, see Donald J. Pisani, "State v. Nation: Federal Reclamation and Water Rights in the Progressive Era," in *Water, Land, and Law in the West: The Limits of Public Policy, 1850–1920* (Lawrence: University Press of Kansas, 1996), 38–49.

75. "Breed the best in every class and you will own better farms, better

barns, better homes and have better wives and children" (John Springer, "Inaugural Address," *Proceedings, 1898,* 22).

76. Governor William A. Richards, "The Cession of Public Lands to the States," *Proceedings, 1898,* 93.

77. In fact, Richards anticipated what would later be called the principle of "commensurability" in federal grazing administration—that is, permitting a livestock owner to graze only as many animals as he or she was able to take care of through the winter with feed grown on private or leased lands. "The ratio between the quantities of each kind of land to be held together would be naturally fixed, no one wanting more grazing land than sufficient for the stock that his irrigable land would supply with feed for the winter," Richards said (ibid.).

CHAPTER 2. THE PROPERTIES OF THE HOMEBUILDER

Epigraph: *Proceedings of the National Live Stock Association* (Denver: Smith-Brooks Printing Co., 1903), 125. Reed was the mayor of Kansas City, Missouri, where the convention was held that year. Hereafter, the conventions will be cited as *Proceedings,* with the year.

1. Sam Cowan, *Proceedings,1907,* 96–97.

2. See Charles E. Ball, *Building the Beef Industry: A Century of Commitment* (Denver: National Cattlemen's Foundation, 1998), 42.

3. *Proceedings, 1916,* 32.

4. Written statement from A. E. de Ricqles in U.S. Congress, House, Committee on Public Lands, *A Bill to Provide for the Disposition of Grazing Lands under the Homestead Laws and for Other Purposes,* Hearings on H.R. 9582 and H.R. 10539, 63d Cong., 2d sess., pt. 1 (1914), 253 (hereafter cited as *Hearings* on H.R. 9582 and H.R. 10539).

5. Stanford Layton has argued that the country life movement and the back-to-the-land movement formed a kind of "matrix" from which the early twentieth-century homesteading acts emerged. *To No Privileged Class: The Rationalization of Homesteading and Rural Life in the Early Twentieth-Century West* (Provo, Utah: Brigham Young University, Charles Redd Center for Western Studies, 1988). On the country life movement itself, see David Danbom, *The Resisted Revolution: Urban America and the Industrialization of Agriculture, 1900–1930* (Ames: Iowa State University Press, 1979). On the Country Life Commission, which Roosevelt appointed, see *U.S. Congress, Senate, Report of the United States Country Life Commission,* 60th Cong., 2d sess., Senate Doc. 705 (1909).

6. David Emmons, *Garden in the Grasslands: Boomer Literature of the Central Great Plains* (Lincoln: University of Nebraska Press, 1971), 188.

7. William E. Smythe, *The Conquest of Arid America* (New York: Harper & Bros., 1900), 9. Patricia Nelson Limerick has characterized Smythe's vision of irrigation in the following way: "Most people fail to see transcendent meaning in irrigated agriculture, but the idea came easily to William Ellsworth Smythe. . . . The experience of watching farms wither from lack of rain, while water flowed in untapped streams, changed the direction of Smythe's life. He con-

verted to reclamation." Limerick, *The Legacy of Conquest: The Unbroken Past of the American West* (New York: Norton, 1987), 135.

8. The most extensive examination of dry farming remains Mary Wilma Hargreaves, *Dry Farming in the Northern Great Plains, 1900–1925* (Cambridge, Mass.: Harvard University Press, 1957).

9. Address by Hon. Alva Adams, *Sixth Annual International Dry Farming Congress*, 1911, 57.

10. Ibid., 56. "Home building is the best business in the world. The home is the seat of the happiness and the sheet anchor of free government. In the family fireside is planted deep the flag of this republic. Those who broaden the domain of homes are the true patriots and our greatest men," Adams also said.

11. Edward Everett Dale, *The Range Cattle Industry: Ranching on the Great Plains from 1865 to 1925* (1930; repr., Norman: University of Oklahoma Press, 1960), 176.

12. Quoted in Danbom, *Resisted Revolution*, 22.

13. E. Louise Peffer, *The Closing of the Public Domain: Disposal and Reservation Policies, 1900–1950* (Stanford, Calif.: Stanford University Press, 1951), 141.

14. "A reading of the two reports of the commission suggests that it was created to give support to views already well crystallized in the minds of Pinchot and Newell," Paul Gates writes (*The History of Public Land Law Development* [Washington, D.C.: Zenger Publishing Co., 1968], 489).

15. See "Proceedings of Conference between Special Land Commission . . . and Prominent Stockmen of the West." Attached to *Proceedings, 1905.*

16. This was to repeal a provision that had allowed those people who had patented land within forest reserves to exchange it for public land outside the reserves; this repeal, it was presumed, would cut down on continued land fraud. Peffer, *Closing of the Public Domain,* 47.

17. *Report* of the Public Lands Commission, 58th Cong., 3d sess., Senate doc. no. 189, (1905), 18.

18. Ibid., 20.

19. Ibid., xii.

20. The commission argued that "under the present conditions, speaking broadly, the large estate usually remains in a low condition of cultivation, whereas under actual settlement by individual home makers the same land would have supported many families in comfort and would have yielded far greater returns" (ibid., 14).

21. "[I]t appears that the chief influence lay in the fact that the lease acted as an advertisement of the land" (ibid., 47). Texas retained its public lands when it was admitted as a state in 1845.

22. Samuel Hays, *Conservation and the Gospel of Efficiency: The Progressive Conservation Movement* (1959; repr., New York: Atheneum, 1980), 55.

23. George K. Bowden, an attorney in the 1920s for a Senate subcommittee to the Committee on Public Lands and Surveys, counted sixty-five grazing bills that came before Congress between the end of the nineteenth century and 1926. "Not one of those bills has ever been reported out of committee" ("Grazing on National Forests and the Public Domain," *Proceedings, 1926,* 51).

24. William D. Rowley, *U.S. Forest Service Grazing and Rangelands: A History* (College Station: Texas A&M University Press, 1985), 36–37.

25. Pinchot wrote years later, "I hate a sheep, and the smell of a sheep. . . . Yet I recognize (with regret) that sheep are necessary, and (with satisfaction) that good handling can make and keep them harmless." *Breaking New Ground* (New York: Harcourt, Brace, 1947), 270.

26. Ibid., 177; Rowley, *U.S. Forest Service Grazing,* 38.

27. Pinchot, *Breaking New Ground,* 177–78.

28. Ibid., 181–82.

29. The most prominent stockman, in addition to Potter, who joined the Forest Service was Will C. Barnes, who had managed the Esperanza Cattle Co. in Arizona. Barnes was devoted both to the cause of the service and to western cattlemen, and was a prolific contributor to the ANLSA's trade journal, the *Producer.*

30. Although the National Wool Growers Association was generally skeptical of Forest Service policy in the Progressive period, its trade association journal, the *National Wool Grower* (hereafter cited as *NWG*), often featured articles by Forest Service personnel. As just a sample, see C. S. Chapman, "Range Development and Improvement on National Forests," *NWG,* May 1911, 22–24, and articles by Potter himself: "Relation of Forest to Flockmaster," *NWG,* January 1912, 19–21, and "Co-operation in Range Management," *NWG,* January 1913, 15–17.

31. John C. MacKay, *Proceedings, 1900,* 273.

32. Morton Keller, *Regulating a New Economy: Public Policy and Economic Change in America, 1900–1933* (Cambridge, Mass.: Harvard University Press, 1990), 150.

33. *Proceedings, 1905,* 325–26.

34. Ibid., 326.

35. *Proceedings, 1903,* 250.

36. *Proceedings, 1900,* 202–3, 302. Or, as another speaker put it baldly in 1907: "You fellows don't care about the settler, except that you are going to become one yourself on a piece of land you have got your eye on. There is no use to mince words, and make false pretenses. What you want is to get as much grass for your stock as you can." *Proceedings, 1907,* 97.

37. *Proceedings, 1900,* 300–301.

38. Certainly, this was a reputation that ranchers would continue to carry with them from the outside. For instance, at the American National Live Stock Association's 1915 convention, the cattlemen were welcomed by a California state government representative who remarked that the cattlemen "represent the sort of life that keeps us virile—outdoor life. . . . [A]s long as we can have an outdoor life, and outdoor men to live it and lead it, there is no danger of our civilization becoming decadent." *Proceedings, 1915,* 8–9.

39. *Proceedings, 1900,* 270.

40. *Proceedings of the Public Land Convention* (Denver: Press of the Western Newspaper Union, 1907), 55. Wilson's fellow Wyoming sheep rancher Francis E. Warren also thought about settling farmers on his property, implying that this would be good for his image. See Francis E. Warren to Fred Warren,

December 14, 1908, Francis E. Warren Papers, box 9, American Heritage Center, University of Wyoming, Laramie.

41. *Proceedings, 1905,* 295–96.

42. *Proceedings, 1903,* 141.

43. *Proceedings, 1900,* 304.

44. *Hearings* on H.R. 9582 and H.R. 10539, 437.

45. *Proceedings, 1908,* 86.

46. Ibid., 115. Carey in fact noted that he had changed his mind on the leasing question, having previously favored continued homesteading.

47. Likewise, the western livestock industry began having more public discussions with government officials. In the 1908 convention, the ANLSA's executive committee noted that it was pleased that President Roosevelt "appropriately recognized this Association" in making appointments to a committee to discuss the public lands. "Some of the members of our Committee on Forest Reserves and Grazing Lands met with this special committee appointed by the President," and advised getting "federal administration of the open range" (*Proceedings, 1908,* 58).

48. *Proceedings, 1904,* 243–44.

49. Peffer, *Closing of the Public Domain,* 65, 97.

50. *Public Land Convention,* 136–37.

51. Theodore Roosevelt, "Annual Message to Congress," 1907, in *Documents in American History,* ed. Henry Steele Commager, 7th ed. (New York, 1963), 50.

52. *Proceedings, 1908,* 50–51.

53. *Hearings* on H.R. 9582 and H.R. 10539, 135.

54. Ibid., 85.

55. Hearings on H.R. 9582 and H.R. 10539, 152. Perhaps one of the most ludicrous moments of the hearings came when Congressman John Raker of California, who was a tireless defender of the homesteader, pressed leasing supporter J. B. Killian about his knowledge of land tenure and human history. Raker was concerned that if ranchers were allowed to lease government land, they would also be allowed to fence it, which would discourage homesteading. "Do you know," he asked Killian, "from your examination from the beginning of history down to the present time of any place or any condition where men have been permitted to inclose [*sic*] their land" and other men were then able to "establish homes or mining camps" on them? Clearly stymied, Killian answered, "Well—"; at which point Congressman Charles Thomson of Illinois rescued him by asking, "Is this B.C. or anno Domini?" (124).

56. Ibid., 57

57. Ibid., 103.

58. *Proceedings, 1915,* 57. On William Kent's progressivism, see Anne Hyde, "William Kent: The Puzzle of Progressive Conservationists," in *California Progressivism Revisited,* ed. William Deverell and Tom Sitton (Berkeley and Los Angeles: University of California Press, 1994), 34–56.

59. Robert H. Wiebe, *Businessmen and Reform: A Study of the Progressive Movement* (Cambridge, Mass.: Harvard University Press, 1962), 179. "If one were to read the pages of the Congressional Record he would find there more

words uttered in behalf of the homesteader within the National Forests than in behalf of any other class of our citizens," the *National Wool Grower* editorialized at the height of the debate over how to admit homesteaders to the national forests ("Homesteading the Forests," *NWG*, February 1913, 28).

60. Carol Rose, *Property and Persuasion: Essays on the History, Theory, and Rhetoric of Ownership* (Boulder, Colo.: Westview Press, 1994), 296–97.

61. Like Rose, C. B. Macpherson uses the notion of sight, although in a fairly unexplored way, to explain how meanings of property are formed: "How people see the thing—that is, what concept they have of it—is both effect and cause of what it is at any time. What they see must have some relation (though not necessarily an exact correspondence) to what is actually there; but changes in what is there are due partly to changes in the ideas people have of it. This is simply to say that property is both an institution and a concept and that over time the institution and the concept influence each other." *Property: Mainstream and Critical Positions*, ed. C. B. Macpherson, (Toronto: University of Toronto Press, 1978), 1.

62. *Public Land Convention*, 11.

63. "The property system in U.S. history is one that promotes the dispersal of ownership. This dispersal of ownership allows a well-functioning competitive market to exist; disperses power; grants widely the benefits of independence, stability, and liberty that are associated with property ownership; and promotes access to the means necessary for a dignified human life. . . . [O]ur political history is replete with government action, such as the homestead laws, designed to ensure widespread dispersal of ownership," Joseph Singer writes (*The Edges of the Field: Lessons on the Obligations of Ownership* [Boston: Beacon Press, 2000], 26).

64. Rowley, *U.S. Forest Service Grazing*, 59.

65. Ibid.

66. Ibid., 61, 90. During the Depression, grazing permits were even accepted as collateral by some banks in the West (ibid., 162).

67. Ibid., 72–73.

68. *Proceedings, 1907*, 100.

69. *Breaking New Ground*, 259.

70. See Rodgers, *Atlantic Crossings*, 95–111.

71. 220 U.S. 523–38 (1911).

72. Quoted at p. 536; See also *Camfield v. United States*,167 U.S. 524 (1897).

73. I say "loosely" because the language of trusteeship is very different from that used in establishing policy for the state trust lands, also known as the "school lands." These were lands granted to the states upon their admission to the United States. As Jon Souder and Sally Fairfax write, these lands, "in combination with the revenues and permanent funds they produce, are generally viewed as a trust; hence, trust land managers approach their management responsibilities under the same array of rules and enforcement mechanisms that surround any trustee, such as a banker managing funds for a client's grandchild." This arrangement, they argue, provides a much stricter set of guidelines for managing state lands than the principles established for managing public

land use. Souder and Fairfax, *State Trust Lands: History, Management, and Sustainable Use* (Lawrence: University Press of Kansas, 1996), 1. Moreover, there is a stricter interpretation of trusteeship to be found in the public trust doctrine, which has long been used by states to protect tidelands and submerged lands for certain public uses, such as navigation and fishing. The public trust doctrine is a unique legal principle that binds the states' regulatory authority with property. "[B]ecause the public trust doctrine is fundamentally a property- or ownership-based doctrine, a state's authority under the public trust doctrine is not limited to the power to regulate but also includes the power to protect the state's fundamental rights in its property, and the rights of all members of the public to use such property, even when the property has been conveyed into private ownership," Jack H. Archer et al. observe in *The Public Trust Doctrine and the Management of America's Coasts* (Amherst: University of Massachusetts Press, 1994), 4. Carol Rose also discusses the public trust doctrine in *Property and Persuasion*, 111–16, where she describes it as a "strong" doctrine for protecting public property, compared to "weak" doctrines that emerged from the public's customary use of certain properties.

74. *United States v. Grimaud,* 220 U.S. 517 (1911).

75. Rose, *Property and Persuasion,* 121–22; *Property,* ed. Macpherson, 4–6.

76. The decision quotes from *United States v. Trinidad Coal Co.,* 137 U.S. 160: "All the public lands of the nation are held in trust for the people of the whole country." It goes on: "And it is not for the courts to say how that trust shall be administered. That is for Congress to determine" (220 U.S. 537). One of the reasons this is complicated is that the only other place in the Constitution that mentions federal property is in Article I, which gives " 'exclusive' federal jurisdiction over the District of Columbia and other places for government if the states agree to cede jurisdiction." George Cameron Coggins and Robert L. Glicksman, "Power, Procedure, and Policy in Public Lands and Resources Law," *Natural Resources and Environment* 10 (Summer 1995): 3.

77. U.S. Constitution, Article IV, section 3, clause 2.

78. *Light v. United States,* 536–37; *Kansas v. Colorado,* 206 U.S. 89.

79. Morris Cohen, "Property and Sovereignty," in *Property,* ed. Macpherson, 159. Cohen's piece was originally given at the Cornell Law School and was reprinted in *Cornell Law Quarterly* 13 (1927). As for the ingrained distinction between the two, Cohen writes that "[s]overeignty is a concept of political or public law and property belongs to civil or private law."

80. Quoting from *Van Brocklin v. Tennessee,* 117 U.S. 158.

CHAPTER 3. THE LESSONS OF THE MARKET

Epigraph: Address of Clay Tallman, *Proceedings* of the American National Live Stock Association (Denver: Smith-Brooks Printing Co., 1919), 24. Hereafter cited as *Proceedings,* with year.

1. For a detailed look at work on planning in World War I, and beyond, see Patrick D. Reagan's bibliographic essay "American Planning," in *Voluntarism, Planning, and the State: The American Planning Experience, 1914–1946,* ed.

Jerold E. Brown and Patrick D. Reagan (New York: Greenwood Press, 1988), 141–62. It should be noted that while Hoover mobilized state power in the economy as food administrator, he saw "price-fixing as at best a necessary evil in time of war" and sought to develop voluntary, associational relationships between the government and farmers in the 1920s. See Joan Hoff Wilson, "Herbert Hoover's Agricultural Policies, 1921–1928," in *Herbert Hoover as Secretary of Commerce: Studies in New Era Thought and Practice,* ed. Ellis W. Hawley (Iowa City: University of Iowa Press, 1981), 125. It was Hoover's associational philosophy that guided his policy agenda for the public domain when he became president.

2. These contests over administrative authority were a hallmark of 1920s, or "New Era," planning. The immediate postwar years saw "the transfer of public policy making from the political to the administrative arena," Guy Alchon notes. A variety of new "technocratic" institutions emerged right after the war, which "were clearly portents of things to come, since they contained the rudiments of the modern managerial constellation of business, foundation, social science, and government elites." Alchon, *The Invisible Hand of Planning: Capitalism, Social Science, and the State in the 1920s* (Princeton, N.J.: Princeton University Press, 1985), 51. At the same time, as secretary of commerce (and later as president), Herbert Hoover encouraged government agencies to work with voluntary trade and marketing associations.

3. The Forest Service allowed 188,000 more cattle and 876,000 more sheep in the national forests (U.S. Congress, Senate. *The Western Range . . . : A Report on the Western Range—A Great but Neglected Resource,* 74th Cong., 2d sess., 1936, doc. no. 199, 265). It took some time before the Stock-Raising Homestead Act was actually up and running, and by the early 1920s, it was widely considered a failure. See Paul W. Gates, *The History of Public Land Law Development* (Washington, D.C.: Zenger Publishing Co., 1968), 516–22.

4. Will C. Barnes, "The Work of the Forest Service in War Time," *Proceedings, 1918,* 142; William D. Rowley, *U.S. Forest Service Grazing and Rangelands: A History* (College Station: Texas A&M University Press, 1985), 112.

5. Frank Hagenbarth, "The Relation of Federal Government to the Producer in the Present Emergency," *Proceedings, 1918,* 28.

6. "We trust that the Food Administrator will select the best cattleman, the best sheepman, and the best hogman in the United States, and invite them to Washington to stay there in the Food Administration Building, organize a proper force, and go to work with plenty of authority and a free hand on some of these issues" (A. E. de Ricqles, "A Live-Stock Policy for Washington," *Proceedings, 1918,* 59).

7. Hagenbarth, "Relation of Federal Government," *Proceedings, 1918,* 32.

8. Gates, *History of Public Land Law Development,* 519–22.

9. Lynn Ramsay Edminster, *The Cattle Industry and the Tariff* (New York: Macmillan, 1926), 304–5.

10. *National Wool Grower,* May 1920, 16. Hereafter cited as *NWG.*

11. Will C. Barnes, "Sheepmen on the National Forests, *NWG,* February 1921, 22, 33.

12. Ibid., 34.

13. "The efficient live-stock unit—as a business enterprise—should, I believe, become more and more the key-point in the grazing management of the national forests, including the ranch property and equipment needed to supplement public range allotments," W. B. Greeley told the 1923 ANLSA convention. "The government should encourage such well-established and well-equipped live-stock enterprises" (Greeley, "Stabilizing the Use of Public Ranges," *Proceedings, 1923,* 35).

14. U.S. Department of Agriculture, *Agriculture Yearbook, 1923* (Washington, D.C.: GPO, 1923), 58.

15. It should be remembered at this point that the national forests were transferred out of the Department of the Interior in 1905. In that year, the Forest Service actually proposed that the national parks should be transferred out of Interior and "come under the supervision" of the service. The parks stayed in the Interior Department, of course, and in 1916 Congress passed a law creating the National Park Service under that department. E. Louise Peffer, *The Closing of the Public Domain: Disposal and Reservation Policies, 1900–1950* (Stanford, Calif.: Stanford University Press, 1951), 175–76.

16. In addition to differentiating themselves as indicated, the two departments managed geographically different lands, which had different functions for ranchers. Forest Service grazing lands lay mostly at higher elevations and were used as summer forage; livestock owners herded their animals to these pastures in late spring and brought them down in early fall. The grass on these lands was generally of much higher quality than that left on the remaining public domain.

17. David F. Houston, "Address," *Proceedings, 1919,* 82–83. Emphases added.

18. Ibid, 83. Houston also noted that "this meeting has seemed to me to be a sort of conference of the Department of Agriculture. A considerable part of the speech of your President dealt with the Department of Agriculture. Most of your speakers . . . have been drawn from its staff."

19. U.S. Congress, Senate, Subcommittee of the Committee on Public Lands and Surveys, *National Forests and the Public Domain,* 69th Cong., 1st sess., vol. 1 (1925), Hearings on S. Res. 347, 139. Hereafter cited as *Hearings* on S. Res. 347.

20. Ibid., 140.

21. Gifford Pinchot first showed up at an ANLSA convention in 1904; thereafter, USDA and especially Forest Service officials were routine presences at the annual conventions. During the teens, Albert F. Potter and Will C. Barnes both participated in the ANLSA's annual programs.

22. Quoted in Peffer, *Closing of the Public Domain,* 199.

23. Will C. Barnes, "Grazing on National Forests," *Proceedings, 1921,* 98.

24. Quoted in Peffer, *Closing of the Public Domain,* 175.

25. Clay Tallman, "Address," *Proceedings, 1919,* 25.

26. Peffer, *Closing of the Public Domain,* 181–82.

27. Gary D. Libecap, *Locking Up the Range: Federal Land Controls and Grazing* (Cambridge, Mass.: Ballinger, 1981), 39.

28. Ibid., 8.

29. In 1920, the General Land Office in the Department of the Interior re-

ceived approximately $3,000,000 in congressional appropriations, compared to the Forest Service's $6,000,000. For more figures on these annual appropriations, see Libecap, *Locking Up the Range,* 40.

30. William Greeley, "Stabilizing the Use of Public Ranges," 30.

31. Ibid., 31.

32. See David E. Hamilton, *From New Day to New Deal: American Farm Policy from Hoover to Roosevelt, 1928–1933* (Chapel Hill: University of North Carolina Press, 1991), 4–6.

33. Houston, "Address," *Proceedings, 1917,* 95–96.

34. See, e.g., G. S. Klemmedson, "Costs and Methods in Carrying Cattle on National Forest Ranges in Colorado, Wyoming, Montana, Utah and Idaho in 1923" (July 1924), in Colorado Stockgrowers Association Papers, Colorado Historical Society, file #372. Klemmedson was an assistant farm economist with the Bureau of Agricultural Economics. See also Division of Range Research, Forest Service, United States Department of Agriculture, "The History of Western Range Research," *Agricultural History* 18 (July 1944): 127–43; C. L. Forsling, "Range Studies as an Aid in Live-Stock Production," *Producer,* December 1924, 2–7; and Glynn Bennion, "A School for Graziers," *NWG,* October 1924, 13–14, 41–42.

35. Greeley, "Stabilizing the Use of Public Ranges," 32.

36. Ibid.

37. In proposing this direction, Greeley noted that he would discuss the policy with livestock owners, who were in fact ambivalent at this point about shouldering the burden of building improvements on public lands; as the secretary for the Arizona Woolgrowers Association believed, "the stockmen do not believe that they should bear any part of the cost of [fencing in the national forests] as it is built on Government property and when they leave it it belongs to the Government." Others saw the investment as a positive thing, especially since improvements built by a permittee would be figured into the grazing fee. By the following year, however, Greeley had given up the proposal, and the 1924 *Forest Manual* primarily discusses the procedures for improvements built by the permittees, although the question of who would build improvements has continued to be a live one to the very present. *National Forest Manual—Grazing* in Hearings on S. Res. 347, pt. 1, 89–94. Greeley, "Stabilizing the Use of Public Ranges," 35, and "Grazing Administration and Range Fees," *Proceedings, 1924, 133.*

38. Greeley, "Stabilizing the Use of Public Ranges," 35.

39. Greeley, "Grazing Administration and Range Fees," 133.

40. Peffer, *Closing of the Public Domain,* 187. See also Rowley, *U.S. Forest Service Grazing and Rangelands,* 118–20.

41. "I never have been able to see any reason why the government of the United States should grant some special privilege to some special persons who were fortunate enough to obtain grazing permits in certain forest reserves," one congressman noted. "Everybody who raises sheep and cattle cannot obtain these permits, if they are lower than would be charged upon other land." Quoted from *Congressional Record,* January 5, 1917, in A. F. Potter, "Grazing Fees on the National Forests," *Proceedings, 1917,* 120.

42. C. E. Rachford, "Range Appraisal Report," in *Hearings* on S. Res. 347, pt. 1, 17–39.

43. Ibid., 33.

44. Every issue of the *National Wool Grower* and the *Producer* between late 1923 and through 1925 included pieces on the grazing fee battle. Of the more illuminating articles, see William Sharp, "The Price of Grass, *NWG*, March 1924, 13–15; Glynn Bennion, "Grazing Land Values," ibid., 19–21; and Richard Dillon, "Comes Now the Plaintiff," *Producer*, April 1924, 5–9.

45. Quoted in Rachford, "Range Appraisal Report," 17.

46. Ibid., 18.

47. Ibid., 17. The problem was not simply that the grazing lands within the national forests varied tremendously across the West; there were also "wide fluctuations in prices for similar rangeland from locality to locality" on the private market. Rowley, *U.S. Forest Service Grazing and Rangelands*, 123.

48. *Producer*, December 1925, 17.

49. Rachford, "Range Appraisal Report," 33. Secretary of Agriculture Henry C. Wallace acknowledged that "a small percentage of grazing permittees, particularly in the Southwest, have been unable to pay the fees required by the Forest Service" (*Agriculture Yearbook, 1923, 57*).

50. Rachford, "Range Appraisal Report," 36.

51. For instance, in his annual address to the National Wool Growers' Association in 1924, President Frank Hagenbarth said: "Congress has not authorized directly or indirectly the commercialization of the grazing resource. The present proposal of the Department of Agriculture has the effect of changing national policy. We cannot accept or abide by such a change unless or until it is specifically and clearly required or authorized by Congress" ("Address of F. J. Hagenbarth," *NWG*, February 1924, 28). Unfortunately, Hagenbarth always had a short memory: here he forgot that four years earlier the House Agriculture Committee had wanted to raise grazing fees much higher than now proposed by the Forest Service.

52. F. R. Marshall, "Higher Grazing Fees on National Forests," *Producer*, November 1923, 7.

53. Rachford, "Range Appraisal Report," 33.

54. A 1923 survey of ranching in Colorado, Wyoming, Montana, Utah, and Idaho indicated that ranchers who grazed their animals in the national forests experienced the greatest animal losses when their stock were in the forests. See Klemmedson, "Costs and Methods of Carrying Cattle," 7–9.

55. William Sharp, "The Price of Grass," *NWG*, March 1924, 14.

56. Ibid.

57. This claim emerged in all sorts of shapes. When asked during the Stanfield Hearings why the government should not get "full value" for the forage on national forests—especially since the Forest Service argued it did for timber—the secretary of Arizona Woolgrowers Association, H. B. Embach, said: "The lumberman finds the trees growing; he has not contributed anything to the growth of it. The grass can not be used in its native state; it has to go through an animal before it can be made into beef or mutton." *Hearings* on S. Res. 347,

115 7. Not surprisingly, perhaps, ranchers never mentioned the labor of others, such as lumbermen, when making this argument.

58. But that transfer was then subject to a reduction of 10 percent. *See National Forest Manual—Grazing*, 71.

59. Rachford, "Range Appraisal Report," 33.

60. Ibid., 21, 37. For another take on the law of supply and demand, see Will Barnes's characterization in William MacLeod Raine and Will C. Barnes, *Cattle* (Garden City, N.J.: Doubleday, Doran, 1930), 226: "Damming and directing the flow of the cattle tide, the Forest Service has helped to change it from a turbulent flood to a placid stream, and has been a factor in transforming the cattle trade from an uncertain adventure to a business dominated by the laws of supply and demand." Here we see the public agency of the federal government directing the livestock industry into the private world of the market.

61. In the years after the war, ranchers saw all facets of the industry in a state of disruption. See, e.g., the very heated discussion at the 1921 ANLSA convention on whether there should be a federal commission formed to regulate the meatpacking industry. Over the years, ranchers had had a rather tormented relationship with meatpackers. When prices were good, as they had been before the war, they were largely on good terms; when prices fell, as they did so dramatically after the war, ranchers accused the packers of unfair business practices. See *Proceedings, 1921,* 187–204. Ranchers also believed that both the market for private land and assessments of that land were tremendously inflated. The secretary of the Colorado Stockgrowers Association, B. F. Davis, wrote a fascinating set of notes about this problem, sometime in 1923, which can be found in Colorado Stock Growers Association papers, box 2, file no. 162, Colorado Historical Society.

62. Rachford, "Range Appraisal Report," 37.

63. Range economics was in its infancy in the 1920s. A ranch economics textbook from 1968 states, "After much initial work in the 1920–1930 period, many of the original group of researchers [in ranch economics] retired or were diverted to other interests. Much of the present interest in ranch economics stems from work of the Bureau of Agricultural Economics in the U.S. Department of Agriculture in the 1940s and from a committee of university economists organized in the 1950s to make studies of ranches." James R. Gray, *Ranch Economics* (Ames: Iowa State University Press, 1968), 2–3.

64. Marion Clawson, *The Western Range Livestock Industry* (New York: McGraw-Hill, 1950), 255. Rachford notes in his report that the Forest Service tried to control for inflated private rents by trying to gather rental data for as many years as possible, and to exclude from the comparison those private tracts of land deemed not representative of lands found in the national forests.

65. Rachford, "Range Appraisal Report," 21.

66. Clawson, *Western Range Livestock Industry*, 271.

67. Greeley, "Grazing Administration and Range Fees," 138.

68. Clawson, *Western Range Livestock Industry*, 254.

69. *Agriculture Yearbook, 1923,* 60. Richard White has explored the pitfalls of relying on the market for guidance in public land policy. See "Contested Terrain: The Business of Land in the American West," in *Land in the American*

West: Private Claims and the Common Good, ed. William G. Robbins and James C. Foster (Seattle: University of Washington Press, 2000), 190–206. This was a common rendering of the Forest Service's argument that it was in the public's interest to have fees raised.

70. This question actually had two components. One was that ranchers wanted grazing to be recognized in writing as a legitimate use of the national forests; as it stood, only timber conservation and watershed protection were specifically set down as the purposes for administering the national forests. The second part of this question had to do with granting ranchers a legal right to their permit.

71. Peffer, *Closing of the Public Domain,* 190.

72. One of the stranger effects of Bowden's presence was that he came off as cross-examining even the "friendly" witnesses, and some were reluctant to stake out much of an opinion at all. This happened with Henry G. Boice, president of the Arizona Cattle Growers Association and future president of the ANLSA. When Boice was encouraged to give any comment at all on the Rachford appraisal, he declined to do so. Bowden's continued provocation simply produced more of the same avoidance or waffling. *Hearings* on S. Res. 347, 448 ff. As for the politicians' pugilism, Ralph Cameron noted to the ANLSA in 1926 that "we have picked a real fight with the bureaucrats in Washington, but at least we are making an honorable fight, and I believe a successful one, to restore to our people of the West a reasonable and sane administration of these great national resources" (letter reprinted in *Proceedings, 1926,* 40).

73. The group added that such a right was "subject to provisions necessary for the protection of other resources of the national forests" and that "the holders of such rights shall be responsible for wilful [*sic*] damage done by them to resources of the forests" ("Stockmen Submit Public-Land Recommendations," *Producer,* September 1925: 8).

74. Ibid.

75. "There is no reason why the users of the forests should not have as a right the position of lessees under the Secretary of Agriculture, and a holding on an area basis would entail less contact with the 'bureaucratic methods' which aroused the ire and eloquence of many delegates" ("The Salt Lake Conference" [editorial], *Producer,* September 1925, 11). As for the NWGA, Frank Hagenbarth had been one of the organizers of the conference ("Stockmen Submit Public-Land Recommendations," 7). On associationalism, see Ellis Hawley, "Herbert Hoover, the Commerce Secretariat, and the Vision of an Associative State," *Journal of American History* 61 (June 1974): 116–40.

76. "Senator Robert N. Stanfield . . . voiced the fear that the time was at hand when the government of the United States would be conducted according to rules and regulations, rather than by law" ("Stockmen Submit Public-Land Recommendations," 7).

77. "We want the Forest Service!" he exclaimed. "Such a vast and important group of resources as the forest contains must be administered. . . . When we say 'administer,' however, that is all we mean" ("Idaho Man Takes Slam at Greeley," *Producer,* March 1926, 10).

78. *Hearings* on S. Res. 347, pt. 1, 187.

79. Ibid., 188–89

80. *NWG,* February 1925, 45.

81. *Hearings* on S. Res. 347, vol. 2, 1846–47.

82. *NWG,* March 1925, 11.

83. Thomas Cooper, "Evils of Federal Control of Range—A Solution," *NWG,* July 1925, 25.

84. Glynn Bennion, "Governmental Relation to Range Use," *NWG,* July 1925, 26–27.

85. Ray Lyman Wilbur, *The Memoirs of Ray Lyman Wilbur,* ed. Edgar Eugene Robinson and Paul Carroll Edwards (Stanford, Calif.: Stanford University Press, 1960), 406.

86. C. Fred Williams, "William M. Jardine and the Foundations for Republican Farm Policy, 1925–1929," *Agricultural History* 70 (Spring 1996): 216–32. The political divide between Hoover and Wallace largely concerned "McNary-Haugenism," the policy passed by Congress to aid American farmers, but vetoed by Coolidge. See also Wilson, "Herbert Hoover's Agricultural Policies, 1921–1928," 115–44.

87. Herbert Hoover, confidential letter to F. R. Marshall, December 19, 1924, "Agriculture Forest Service Policy, 1924–25," Commerce Papers, box 6, Herbert Hoover Presidential Library.

88. F. R. Marshall to Herbert Hoover, December 26, 1924, "Agriculture Forest Service Policy, 1924–25," Commerce Papers, box 6, Herbert Hoover Presidential Library.

89. *Producer,* March 1928, 17.

90. For instance, the secretary of the association, Ovid Butler, also made attacks on the stockgrowers during the fall of 1925 in *American Forests and Forest Life.* The ANLSA's response can be found in "To Save the Forests from Stockmen," 16–17.

91. William Greeley, "The Stockmen and the National Forest," *Saturday Evening Post,* November 14, 1925, 10.

92. *Producer,* December 1925, 18.

93. Ibid., 17.

94. Rachford, "Range Appraisal Report," 35.

95. *Producer,* December 1925, 18.

96. Ibid.

97. *Producer,* July 1932, 17.

98. John Walton, *Western Times and Water Wars: State, Culture, and Rebellion in California* (Berkeley and Los Angeles: University of California Press, 1992), 196.

99. Rowley, *U.S. Forest Service Grazing and Rangelands,* 138–40.

100. Ibid., 135.

101. Ibid.

102. Peffer, *Closing of the Public Domain,* 192.

103. Donald Richberg, quoted in Morton Horwitz, *The Transformation of American Law, 1870–1960: The Crisis of Legal Orthodoxy* (New York: Oxford University Press, 1992), 161. See also Morton Keller, "The Pluralist State: American Economic Regulation in Comparative Perspective, 1900–1930," in

Regulation in Perspective: Historical Essays, ed. Thomas McCraw (Cambridge, Mass.: Harvard University Press), 56–94. Problems like those encountered by Forest Service officials in the 1920s also arose in setting railroad rates in the nineteenth century. In the 1870s, for instance, Charles Francis Adams and Albert Fink, the "father of railroad economics," argued that "the proper basis for a railroad rate was not only the value of the service (a method critics called the doctrine of 'all the traffic will bear'), but also the cost of the service to the corporation and a proper allowance for profit." Thomas K. McCraw, *Prophets of Regulation* (Cambridge, Mass.: Harvard University Press, 1984), 47. Christopher Rachford was relatively unwilling to include costs and allowance for profit in his figures for grazing fees, although he was also, as noted, averse to using the "all the traffic will bear" method of calculating fees.

104. *Producer,* February 1927, 13–14.

CHAPTER 4. THE SOVEREIGNTY OF THE STATE,
OR THE STATES?

Epigraph: Herbert Hoover, *The Challenge to Liberty* (New York: Scribner, 1934), 133. Hoover tempered this statement by saying: "The failure of a minority of States to enforce laws which prevent an abuse of Liberty in employment of children, sweating of labor, manipulation of public markets, bad banking, and such, either compels or gives excuse to Federal invasion of State functions" (133–34).

1. The full text of Wilbur's speech is reprinted in Charles Winter, *Four Hundred Million Acres: The Public Lands and Resources* (Casper, Wyo.: Overland Publishing Co., 1932), 169–70.

2. Reprinted in Winter, *Four Hundred Million Acres,* ch. 18. Of course, the livestock associations greeted Hoover's proposal with a great deal of interest and reprinted much of his letter, too. See, e.g., "President Hoover's Call for Action," *National Wool Grower,* September 1929, 15–16. Hereafter cited as *NWG*.

3. Quoted in Winter, *Four Hundred Million Acres,* 187.

4. Samuel Hays, *Conservation and the Gospel of Efficiency: The Progressive Conservation Movement, 1890–1920* (1959; repr., New York: Atheneum, 1980), 69.

5. The eleven members from the public land states held a variety of titles: for instance, two were state land commissioners, one was listed as an attorney, and one was the director of the experiment station at Utah State Agricultural College. I refer to the body as a committee, rather than a commission, because it was most commonly known as the Garfield Committee. *Report* of the Committee on the Conservation and Administration of the Public Domain, in U.S. Congress, Senate, Committee on Public Lands and Surveys, *Granting Remaining Unreserved Public Lands to the States,* Hearings on S. 17, 2272, and S. 4060, 72d Cong., 1st sess. (1932), 334. The hearings, as distinct from the report, will hereafter be cited as *Hearings* on S. 17, 2272, and 4060. Charles Winter noted that the committee was intended to be smaller than it was. See Winter, *Four Hundred Million Acres,* 186.

6. U.S. Congress, House of Representatives, Committee on the Public Lands,

Granting Remaining Unreserved Public Lands to the States, Hearings on H.R. 5840, 72d Cong., 1st sess. (1932), 179, hereafter cited as *Hearings* on H.R. 5840. That he chose not to speak as a member of the committee clearly irked its secretary, Hugh Brown, who wrote to Garfield that Jenkins's testimony was "a rather peculiar exhibition," and that he had "proceeded to present precisely the same radical views he offered at the first meeting of the Committee on the Conservation and Administration of the Public Domain." Those "radical views" revolved largely around the question of subsurface rights. Hugh Brown to James Garfield, March 22, 1932, "7.0 Correspondence: Committee—Garfield, James R., 1932–33," box 1090, President's Committee on the Conservation and Administration of the Public Domain, 1918–1937, Herbert Hoover Papers, Herbert Hoover Presidential Library, West Branch, Iowa.

  7. The articles in the *National Wool Grower* and the *Producer* show that the associations were not as invested in the mineral rights issue as some western states' rights politicians were. But their position was well expressed by the secretary of the NWGA, S. W. McClure, when he noted at the 1932 national convention: "A public lands commission, consisting partly of inexperienced visionaries, has recommended that the Federal Government after withdrawing everything of value from the remaining public lands, shall turn the worthless residue over to the states, under conditions that would bring heavy expenditures to the unhappy residents" ("Address by Dr. S. W. McClure before the National Convention," *NWG*, February 1932, 46). McClure was not unusual in referring to grazing lands as not having much value, although they were the mainstay of the industry's production.

  8. *Denver Post,* November 24, 1929, n.p., in "2.51 Newspaper Clippings, Colorado, 1929–1931"; *Leadville Herald Democrat,* September 3, 1929, n.p., ibid.; *Bozeman Chronicle,* December 29, 1930, n.p., "2.51 Newspaper Clippings, Montana, 1929–1931"; *Boise Statesman,* March 28, 1932, n.p., "2.51 Newspaper Clippings, 1929–1932," all in box 1080, President's Committee Papers, Hoover Papers, Hoover Library.

  9. Joseph Painter to James Garfield, n.d. [1930], "2.0 Correspondence," box 1077, President's Committee Papers, Hoover Papers, Hoover Library.

  10. See, e.g., "A Discussion of the Open Public Domain," Agricultural Division, Conservation Branch, United States Geological Survey," March 22, 1930, "5.1 Reports of Geological Survey, 1930—April," box 1084, President's Committee Papers, Hoover Papers, Hoover Library. And westerners agreed. As the *National Wool Grower* commented, "It is generally recognized [in the West] that these [lands] could not be expected to produce any considerable revenue through the livestock industry." See "President Hoover's Call for Action on Public Grazing Lands," 17. The *National Wool Grower* was skeptical that the sheep industry could pay for public domain lands. It noted that the livestock industry "is in no position to carry additional financial burdens. If payments are to be made for the use of grazing which now only appears to be free then reduction of taxes upon owned land and livestock must be provided for" ("Members Named for Public Land Commission," *NWG,* November 1929, 15).

  11. *Hearings* on S. 17, S. 2272, and S. 4060, 310.

12. Ray Lyman Wilbur, *Conservation in the Department of the Interior* (Washington, D.C.: GPO, 1931), 45–46.

13. Assistant Secretary of the Interior Joseph Dixon delivered Hoover's address at a meeting of the governors of public land states in Salt Lake City, August 26, 1929. See Herbert Hoover to Joseph Dixon, August 21, 1929, "2.5 Correspondence—Articles, Pamphlets, Speeches, 1924–29," box 1079, President's Committee Papers, Hoover Papers, Hoover Library.

14. *Report* of the Committee on the Conservation and Administration of the Public Domain, 342. Emphases added.

15. As we saw in chapter 2, "ranching" had a troubled relationship with "agriculture," and in fact the most popular view maintained that it was dangerous for ranchers to be allowed too much private land. In a letter to the Senate Committee on Public Lands and Surveys, for instance, the American Farm Bureau Federation complained that the "administrative processes" in the bill would encourage the "hasty transference of the public domain into private hands"—a transfer that would involve "private holdings of [a] large area, thereby defeating the general administration of such lands for the public welfare" (*Hearings* on S. 17, 2272, and 4060, 327).

16. *Report* of the Committee on Conservation and Administration of the Public Domain, 342.

17. Carl Abbott has written that despite Hoover's later reputation "as an advocate of federal inaction during the onset of the Great Depression, it is ironic that, especially before his presidency, Hoover helped to change the federal role in the West from promoter to planner." Abbott, "The Federal Presence" in *The Oxford History of the American West,* ed. Clyde A. Milner II, Carol A. O'Connor, and Martha A. Sandweiss (New York: Oxford University Press, 1994), 475. It is important to note, however, that Hoover would have made a sharp distinction between this interstate planning of the Colorado River Compact and the more centralized planning of an agency like the Forest Service.

18. *Report* of the Committee on Conservation, 340. This position would have enacted at the state level the federal policy of pre-homesteading days, when the government auctioned off its lands. See Paul Gates, *The History of Public Land Law Development* (Washington, D.C.: Zenger Publishing Co., 1968), 127. Gates argues that producing revenue was a primary objective of government land policy even after the Homestead Act. See ibid., 435–62.

19. *Report* of the Committee on Conservation, 352–53. In another place, however, the committee noted that "[t]he policy should be continued of having a central organization to design and build works, but to transfer these works to the control and management of the water users as soon as the projects are settled and developed" (ibid., 341).

20. Ibid., 355.

21. Ibid., 339.

22. "An Editorial—A Dangerous Grant," *American Forests,* April 1931, n.p., "2.5 Correspondence—Articles, Pamphlets, Speeches, 1932," box 1079, President's Committee Papers, Hoover Papers, Hoover Library. Gifford Pinchot and Forest Service Chief R. Y. Stuart, made similar arguments in hearings before

Congress on the question of cession. See *Hearings* on S. 17, 2272, and S. 4060, 202–4, 299–301.

23. Brandjord to Brown, February 10, 1931, "7.0 Correspondence—Committee—Brandjord I. M., 1931–32," box 1090, President's Committee Papers, Hoover Papers, Hoover Library. Brandjord and Perry Jenkins were the most vocal states' rights proponents on the committee.

24. Ibid., 362–63 (emphases added). The report continues, "Rather should we think in terms of practical idealism, relying upon a leadership with ample resources, marshalling the forces of research, of intelligent publicity, of wise instruction on the elimination of waste from production and fabrication, and on sound economics, leading the way to a clear understanding of the reasons why waste is the inevitable companion of the uncontrolled production of any natural resource when carried to an unusable excess above the normal requirements of the consuming public."

25. Ellis Hawley, "Herbert Hoover, the Commerce Secretariat, and the Vision of an 'Associative State,' 1921–1928," *Journal of American History* 61 (1974): 116–40.

26. Joan Hoff Wilson, "Herbert Hoover's Agricultural Policies, 1921–1928," in *Herbert Hoover as Secretary of Commerce: Studies in New Era Thought and Practice,* ed. Ellis Hawley (Iowa City: University of Iowa Press, 1981), 115–44. Wallace's recommendations were given legislative substance in the McNary-Haugen bill, which took different forms in the early 1920s and which was passed by Congress but vetoed by President Coolidge.

27. Ibid., 126. Wallace's plan (McNary-Haugenism) would have made farmers "pay an equalization fee (to make up for any loss incurred when the government sold surpluses at low world prices)" (ibid.).

28. Quoted in ibid., 124.

29. As we shall see in chapter 5, the first director was Farrington Carpenter, a Colorado cattle owner. Within two years after the Taylor Grazing Act, the Grazing Service required all field employees, and the director and assistant director, to have lived at least one year in the particular western state that they would serve. E. Louise Peffer, *The Closing of the Public Domain: Disposal and Reservation Policies, 1900–1950* (Stanford, Calif.: Stanford University Press, 1951), 223.

30. James Muhn, "The Mizpah-Pumpkin Creek Grazing District: Its History and Influence on the Enactment of a Public Grazing Policy, 1926–1934" (M.A. thesis, Montana State University, 1987), 65.

31. The quotations are from a memorandum by Northcutt Ely, the executive assistant to the Secretary of the Interior, to Wilbur, included in the record of *Hearings* on S. 17, 2272, and 4060, 13.

32. See Peffer, *Closing of the Public Domain,* 215.

33. Ibid., 181.

34. *Hearings* on H.R. 5840, 172. The speaker was Thomas Cooper, then president of the Wyoming Wool Growers Association.

35. Ibid., 179–80.

36. "New Public Land Bill," *Producer,* June 1932, 18.

37. "State Control of Public Domain," *Producer,* August 1929, 19. The ar-

ticle also noted correctly that "[t]he leader of the dissenters has been the State of Wyoming, where conditions which are purely local have made both cattle- and sheepmen satisfied with the existing order of things."

38. "The Convention," *Producer,* February 1930, 19.

39. "Address of President F. J. Hagenbarth," *NWG,* February 1932, 31.

40. "Forest Grazing Fees Reduced One-Half for 1932," *NWG,* March 1932, 7.

41. "Report of the Committee on Public Lands," *NWG,* February 1932, 15–16.

42. Ibid.

43. "The Public Domain Bill," *NWG,* April 1932, 7.

44. Robert Wiebe, *Businessmen and Reform: A Study of the Progressive Movement* (Cambridge, Mass.: Harvard University Press, 1962), 201.

45. Ibid., 202.

46. This observation of western political ideology has been made throughout the century, but new western historians have especially emphasized it. See, e.g., Patricia Nelson Limerick, *The Legacy of Conquest: The Unbroken Past of the American West* (New York: Norton, 1987), 134–75; Richard White, "*It's Your Misfortune and None of My Own": A History of the American West* (Norman: University of Oklahoma Press, 1991), 409; and Michael P. Malone and F. Ross Peterson, "Politics and Protests," in *Oxford History of the American West,* 501–34.

47. *Proceedings of the Public Land Convention* (Denver: Press of the Western Newspaper Union, 1907), 150.

48. Ibid., 151.

49. Hearings on S. 17, 2272, and 4060, 150.

50. Paul Gates, "The Federal Lands—Why We Retained Them," in *Rethinking the Federal Lands,* ed. Sterling Brubaker (Washington, D.C.: Resources for the Future, 1984), 35.

51. Quoted in Gates, *History of Public Land Law Development,* 73.

52. Ibid., 6.

53. Quoted in ibid., 9.

54. These were the Morrill Acts of 1862 and 1890 and the Hatch Act of 1887 (ibid., 22–28).

55. Gates concludes that the total acreage granted to public land states was 197,555,625 acres by 1932 (ibid., 27).

56. Gates, "Federal Lands," 50. See also Peffer's discussion of western reactions to the Forest Service in *Closing the Public Domain,* 63–69, 90–98.

57. There were western politicians at the 1907 Public Lands Convention who expressed support for Pinchot's conservation policies. For instance, in advocating federal grazing control of the public domain and approving the existence of national forests, the ANLSA was allied with the conservationist camp (although often disagreeing with Forest Service policy). See Lawrence Rakestraw, "The West, States' Rights, and Conservation: A Study of Six Public Land Conferences," *Pacific Northwest Quarterly* 48 (July 1957): 87–99.

58. *Proceedings of the Public Land Convention,* 84.

59. Ibid., 86.

60. Ibid., 88.

61. "A law allowing certain portions of the public lands to be leased would be a statute conferring on stockmen and settlers a right not now possessed by them, while the legislation for range control is simply the grant of power to a Government official to compel settlers and stockmen to pay for a right and privilege they now enjoy without cost, or to modify or deprive them altogether of those privileges." Range control was an option, he noted, that had "the enthusiastic and vigorous support of Bureau officials. It is in fact a finished product of Bureaucracy." Ibid., 88.

62. "States Challenge Rise of Federal Power," *New York Times,* April 11, 1926, sec. 9, 3.

63. Ibid.

64. Lynn Dumenil, "'The Insatiable Maw of Bureaucracy': Antistatism and Education Reform in the 1920s," *Journal of American History* 77 (September 1990): 500.

65. Charles Winter, *Four Hundred Million Acres.* As to whether Winter's belief in states' rights intensified after leaving Congress, it is difficult to say. That he published a book on it would suggest it did. However, one could argue, the generally sympathetic climate for states' rights (especially Hoover's endorsement of it for the public domain) may have also encouraged Winter to publish the book. On Winter, see T. A. Larson, *History of Wyoming* (Lincoln: University of Nebraska Press, 1965), 426–29.

66. It did, however, pique the interest of Hugh Brown, the secretary of the Garfield Committee. He noted in a letter to Garfield that he had requested, and just received, a copy of the book. Hugh Brown to James Garfield, February 1, 1932, "7.0 Correspondence: Committee—Garfield, James R., 1932–33," box 1090, President's Committee Papers, Hoover Papers, Hoover Library.

67. It is important to note, for instance, that Wyoming Senator John Kendrick, who "trounced" Winter in the 1928 election and rejected the idea of cession in that year, changed his mind and supported cession by the early 1930s (T. A. Larson, *History of Wyoming,* 426–29). That Larson briefly discusses *400 Million Acres* in his history of Wyoming suggests that the book was of some importance to Wyoming's political stance (ibid., 428).

68. Winter, *Four Hundred Million Acres,* 28.

69. Ibid., 36.

70. The only land that Winter believed the government could legitimately own was national parks.

71. Winter, *Four Hundred Million Acres,* 125.

72. Ibid., 163.

73. *Hearings* on S. 17, 2272, 4060, 151.

74. Ibid., 149. It would appear that the questions states' rightists raised about sovereignty could be traced back to foundational issues of sovereignty during the period of early modern state formation. As they saw the locus of American political authority residing primarily in the states, they believed that authority should be grounded in territorial sovereignty, not simply jurisdictional sovereignty. Peter Sahlins wonderfully traces the history and tensions between

these two ideas in *Boundaries: The Making of France and Spain in the Pyrenees* (Berkeley and Los Angeles: University of California Press, 1989).

75. R. Jeffrey Lustig, *Corporate Liberalism: The Origins of Modern American Political Theory, 1890–1920* (Berkeley and Los Angeles: University of California Press, 1982), 213–23.

76. Daniel Rodgers, *Contested Truths: Keywords in American Politics since Independence* (New York: Basic Books, 1987), 162, 166.

77. Ibid., 167.

78. Winter, *Four Hundred Million Acres,* 137.

79. An editorial in the Tucson *Citizen,* for instance, noted that it was wary of the proposed transfer. "Arizona being one of the public land states, our governor is strongly in sympathy with the cession proposal, but he is in error in inferring that the constitutional guarantee of admission into the union on an 'equal footing,' refers to the physical base of the state, i.e., all the land circumscribed by its borders, or that it refers to anything whatsoever but political stature. To avow the contrary in the court of constitutional construction might cause its august members to laugh in their sleeves—made large and flowing for the purpose." "The Public Lands Question," *Citizen,* January 12, 1931, "2.51 Newspaper Clippings, Arizona 1929–31," box 1080, President's Committee Papers, Hoover Papers, Hoover Library.

80. Winter, *Four Hundred Million Acres,* 163.

81. Indeed, an editorial in *American Forests* questioned why the committee recommended a transfer to the states at all. "If private ownership is the ultimate solution why, it may be asked, does the committee recommend first turning the lands over to the states." "The Public Domain Report," *American Forests,* April 1931, in "2.5 Correspondence—Articles, Pamphlets, Speeches, 1931," box 1079, President's Committee Papers, Hoover Papers, Hoover Library.

82. Ibid., 156.

83. Ibid., 90.

84. Ibid., 156.

85. Quoted in ibid., 170.

86. I use "man" very explicitly, because as it should be clear by now, the image of the independent property owner was absolutely gendered male.

87. C. B. Macpherson, *The Political Theory of Possessive Individualism* (Oxford: Oxford University Press, 1962), 3.

88. Joseph Singer has written eloquently on the way that the dominant interpretations of property law have embraced the ideal of the unencumbered title—in other words, that legal rules about property should consolidate all the rights to controlling resources in the hands of the property owner. However, Singer argues that other models of property law are available that emphasize the relations of property rather than identifying the owner. See Joseph William Singer, "The Reliance Interest in Property," *Stanford Law Review* 40 (February 1988): 634.

89. Frank W. Mondell to James R. Garfield, November 4, 1929, "5.5 Reports: Sources Outside Government, 1929–32," box 1089, President's Committee Papers, Hoover Papers, Hoover Library.

90. George Dern, "Public Land Policies: Addresses by Governor George H. Dern," p. 27, in "2.5 Correspondence: Articles, Pamphlets, Speeches, January–May 1930," box 1079, President's Committee Papers, Hoover Papers, Hoover Library.

91. "I am sure you have personally noted the change the last few years has developed in the feeling of many of the people of the West against the everlasting control of the Federal Government, through the Department of the Interior, and Department of Agriculture, over the minerals and forests of the 11 Western public land states." Charles Gilmore to Herbert Hoover, August 29, 1929, "Public Domain—1929, September–October," Ray Lyman Wilbur Papers, Hoover Library.

92. Joseph L. Sax, "The Claim for Retention in the Public Lands," in *Rethinking the Federal Lands,* ed. Sterling Brubaker (Washington, D.C.: Resources for the Future, 1984), 130 (author's emphasis). I assume that by emphasizing "as such," Sax is also trying to get at the construction of land ownership as something experienced more concretely than other forms of governmental activity.

93. Ibid., 131.

94. As Hendrik Hartog has shown, during the first 100 years of the Republic, New York City separated its public functions from its property ownership: "New York City changed from a government insistent on governing through its personal, private estate, to one dedicated to using a public bureaucracy." Indeed, by the turn of the nineteenth century, Hartog notes, New York City was, like the federal government, getting rid of its lands. What land it did hold on to "was radically distinguished from its role as a government." Hendrik Hartog, *Public Property and Private Power: The Corporation of the City of New York in American Law, 1730–1870* (Chapel Hill: University of North Carolina Press), 8.

CHAPTER 5. THE TAYLOR GRAZING ACT
AND THE "VAST NATIONAL ESTATE"

Epigraph: Transcript of Proceedings, Phoenix, Arizona, January 28, 1935, box 1, p. 14, Farrington R. Carpenter Papers, Western History Collection, Denver Public Library. Hereafter cited as FRC Papers.

1. E. Louise Peffer, *The Closing of the Public Domain: Disposal and Reservation Policies, 1900–1950* (Stanford, Calif.: Stanford University Press, 1951), 224.

2. Grant McConnell, *Private Power and American Democracy* (New York: Vintage Books, 1966), pp. 200–211. McConnell's analysis borrows heavily from Wesley Calef, *Private Grazing and Public Lands: Studies of the Local Management of the Taylor Grazing Act* (Chicago: University of Chicago Press, 1960), and Phillip Foss, *Politics and Grass: The Administration of Grazing on the Public Domain,* (Seattle: University of Washington Press, 1960).

3. See Gary D. Libecap, *Locking up the Range: Federal Land Controls and Grazing* (Cambridge, Mass.: Ballinger, 1981), and, for a more contemporary account, Karl Hess, Jr., *Visions upon the Land: Man and Nature on the Western Range* (Washington, D.C.: Island Press, 1992).

4. Richard Lowitt, *The New Deal and the West,* (Bloomington: Indiana University Press, 1984), 21–22;

5. Transcript of Proceedings, Statewide Meeting for Idaho, Boise, Idaho, December 17, 1934, box 1, p. 5, FRC Papers. I have corrected minor grammatical and spelling errors in the typed transcripts.

6. Ibid., 6.

7. U.S. Congress, House of Representatives, Committee on Public Lands, *Grazing on Public Domain,* Hearings on H.R. 11816, 72d Cong., 1st sess. (1932), 15 (hereafter cited as *Hearings* on H.R. 11816).

8. Taylor's bill was substantially the same as the bill that Donald Colton had gotten through the House, but not through the Senate, by the time Franklin Roosevelt moved into the White House. As the later head of the Grazing Service noted, "Except for the intervention of an election, [the Taylor Grazing Act] would now be known as the Colton Act." Comments by Clarence Forsling in *Public Land Policy: Proceedings of the Western Resources Conference,* ed. Phillip O. Foss (Boulder: Colorado Associated University Press, 1968), 90.

9. Quoted in Peffer, *Closing of the Public Domain,* 217.

10. U.S. Congress, House of Representatives, Committee on the Public Lands, *To Provide for the Orderly Use, Improvement, and Development of the Public Range,* Hearings on H.R. 2835 and H.R. 6462, 73d Cong., 2d sess. (1933 and 1934), 31. Hereafter cited as *Hearings* on H.R. 2835 and H.R. 6462.

11. Ibid., 6.

12. Ibid.

13. He noted that "it would be unsound, economically, to include such work in the conservation program in the absence of a satisfactory future control of the lands benefited and the permanency and continued maintenance of such projects." The work would take place after "the late fall and winter when work in the conservation camps in the higher altitudes of the national parks and forests will be impossible." Ibid.

14. Ibid., 9.

15. Ibid., 11.

16. Ibid., 5.

17. The bill also allowed the secretary to withdraw appropriate grazing lands from national forests. The House passed the act without any restriction on the amount of land that could be put into grazing districts. Once it got to the Senate, however, Senator O'Mahoney from Wyoming amended it to restrict grazing districts to 80 million acres, based on the argument that no more was available, because the remaining public domain lands were so scattered that the Department of the Interior could not consolidate them into grazing districts. Many Wyoming ranchers—particularly in the eastern part of the state, where the lands did lie in a very scattered way—were opposed to converting too much land into grazing districts. The Taylor Grazing Act provided for the leasing of these tracts of land, and this was a much more attractive option for these ranchers, who also tended to be more politically prominent than western Wyoming ranchers. The latter generally favored grazing districts, because the public domain lay in larger tracts there. Conference on Amendments to the Taylor Bill, Denver, Colorado, February 13, 1933, box 1, pp. 14–19, FRC Papers.

18. Excerpts from the bill are taken from U.S. Congress, Senate, *The West-ern Range: . . . A Report on the Western Range—A Great But Neglected Re-source,* 74th Cong., 2d sess., doc. 199 (Washington, D.C.: GPO, 1936), 290.

19. Ibid., 291.

20. Ibid., 293.

21. Ibid., 292.

22. Quoted in ibid.

23. Roosevelt brought in Attorney General Homer Cummings to provide a third opinion on this question. Cummings ended up agreeing with the Depart-ment of Interior that the act did secure federal authority over the range. On this, and the Taylor Grazing Act generally, see T. H. Watkins, *Righteous Pilgrim: The Life and Times of Harold L. Ickes* (New York: Holt, 1990), 477–83. See also Henry Wallace's letter to Roosevelt of June 27, 1934, which notes the disagree-ment between the two solicitors, in *Franklin D. Roosevelt and Conservation, 1911–1945,* ed. Edgar B. Nixon (Washington, D.C.: GPO, 1957), 1: 307–8.

24. Ferdinand A. Silcox to Henry A. Wallace, June 21, 1934, in *Franklin D. Roosevelt and Conservation,* ed. Nixon, 308–13.

25. Statement by Franklin Roosevelt on signing the Taylor Grazing Act, June 28, 1934, in ibid., 313.

26. All quotations are from *Hearings* on H.R. 2835 and H.R. 6462, 10–11. On p. 17, Ickes continued to make the analogy between the government's land-holding and an individual's property ownership, referencing the rules of pre-scriptive easements, which hold that a non-owner who has come to rely on us-ing a particular property without the permission of the owner may have generated a right to continued use of it; or to put it another way, the owner has lost "the right to prevent another from using her property in a specific way." Jo-seph Singer, "The Reliance Interest in Property," *Stanford Law Review* 40 (Feb-ruary 1988): 669.

27. Wallace also used the term "empire." See his letter to Harold Ickes of November 13, 1936, in ibid., 602: "The fundamental difference between your Department and mine in relation to the legislation for regulating grazing on the public domain has centered largely around the question of the degree to which that legislation will permit establishment of vested or prescriptive rights under which public interests in a vast empire legally will be subordinated to interests of a comparatively small number of livestock growers and owners of range lands."

28. The claim about Ickes's "dictatorship" can be found in many sources from organized ranchers at this time, but see in particular Vincent Carter's tes-timony in *Hearings* on H.R. 2835 and 6462, 101.

29. Letter reprinted in "President Roosevelt's Veto and Secretary Ickes' Memorandum," *American Cattle Producer,* October 1935, 7.

30. "Administration of the Taylor Public Domain Act," *National Wool Grower,* July 1934, 10.

31. Ibid.

32. Transcript of Proceedings, Bakersfield, California, January 17, 1935, box 1, pp. 9–10, FRC Papers.

33. *Hearings* on H.R. 2835 and H.R. 6462, 141. Part of the problem here is

that Carpenter's categories of what constitutes "small" kept shifting. Small cattlemen were those that simply grazed domestic stock on the national forests, in Carpenter's public statements, or they were also those who grazed 200 to 300 cattle, "that being the smallest unit that a man can operate and call himself a cow man or really subsist on from cattle" (ibid.). "We know a man cannot successfully operate a herd of, say, less than 100 head of cattle, or of less than one or two thousand head of sheep, depending on the area," Rufus Poole, the assistant solicitor of the Interior Department, told the House Committee on Public Lands. U.S. Congress, House of Representatives, *To Provide for the Orderly Use, Improvement, and Development of the Public Range,* 74th Cong., 1st sess. (1935), Hearings on H.R. 3019, 22. Hereafter cited as *Hearings* on H.R. 3019.

34. *Hearings* on H.R. 2835 and H.R. 6462, 143–44.

35. Ibid., 144.

36. Transcript of Proceedings, Billings, Montana, December 7, 1934, box 1, p. 3, FRC Papers.

37. Transcript of Proceedings, Boise, Idaho, box 1, pp. 27, 8, FRC Papers.

38. Transcript of Proceedings, Bakersfield, California, January 17, 1935, box 1, p. 26, FRC Papers. Carpenter had said essentially the same thing a month earlier in Billings, although as soon as he blurted it out, he backtracked, adding, "The picture I presented of the T.V.A. is not true." Perhaps in the later meeting, in California, he had stopped worrying about any adverse reaction to such unorthodoxy in the New Deal. Transcript of Proceedings, Billings, Montana, box 1, p. 25, FRC Papers.

39. Transcript of Proceedings, Statewide Meeting for Arizona, Phoenix, Arizona, January 28, 1935, box 1, p. 40, FRC Papers; Transcript of Proceedings, Bakersfield, California, box 1, pp. 46–47, FRC Papers.

40. Transcript of Proceedings, Billings, Montana, box 1, p. 31, FRC Papers.

41. Transcript of Proceedings, Boise, Idaho, box 1, p. 36, FRC Papers.

42. Transcript of Proceedings, Billings, Montana, box 1, p. 38, FRC Papers.

43. Peffer, *Closing of the Public Domain,* 225.

44. Transcript of Proceedings, Statewide Meeting for Nevada, Reno, Nevada, January 24, 1935, box 1, p. 23, FRC Papers.

45. "Everybody who could ever hope to have a permit on this district can vote, whether he lives here or not," Carpenter said initially, but he denied a few moments later that he really meant what that seemed to suggest, as only those who had run stock on the public domain would be able to vote. Transcript of Proceedings, Grand Junction, Colorado, September 17, 1934, box 1, pp. 8, 10, FRC Papers.

46. Ibid., p. 8.

47. Transcript of Proceedings, Boise, Idaho, box 1, pp. 116–21, FRC Papers.

48. Ibid., p. 121.

49. McConnell, *Private Power,* 204.

50. The impression was that the Forest Service would be able to buy this land under the Agriculture Department's program of buying up submarginal land. Transcript of Proceedings, Bakersfield, California, box 1, p. 83, FRC Papers.

51. Ibid., p. 87.

52. Ibid., pp. 87–106.

53. McConnell, *Private Power,* 210–11.

54. Conference on Amendments, box 1, pp. 53–54, FRC Papers.

55. Ibid., p. 57.

56. Transcript of Proceedings, Boise, Idaho, box 1, p. 18, FRC Papers.

57. Transcript of Proceedings, Phoenix, Arizona, box 1, pp. 76, 29, FRC Papers.

58. Transcript of Proceedings, Malta, Montana, December 4, 1934, box 1, p. 22, FRC Papers.

59. When an Arizona rancher asked Carpenter for his definition of "commensurability," he gave this convoluted, though correct answer: "Commensurability is reducing to a common denominator in terms of feed units per animal per month, the means by which you are able to care for your livestock in the locality in which you live and under the conditions there, during the time which it is not possible to grant you grazing privileges on the public domain range lands." Transcript of Proceedings, Phoenix, Arizona, box 1, p. 81, FRC Papers.

60. Transcript of Proceedings, Malta, Montana, box 1, p. 29, FRC Papers. See also the proceedings at Boise, Idaho, box 1, pp. 81–82, and Reno, Nevada, box 1, p. 126.

61. Transcript of Proceedings, Phoenix, Arizona, box 1, p. 81, FRC Papers

62. Transcripts of Proceedings, Boise, Idaho, box 1, pp. 97, 108–9, FRC Papers.

63. Transcript of Proceedings, Reno, Nevada, box 1, p. 81, FRC Papers.

64. Transcript of Proceedings, Billings, Montana, box 1, pp. 18, 38, FRC Papers.

65. Ibid., pp. 38–39. Emphases added.

66. See *National Forest Manual—Grazing* in U.S. Congress, Senate, Subcommittee of the Committee on Public Lands and Surveys, *National Forests and the Public Domain,* 69th Cong., 1st sess., pt. 1 (1925), Hearings on S. Res. 347, 62. Of course, once administrative rules were established, ranchers had certain "rights" within the specified permit, but these were not the same thing as having property rights in the range.

67. Carpenter also talked about how the government would "take a 'bankerlike' attitude" as it decided who would and would not attain range rights—that is, looking at ranchers' "complete setup." See Transcript of Proceedings, Boise, Idaho, box 1, p. 65, FRC Papers.

68. Transcript of Proceedings, Boise, Idaho, box 1, pp. 65–66, FRC Papers.

69. By talking about permits as covenants that ran with the land, Carpenter clearly wanted to reinforce the fact that the permit was attached to the private, dependent property—not to the person. There was, however, a distinction between running covenants and easements that property theorists were discussing during the very period in which the Taylor Grazing Act was being discussed. Like easements, covenants that ran with the land involved one person's promise "to another to do or to refrain from doing something"; this was a promise that could be legally enforced and, also like easements, touched on land "with which the covenantor or covenantee, or both, were connected." The legal debate concerned whether running covenants fell under contract law or, like easements, under property law. Most property law teachers have tended to see them as

falling under the latter category. See Roger A. Cunningham, William B. Stoebuck, Dale A. Whitman, *The Law of Property* (St. Paul, Minn.: West., 1984),
467, 487, and Charles E. Clark's *Real Covenants and Other Interests Which
"Run with the Land,"* 2d ed. (Chicago: Callaghan, 1947), 171–86.

70. Readers familiar with the literature on public grazing lands will see by
now that I sharply disagree with the interpretation of the Taylor Grazing Act
that Debra Donahue has given in *Western Range Revisited: Removing Livestock
from Public Lands to Conserve Native Biodiversity* (Norman: University of Oklahoma Press, 1999). Through very attenuated historical reasoning, Donahue
argues that "grazing was not intended to be the predominant use of public lands
under the Taylor Act; in fact grazing was at best a co-equal use of the public domain, where it was not actually subordinated to other uses" (203). Although she
is correct in saying that the act allowed for other uses of the land, and that some
uses were seen as "higher" or more valuable than grazing—such as agriculture—the Taylor Grazing Act was nonetheless intended to "stabilize" the livestock industry, while also protecting the land from overgrazing. I also would
agree fully with her that the Taylor Grazing Act allows room to reevaluate the
place of domestic livestock on the public lands, and that socioeconomic changes
may compel substitution of other uses for those of the livestock industry. However, her understanding of the intentions behind the act is based on a very
pinched reading of it and of the historical context surrounding its passage.

71. Peffer, *Closing of the Public Domain,* 236.

72. U.S. Congress, Senate, *The Western Range,* v.

73. Because several Forest Service officials wrote each chapter of *The Western Range,* and because it clearly represented official policy at the highest level,
I refer to the service as the author.

74. U.S. Congress, Senate, *The Western Range,* 468.

75. This emphasis was reflected, of course, in the USDA's signal program,
the Agricultural Adjustment Act. As a trope for departmental discourse, "adjustment" had several meanings. The most fundamental adjustment was between farmers' production and the nation's consumption. But it was also used
to signify the need to adjust farmers to more modern distribution and marketing techniques and even to address the supposed "cultural lag" between farm
families' attitudes and modern American life; indeed, much of the study of rural
sociology in these years was taken up with the question of farmers' adjustment
to modern life. See, e.g., Edmund de S. Brunner and J. H. Kolb, *Rural Social
Trends* (New York: McGraw-Hill, 1933), 62. For the ideas behind agricultural
adjustment generally, see Richard S. Kirkendall, *Social Scientists and Farm Politics in the Age of Roosevelt* (Columbia: University of Missouri Press), 1967.

76. U.S. Congress, Senate, *The Western Range,* 469.

77. Ibid., 471.

78. Ibid.

79. Ibid., 472.

80. U.S. Congress, Senate, *The Western Range,* 471. Emphases added.

81. Ibid., 470. Including ranchers under the term "agriculturalists" was not
unique to the Forest Service, but its repeated use of it reflects, I think, the USDA's
attempt to bring all aspects of western ranching under its umbrella. The term

"tilled forage-crop" was another product of this attempt: here, the centerpiece of ranchers' production, "forage," appears in a kind of agricultural sandwich.

82. U.S. Congress, Senate, *The Western Range*, v.

83. This is, at least, how I interpret a somewhat confusing section under the chapter "The Administration of Public Range Lands." In discussing the Forest Service's success in handling the multiple uses of the forests, the authors wrote: "The high degree of correlation necessary to obtain effective conservation and use of the associated resources on the land emphasizes the need for territorial rather than functional jurisdiction in administration of range land. The expert services of other agencies should be used as needed, but in order to accomplish the necessary correlation and to keep down the cost of administration, a single agency must retain responsibility on a given body of land," the chapter on "The Administration of Public Range Lands" says in discussing the Forest Service's success in handling the multiple uses of the forests (U.S. Congress, Senate, *The Western Range*, 453).

84. Henry A. Wallace to Harold L. Ickes, November 13, 1936, in *Franklin D. Roosevelt and Conservation*, ed. Nixon, 602.

85. Watkins, *Righteous Pilgrim*, 559.

86. In October 1937, Pinchot remarked at a meeting of the Izaak Walton League that "with the possible exception of the national parks, and I underline the word 'possible,' the Interior Department has never had control of a single publicly owned natural resource that it has not devastated, wasted, and defiled" (ibid., 585).

87. Quoted in ibid., 586. Watkins, too, labels Ickes's interest in garnering the forests a kind of "obsession" (556). The entire plan for reorganizing the government was coming under direct fire from an emboldened and more conservative Congress. See James T. Patterson, *Congressional Conservatism and the New Deal: The Growth of the Conservative Coalition in Congress, 1933–1939* (Westport, Conn.: Greenwood Press, 1967), 314–29, 299–302.

88. In his letter to Henry Wallace condemning *The Western Range*, Ickes wrote: "The report also insists that management of the public domain should be centered in one department, and that, the Department of Agriculture. Such activities as relate to power reserves, reservoir site reserves, irrigation projects, recreation and scenic withdrawals, stock water reserves, stock driveway withdrawals, mineral reservations, public range reserves, grazing districts, leasing or other disposal of isolated tracts of public lands, and various miscellaneous purpose reservations on the public domain are now largely centered in the Interior Department. They contemplate conservation of every natural resource on the Federal domain except timber in national forests and wild life in Federal game reservations." Harold Ickes to Henry Wallace, August 19, 1936, in *Roosevelt and Conservation*, ed. Nixon, 552.

89. *Annual Report of the Secretary of the Interior* (Washington, D.C.: GPO, 1936), vii.

90. Watkins, *Righteous Pilgrim*, 447–51.

91. The Department of the Interior did have some bureaus that performed functions outside the West, such as the Office of Education, but it had since its inception been primarily an agency of the western public domain. This was sym-

bolically established in many ways. For instance, in the Hoover administration, Secretary of the Interior Ray Lyman Wilbur made a significant change in the department's stationery. "It seemed to me that the coat of arms of the Interior Department, an eagle with outspread wings, was not particularly characteristic of the Department and its responsibilities," Wilbur notes in his memoirs. "I selected one of the best pictures I could find of an American bison and had that put on our stationery and official correspondence . . . the revamped letterhead gave a lift to staff morale, emphasizing as it did a fresh start, making us more aware of the fact that ours was a distinctive department with unique . . . functions to perform." Ray Lyman Wilbur and William Atherton Du Puy, *Conservation in the Department of the Interior* (Washington, D.C.: GPO, 1931), 406–7. That distinctiveness, I would argue, was its increasing administrative association with the West.

92. Farrington R. Carpenter, "Range Stockmen Meet the Government," in *The 1967 Denver Westerners Brand Book,* ed. Richard A. Ronzio, vol. 23 (Denver: The Westerners, 1968), 333. Carpenter had been telling this story since he'd left the Grazing Division.

93. My thinking here has been influenced by Margaret Jane Radin's influential essay "Property and Personhood," which can be found in her collection of essays, *Reinterpreting Property* (Chicago: University of Chicago Press, 1993). Radin's work explores how property law has implicitly acknowledged that "to achieve self-development—to be a person—an individual needs some control over resources in the external environment. The necessary assurances of control take the form of property rights" (35). And it does not require a long leap to note that Americans have nearly sacralized the ownership of real property, or *land*. But can land become constitutive of a governmental agency's sense of "self"? "Property and Personhood" does not answer this question, but in the introduction to her collection, Radin notes that much more attention should be paid to the question of how property is "constitutive of group identity." Although she notes that it would be hard to say that corporations could become attached to land, for instance, since the company would sell any property that became too expensive to carry, she also suggests that "[c]ertain groups other than business entities . . . might claim their group's substantive existence as a group is bound up with property" (13). Given that the public lands produced the very existence of the Forest Service and the Department of the Interior, I would argue that the agency and the department developed very strong attachments to the properties under their regulatory control.

94. Gifford Pinchot, *Breaking New Ground* (New York: Harcourt, Brace, 1947), 259.

CHAPTER 6. PROPERTY RIGHTS AND POLITICAL MEANING

Epigraph: The Stockmen's Grazing Committee, *The Federal Grazing Problem and the Stockman's Solution* (pamphlet, n.d. [c. 1952?]), American National Cattlemen's Association Papers, box 28, "Public Land," American Heritage Center, University of Wyoming, Laramie.

1. Ickes did acknowledge that Carpenter used the Geological Survey.

2. Harold Ickes to Farrington R. Carpenter, October 31, 1935, box 2, Farrington R. Carpenter Papers, Denver Public Library. Hereafter cited as FRC Papers.

3. It is also true that Ickes wrote initially that he was "very well satisfied with [Carpenter's] work." Harold Ickes, *The Secret Diary of Harold L. Ickes*, vol. 1: *The First Thousand Days, 1933–36* (New York: Simon & Schuster, 1953), 229. Carpenter claimed at one point that when he and Ickes were discussing the role of advisory boards, Ickes bellowed, "'I want to know what they are doing for *me*,' pointing his finger to himself. I was so taken aback, that I got up and left the room without replying." Farrington R. Carpenter, "The Taylor Grazing Act: The Story of Its Early Operation in the Far Western 'Public Land States,'" box 2, p. 15, FRC Papers. I do not have reason to doubt Carpenter's account, but it was written some time after his tenure in the Interior Department, and he also was never impelled to paint Ickes in positive light.

4. Carpenter refused literally to hand over a signed letter of resignation until he had received a letter from Ickes "stating my services had been satisfactory," and he claims that Ickes initially replied that "that would be a 'hell of a long time.'" Several days passed before Ickes agreed to it, but Carpenter was still very wary of how the deal would transpire, given their mutual animosity. By this time Oscar Chapman, the assistant secretary, and E. K. Burlew, an administrative assistant, were also involved and helped physically to make the transaction happen: "Finally Burlew asked how I would trade [letters] and I said 'you go over in one corner and Chapman in another and leave Ickes's letter on the desk and I'll open and read it and if it is o.k. I'll hand you my resignation,'" which he did. Ibid., p. 18.

5. E. Louise Peffer, *The Closing of the Public Domain: Disposal and Reservation Policies, 1900–1950* (Stanford, Calif.: Stanford University Press, 1951), 248.

6. To support this position, Carpenter even quoted from a speech Ickes himself had made in Denver in 1935: there, Ickes set out broad responsibilities for the advisory committees, declaring that they "shall have original jurisdiction in promulgating rules and regulations for fair range practices in each district," although this power was "subject to final approval by the Department of the Interior." That balance, of course, lay at the heart of the two worldviews represented by the two men. Farrington R. Carpenter to Harold Ickes, n.d., box 2, FRC Papers.

7. Farrington R. Carpenter to Harold Ickes, n.d., box 2, FRC Papers.

8. Harold Ickes to Director Smith, March 15, 1938, box 2, FRC Papers.

9. Harold Ickes to Farrington R. Carpenter, March 8, 1937, box 2, FRC Papers.

10. Farrington R. Carpenter, "What to Do About Public Lands?" *Western Live Stock*, October 1948, 59.

11. *Red Canyon Sheep Co., et al. v. Ickes*, 98 F. 2d 308 (1938), 315, and "Legal Value of 'Priority' on the Public Domain," *National Wool Grower*, August 1938, 28. The case involved a proposed exchange of land whereby the Red Canyon Sheep Company in New Mexico would have lost access to range for which it had received a temporary license under the Taylor Grazing Act. Such an

exchange would, in the words of the *National Wool Grower,* "diminish, if not destroy, the value of [the company's] commensurate holdings" (26). *National Wool Grower* is hereafter cited as *NWG.*

12. *Red Canyon Sheep Company, et al. v. Ickes,* 314.

13. It is possible that in mentioning "grazing rights" here, the court was referencing rights in a contractual sense, because it notes in another part of the decision that the grazing privilege is not "an interest in the land itself" (316). Yet its statement about the act's importance in defining grazing rights is immediately followed by its description of the Interior Department's position, which was that "the appellants have no rights which are the proper subject of equitable protection" (ibid.). The court then declared that none of the cases that the appellees were relying on were "determinative," therefore implying that the appellants might be afforded equitable protection. Moreover, it held, in agreement with a 1918 Supreme Court decision, that "any civil right of a pecuniary nature" should be treated as a property right to be protected by the law (317). Thus, the court continually slips into the language of property rights, even if it also refused to name the grazing privilege as a right. When the case was quoted in the livestock industry's press, it was seen absolutely as articulating a property right in grazing on the Taylor lands. See "Legal Value of 'Priority' on the Public Domain," 26.

14. Farrington R. Carpenter to Nathan Margold, September 12, 1934, box 2, FRC Papers.

15. Margold to Farrington R. Carpenter, September 21, 1999, box 2, FRC Papers.

16. *Brooks v. Dewar,* 313 U.S. 354. The petitioner, L. R. Brooks, a regional grazing supervisor, turned to early Court decisions concerning the Forest Service for precedent. Section 2 of the Taylor Grazing Act, he argued, "is a replica of the statute involved in *United States v. Grimaud,* 220 U.S. 506, and there held to authorize similar rules and regulations" (360). A discussion of that decision may be found in chapter 1.

17. During Carpenter's tenure as director of grazing, what criticism the associations made of the grazing program they directed at the Grazing Division as a whole, not at Carpenter, and he enjoyed wide support. See, e.g., B. H. Stringham, "The Taylor Grazing Administration," *National Wool Grower,* March 1938, 17–18.

18. For example, McCarran thought it was the government's responsibility to "remove" excess wild game animals that were competing with domestic livestock on the federal range. Speaking of the problem of overpopulation among game animals he said, during hearings on S. Res. 241, "I think the Federal Government can step in, and because the Federal Government can claim sovereignty over the land, so much so that it spends vast sums of money for the supervision of the land, it can certainly protect that range from destruction." A witness then asked McCarran, "Would you have them remove the game themselves?" McCarran responded, "Remove the game, or kill the game off, sufficiently to protect the forests for the higher purpose of the sustenance of mankind." Given that McCarran often questioned the government's sovereignty over the federal lands, this response was obviously inconsistent. U.S. Congress, Senate, Subcommittee

of the Committee on Public Lands and Surveys, *Administration and Use of Public Lands,* Hearings on S. Res. 241, 77th Cong., 2d sess. (1942), pt. 5, 1878. The McCarran hearings went on for six years and thus through different congressional sessions. However, I shall cite them hereafter as *Hearings* on S. Res. 241, referring specifically to the volume and the year of the particular hearing from which the citation comes.

19. "The ancient phrase 'incorporeal hereditaments' is still sometimes used to refer to easements and profits. 'Hereditament' signified in medieval law that the interest was inheritable, thus a species of real property. The word 'incorporeal' in old law denoted that such interests, being non-possessory . . . lay in grant by a written, originally sealed instrument." Roger A. Cunningham, William B. Stoebuck, and Dale A. Whitman, *The Law of Property* (St. Paul, Minn.: West, 1984), 435. For more on incorporeal hereditaments and early origins of rights of common, see A. W. B. Simpson, *A History of the Land Law,* 2d ed., (Oxford: Clarendon Press, 1986), 106–8.

20. Patrick McCarran, "Current Legislative Problems," *American Cattle Producer,* March 1939, 13–14.

21. Ickes's speech was printed in both the *American Cattle Producer* and the *National Wool Grower.* Quotations are cited from the March 1939 issue of the latter, under "Public Domain Grazing Policies," 20, 39.

22. Brock's interest in the Taylor Grazing Act was solely in securing the right to lease isolated tracts of land; he was much opposed to the expansion of grazing districts—and therefore more federal oversight—particularly into his home state of Wyoming. See Transcript of Proceedings, Conference on Amendments to the Taylor Bill, Denver, Colorado, February 13, 1935, box 1, pp. 14–15. 58–59, FRC Papers.

23. Charles E. Ball, *Building the Beef Industry: A Century of Commitment* (Denver: National Cattlemen's Foundation, 1998), 99. The ANLSA is now known as the National Cattlemen's Beef Association.

24. J. Elmer Brock, "Inquiry into Public Domain Law Sought," *American Cattle Producer,* April 1940, 14. Historians have not to my knowledge commented on the ANLSA's role in nudging McCarran to instigate the hearings, but not only did the ANLSA take specific credit for getting them under way but the language of its grievances and of McCarran's points for investigation is virtually the same. See F. E. Mollin, "Annual Report of Secretary Mollin," *American Cattle Producer,* February 1941, 10.

25. James T. Patterson, *Congressional Conservatism and the New Deal: The Growth of the Conservative Coalition in Congress, 1933–1939* (Westport, Conn.: Greenwood Press, 1967), 288–324.

26. Quoted in Phillip O. Foss, *Politics and Grass: The Administration of Grazing on the Public Domain* (Seattle: University of Washington Press, 1960), 176, from *Congressional Record,* 76th Cong., 3d sess., vol. 86 (1940–41), 2593. This last grievance went on that "there has been a disregard of the principles which are essentially necessary for the purpose of providing stability of the range-livestock industry which is in competition with non-range-livestock operations not under Government supervision."

27. An "animal unit month" is the amount of forage needed to supply one cow or five sheep for one month.

28. Foss, *Politics and Grass,* 179.

29. A. F. Vass, "Values of Range Grazing Lands," *American Cattle Producer,* (May 1940), 3–4, 32; A. D. Brownfield, "Effect of Federal Land Purchases on Counties," *American Cattle Producer,* July 1940, 9–11, and "Annual Address of President Brock," ibid., February 1942, 6, 12.

30. Farrington R. Carpentet to Harold Ickes, n.d., box 2, FRC Papers.

31. U.S. Congress, Senate, Committee on Public Lands and Surveys, *To Provide for Orderly Use, Improvement, and Development of the Public Range,* Hearings on H.R. 2835 and H.R. 6462, 73d Cong., 2d sess. (1933 and 1934), 9.

32. Transcript of Proceedings, Reno, Nevada, January 24, 1935, box 1, p. 77, FRC Papers. These are Carpenter's words.

33. See Peffer's table on this in *Closing of the Public Domain,* 253.

34. "McCarran Appeals for Open Public Domain," *American Cattle Producer,* February 1942, 19–20.

35. *Hearings* on S. Res. 241, pt. 1 (1941), 99.

36. There are a number of good accounts of the political battle that followed; I shall provide a condensation of these, but for those readers wanting more detail, see Peffer, *Closing of the Public Domain,* 247–78, and Foss, *Politics and Grass,* 171–93.

37. Forsling was quoted as saying he was in a "squeeze" in "Salt Lake Grazing Hearings," *NWG,* June 1945, 8.

38. Peffer, *Closing of the Public Domain,* 265.

39. *Hearings* on S. Res. 241, pt. 1, 9.

40. Ibid., 16.

41. *Hearings* on S. Res. 241, pt. 17, 5200.

42. "Recommendations approved [in 1933] provided for a yearly adjustment of the basic rate in accordance with changes in the average price received by livestock producers in the 11 Western States. The amount of the adjustment will be determined by the ratio that this average price bears to the corresponding average price during the period 1921–32, inclusive, for cattle, and during the period 1921–30, inclusive, for sheep." Secretary of Agriculture Henry A. Wallace, quoted in Marion Clawson, *The Western Range Livestock Industry* (New York: McGraw-Hill, 1950), 263.

43. *Hearings* on S. Res., 241, pt. 17, 5211.

44. Ibid., 5176–77.

45. "The Grazing Land Problem: What's the Solution?" *NWG,* August 1946, 12.

46. In addition to pressing Interior Department officials on the appropriation increase, members of the Committee on the Public Lands pressed them on why a "separate bureau," i.e., the Grazing Division, had been set up in the department. U.S. Congress, House of Representatives, Committee on the Public Lands, *To Provide for the Orderly Use, Improvement, and Development of the Public Range,* Hearings on H.R. 3019, 74th Cong., 1st sess. (1935), 25–27.

47. Quoted in "Secretary Ickes on Grazing Affairs," *NWG*, April 1945, 12.

48. "President Winder's Statement," *NWG*, June 1945, 24. This was an excerpt from Winder's testimony in McCarran's hearings in Salt Lake City, May 29, 1945.

49. "Salt Lake Grazing Hearings," *NWG*, June 1945, 8.

50. Typically, one is seen to have a legal privilege in a license and a right in an easement. Charles Clark summarized the thinking on this difference as follows: "the distinction between an easement and a 'license privilege' is primarily in the fact that the licensee has a privilege and nothing more, while the holder of an easement has not only a privilege, but rights against interference with its exercise or enjoyment." *Real Covenants and Other Interests Which "Run with Land,"* 2d ed. (Chicago: Callaghan, 1947), 20. For an exploration of public land ranchers' position on the question, see Frank J. Falen and Karen Budd-Falen, "The Right to Graze Livestock on the Federal Lands: The Historical Development of Western Grazing Lands," *Idaho Law Review* 30 (1993–94): 505–24. The authors argue that the federal land grazing preference (as opposed to the permit itself) is "a type of property right" (506). However, they never address such critical cases as *Light v. United States* or *Grimaud v. United States*.

51. Joseph William Singer, "The Reliance Interest in Property," *Stanford Law Review* 40 (February 1988): 615–26, 657–58, 678–79. And yet, as I have argued in earlier chapters and shall have occasion to note again, that economic dependence did not mean ranchers operated politically from a stance of vulnerability. Not only had they built an impressive lobbying force, but in legitimizing ranchers' access to the public domain, the Taylor Grazing Act also appeared to them to legitimize their property claims on the lands.

52. Peffer, *Closing of the Public Domain*, 270–78.

53. "Grazing Land Problem," 10.

54. For a recent look at DeVoto's campaign against western stockmen, see John L. Thompson, *A Country in the Mind: Wallace Stegner, Bernard DeVoto, History, and the American Land* (New York: Routledge, 2000), 129–38.

55. Bernard DeVoto, "The West against Itself," *Harper's Magazine* 194 (January 1947): 1–5.

56. Ibid., 10–11.

57. And this kind of argument would be picked up more and more by "wilderness lovers" in the following years. In 1953, a former member of the Forest Service wrote that, with another "stockmen's bill" on the congressional docket, the "users" of the public grazing lands "would, in effect, be able to sell the right to use the people's property with the people having virtually no voice in the matter." In even stronger language, he argued that "the people—the owners of the national forests—must, like the defenders at Verdun, declare that 'they shall not pass,' lest the people lose part of the control of their own property and lay that property open to even graver impairment or capture." See Christopher M. Granger, "The Stockmen's Bill and the Public Interest," reprint from *The Living Wilderness*, Spring 1953, n.p., box 28, "Public Land," American National Cattlemen's Association Papers, American Heritage Center, University of Wyoming, Laramie. Hereafter cited as ANCA Papers.

58. Peffer, *Closing of the Public Domain*, 282.

59. A. F. Vass, "Control and Value of Western Grazing Lands: A Comprehensive Statement That Should Be Read by Every Live Stock Rancher in the Range States," American National Live Stock Association, 1941, box 19, p. 1, ANCA Papers.

60. Ibid., 4, 5, 15, 18.

61. "Annual Address of President Brock," *American Cattle Producer,* February 1942, 6.

62. Letter of August 26, 1946, box 25, "Joint Committee on Public Lands," ANCA Papers. Dan Hughes and Elmer Brock were the first chairmen of the committee, which also included A. D. Brownfield (past president of ANLSA), Victor Christensen of California, and Vernon Metcalf of Nevada—all of whom were very visible witnesses throughout McCarran's hearings.

63. James Muhn and Hanson R. Stuart, *Opportunity and Challenge: The Story of BLM* (Washington, D.C.: U.S. Department of Interior, 1988), 55.

64. William D. Rowley, *U.S. Forest Service Grazing and Rangelands: A History* (College Station: Texas A&M Press, 1985), 197. Rowley's quotation actually begins with "[t]he Forest Service's *new* forthrightness" (emphasis mine), but I would argued that their forthrightness was simply reasserted. In fact, it would seem that it was reasserted about every ten years, as the grazing fee battle was fought in the mid 1920s, the publication of *The Western Range* came in 1936, and its push for reductions came in the mid 1940s.

65. "Public Domain Conference," *NWG,* September 1946, 37.

66. Ibid., 9.

67. See, for instance, the editorial under "Important Problems" in *NWG,* March 1947, 5.

68. "Public Domain Conference," 38.

69. "The National's 1949 Platform and Program," *NWG,* March 1949, 7–8.

70. "Grazing Land Problem," 10.

71. I am quite convinced that this is the meaning that Dan Hughes intended in testifying at the hearings; unfortunately, Hughes's unscripted comments often came out garbled. Here is what he actually said, from the published record of the hearings: "[T]he individual who is recognized as a priority user, or whose right to use is recognized in that bill [the Taylor Grazing Act] has a right which he may go into court and enforce. Prior to the passing of the Taylor Grazing Act I seriously question whether there was a vested right which the courts would undertake to protect, and any user of the public domain or public lands—the thought, of course, is largely that if that right has been recognized, if there is a vested right in a portion of Federal lands, there should be a vested right in the other portion, the forest areas of public lands, and that we should have a bill which recognizes on some broad base the continued right to use that land." *Hearings* on S. Res. 241, pt. 5, 1848.

72. See, for instance, the testimony quoted below from Edwin Magagna in Hearings on S. Res. 241, pt. 19, 5683–92, 5708–10.

73. "While pending consideration it was strongly asserted [that the Taylor Grazing Act] gave no rights whatever, no property or vested rights, yet only yesterday it was cited as a bill which had established such rights," L. F. Kneipp, the

assistant chief of the Forest Service, noted at the hearings in Glenwood Springs, Colorado, referring to Hughes's testimony. *Hearings* on S. Res. 241, pt. 5, 1929.

74. *Hearings* on S. Res. 241, pt. 19, pp. 5707–9. Emphases mine.

75. The quotation is taken from an excerpt from Reich's lengthy article, "The New Property," which can be found in *Property: Mainstream and Critical Positions,* ed. C. B. Macpherson (Toronto: University of Toronto Press, 1978), 202.

76. Meg Jacobs, "'How About Some Meat?': The Office of Price Administration, Consumption Politics, and State Building from the Bottom Up," *Journal of American History* 84 (December 1997): 920–21.

77. *Congressional Record,* 80th Cong., 1st sess., vol. 93, pt. 3, 3642–43.

78. Singer, "Reliance Interest," 634.

79. Ibid., 657.

EPILOGUE

1. "The Federal Estate," in *Private Rights and Public Lands* (Washington, D.C.: Heritage Foundation, 1983), 39. The BLM's former director Marion Clawson was also at this conference, and his paper was included in the collection from the conference. He favored innovation in public land policy, but did not solely support either privatization or a transfer of federal lands to the states.

2. Charles Wilkinson, *Crossing the Next Meridian: Land, Water, and the Future of the West* (Washington, D.C.: Island Press, 1992), 97–98.

3. 43 U.S.C. § 1701 (a) (1) (1988).

4. For two accounts of the rebellion, see R. McGreggor Cawley, *Federal Land, Western Anger: The Sagebrush Rebellion and Environmental Politics* (Lawrence: University Press of Kansas, 1993), and C. Brant Short, *Ronald Reagan and the Public Lands: America's Conservation Debate, 1979–84* (College Station: Texas A&M University Press, 1989).

5. Wilkinson, *Crossing the Next Meridian,* 99

6. Denzel and Nancy Ferguson, *Sacred Cows at the Public Trough* (Bend, Ore.: Maverick Publications, 1983), 228.

7. Quoted in Debra L. Donahue, *The Western Range Revisited: Removing Livestock from Public Lands to Conserve Native Biodiversity* (Norman: University of Oklahoma Press, 1999), 189. Just as an indication of this, Donahue, like other range ecologists, wants to use physical characteristics of the range to understand its suitability (or lack thereof) for livestock grazing: "Although domestic livestock grazing of all public lands could easily be challenged on economic and public policy grounds, the focus [of her book] is on arid rangelands receiving 12 inches of precipitation or less annually" (6).

8. Donahue, *Western Range Revisited,* 174–76. Donahue notes that "[e]victing livestock will be essential" to restoring biodiversity on the arid public lands (192).

9. George Cameron Coggins and Robert L. Glicksman, "Power, Procedure, and Policy," in *Public Lands and Resource Law, Natural Resources and Environment* (Summer 1995): 4; *Kleppe v. New Mexico* 426 U.S. 529, 540 (1976).

10. See, for instance, Dan Dagget, *Beyond the Rangeland Conflict: Toward a West That Works* (Flagstaff, Ariz.: Grand Canyon Trust, 1995), for accounts of some successes in this area.

11. See Harvey M. Jacobs, "The 'Wisdom,' but Uncertain Future, of the Wise Use Movement," in *Who Owns America? Social Conflict over Property Rights,* ed. Harvey M. Jacobs (Madison: University of Wisconsin Press, 1998), 29–44. Donald Last speaks of a "land rights advocacy movement" to talk about these ideas. See "Private Property Rights with Responsibilities: What Would Thomas Jefferson Say About the 'Wise Use' Movement?" in ibid., 45–53. See also John Echeverria and Raymond Booth Eby, *Let the People Judge: Wise Use and the Private Property Rights Movement* (Washington, D.C.: Island Press, 1995.)

12. Karl Hess, Jr., "Wising up to the Wise Use Movement," in *A Wolf in the Garden: The Land Rights Movement and the New Environmental Debate,* ed. Philip D. Brick and R. McGreggor Cawley (Lanham, Md.: Rowman & Littlefield, 1999), 168, 164.

13. Ibid., 164.

14. And I would agree with Richard White that the problems of administering the public lands "will not be adequately confronted—nor will public lands be preserved in any meaningful form—unless Americans forthrightly face the issue of resurrecting 'public' as a meaningful category." See "Contested Terrain: The Business of Land in the American West," in *Land in the American West: Private Claims and the Common Good,* ed. William G. Robbins and James C. Foster (Seattle: University of Washington Press, 2000), 204. The preceding pages, however, should underscore how deeply the category of "public" was imbued before 1950, with ideas about private control and ownership.

Bibliographic Essay

The relevant literature on the public grazing lands seemed at times nearly as vast as the acreage itself, largely because these lands have been an arena of intense governmental interest since the early twentieth century. As everyone knows, the federal government excels in the production of the written word, and it spilled forth reams of paper on the subject from 1900 to 1950 (though nothing like what it would produce from the 1960s onward). But despite their image as men of few words, organized ranchers did their share, too, both in their own publications and in their support for anti-administration congressional hearings. And needless to say, the depth of the conflict between the two sides has inspired plenty of scholarly and journalistic commentary.

In some ways, the heart of this project lay in reading what organized ranchers said and wrote, particularly but not exclusively in public. Public land historians have turned to these documents before, but no one had ever read them systematically or attempted to understand what patterns existed in their political discourse. As with all kinds of trade association documents, one could find plenty of dissembling and disingenuousness, of course. However, they also contained many more frank discussions of policy than I had expected—especially during the Progressive period when western ranchers had not yet coalesced into a powerful political force—and when frankness was in short supply, I still found it fairly easy to ferret out the sources of ideological conflict within the organizations. For western cattle ranchers, I relied on the annual *Proceedings* of the American National Live Stock Association from the organization's birth in 1898 to 1950. Again, the early years of the *Proceedings* were by far the most interesting, in part because the group was so focused on the public land question, but also because the ANLSA was involved in so many political activities during and after the New Deal that took away from its earlier focus on the public domain. I also examined every issue of the ANLSA's journal, the *Producer* (it eventually changed its name to the *American Cattle Producer*) from its start in 1919 to 1950. While this book devotes more attention to the cattle industry than to the sheep industry, I did look through every issue of the trade association journal for the National Wool Growers Association, the *National Wool Grower*, between 1911 and 1950. The *Wool Grower* provided terrific coverage on public land issues and also published the speeches at their conventions. Charles Winter was not a livestock producer, but the discovery of his book *Four Hundred Million Acres: The Public Lands and Resources* (Casper, Wyo.: Overland Publishing Co., 1932) opened up a whole new way of understanding ranchers' political opinions and particularly their attraction to states' rights.

The other place in which ranchers loved to hear themselves talk was in congressional hearings. They weren't alone, of course, as there were plenty of western politicians and administrators who also wanted to take part in this "governmental theater," although during the flare-ups of the 1920s and 1940s, the administrators were much less enthusiastic participants, for obvious reasons. Full citations to these hearings may be found in the notes, but I examined most thoroughly the following hearings: those that preceded the Stock-Raising Homestead Act (hearings on H.R. 9582 and H.R. 10539, especially part 1, 63d Cong., 2d sess., 1914); the so-called Stanfield Hearings in the Senate after the grazing fee battle (hearings on S. Res 347, 3 vols., 69th Cong., 1st sess., 1926); those that investigated the Hoover proposal and also began considering permanent administration of the public domain (hearings on H.R. 7950, 70th Cong., 1st sess., 1929; on H.R. 11816, 72d Cong., 1st sess., 1932, and 72d Cong., 2d sess., 1933; and on H.R. 5840, 72d Cong., 1st sess., 1932; and on the Senate side, Hearings on S. 17, 2272, and S. 4060, 72d Cong., 1st sess., 1932). For discussion of the Taylor Grazing Act, see hearings on H.R. 2835 and H.R. 6462, 73d Cong., 1st sess., 1933, 1934. Finally, the hearings that showcased Senator Patrick McCarran and later Frank Barrett may be found as Hearings on S. Res. 241, 20 vols., 1941–47. Two other important government documents included the *Report* of the Public Lands Commission, 58th Cong., 3d Sess., 1905, Senate Doc. 189, and certainly *The Western Range: . . . A Report on the Western Range —A Great But Neglected Resource* (74th Cong., 2d sess., 1936, S. Doc., 199) was one of the more important government documents to emerge in the period under study.

Of my archival research, the following collections proved the most fruitful. At the American Heritage Center, the papers of the American National Cattlemen's Association (a later name for the American National Live Stock Association) were especially strong sources for the very end of my study. Those interested in the evolution of the association's position in the latter half of the twentieth century will find a rich store of material for the years in which the association began to confront environmental legislation. The papers of the Wyoming Stock Growers Association and the Wyoming Wool Growers Association also contained some amount of discussion about national issues, as did the Frank Mondell Papers and the Francis Warren Papers. At the Herbert Hoover

Presidential Library, the papers from the President's Committee on the Conservation and Administration of the Public Domain were extensive and enlightening, as were the Ray Lyman Wilbur Papers. At the Colorado Historical Society, the papers of the Colorado Stock Growers Association contained several critical unpublished studies that helped me to think through some of the economic issues of public land ranching. And while many scholars have used the Farrington R. Carpenter Papers at the Denver Public Library, to my knowledge, no one had previously read carefully through the transcripts of his meetings with ranchers to grasp how he employed a language of property rights under the Taylor Grazing Act.

The two works on which I most relied for the history of the public lands were Paul Gates, *The History of Public Land Law Development* (Washington, D.C.: Zenger Publishing Co., 1968), and E. Louise Peffer, *The Closing of the Public Domain: Disposal and Reservation Policies, 1900–1950* (Stanford, Calif.: Stanford University Press, 1951). Marion Clawson's work also deserves special mention. As a former BLM chief, he brought to his writings his governmental experience, good historical sense, and balanced analyses. I depended on his *Western Range Livestock Industry* (New York: McGraw-Hill, 1950) to explain numerous points. In the early stages of my research, I also found *The Federal Lands Revisited* (Washington, D.C.: Resources for the Future, 1983) very helpful. In addition, William D. Rowley's *U.S. Forest Service Grazing and Rangelands: A History* (College Station: Texas A&M University Press, 1985) provides an excellent overview of the Forest Service's grazing policy, as well as the politics of its relationship with organized ranchers. Debra Donahue's recent book, *The Western Range Revisited: Removing Livestock from Public Lands to Conserve Native Biodiversity* (Norman: University of Oklahoma Press, 1999) is one of the most comprehensive books to have come out on the public grazing problem. While our views diverge greatly over the meanings of the Taylor Grazing Act, her combined skills as a wildlife biologist and a law professor allow her to examine the ecological implications of grazing policy with particular insight. Paul Starrs's ambitious and comparative study, *Let the Cowboy Live: Cattle Ranching in the American West* (Baltimore: Johns Hopkins University Press, 1998), stands in stark contrast to Donahue's book but, like hers, has helped to reopen the scholarship on public land use.

There are a host of other works that students of public grazing history would want to examine, such as: Wesley Calef, *Private Grazing and Public Lands: Studies of the Local Management of the Taylor Grazing Act* (Chicago: University of Chicago Press, 1961); R. McGreggor Cawley, *Federal Land, Western Anger* (Lawrence: University Press of Kansas, 1993); Phillip O. Foss, *Politics and Grass: The Administration of Grazing on the Public Domain* (Seattle: University of Washington Press, 1960); William L. Graf, *Wilderness Preservation and the Sagebrush Rebellions* (Savage, Md.: Rowman & Littlefield, 1990); Samuel P. Hays, *Conservation and the Gospel of Efficiency: The Progressive Conservation Movement, 1890–1920* (1959; reprint, New York: Atheneum, 1980); Karl Hess, Jr., *Visions upon the Land: Man and Nature on the Western Range* (Washington, D.C.: Island Press, 1992); Benjamin Horace Hibbard, *A History of the Public Land Policies* (1924; reprint, Madison: University of Wisconsin Press,

1965); Christopher McGrory Klyza, *Who Controls Public Lands? Mining, Forestry, and Grazing Policies, 1870–1990* (Chapel Hill: University of North Carolina Press, 1996); Gary Libecap, *Locking up the Range: Federal Land Controls and Grazing* (Cambridge, Mass.: Ballinger., 1981); Grant McConnell, *Private Power and American Democracy* (New York: Vintage Books, 1966); Sharman Apt Russell, *Kill the Cowboy: A Battle of Mythology in the New West* (Reading, Mass.: Addison-Wesley, 1993); Brant C. Short, *Ronald Reagan and the Public Lands: America's Conservation Debate, 1979–1984* (College Station, Tex.: Texas A&M University Press, 1989); William J. Voigt, *Public Grazing Lands: Use and Misuse by Industry and Government* (New Brunswick, N.J.: Rutgers University Press, 1976); Donald Worster, "Cowboy Ecology," in *Under Western Skies: Nature and History in the American West* (New York: Oxford University Press, 1992), 34–52. William deBuys's *Enchantment and Exploitation: The Life and Hard Times of a New Mexico Mountain Range* (Albuquerque: University of New Mexico Press, 1985) provides an incomparable look at the relationships between human communities, nature, and federal land managers. For more polemical works, see Denzel and Nancy Ferguson, *Sacred Cows at the Public Trough* (Bend, Ore.: Maverick Publications, 1983); Lynn Jacobs, *Waste of the West* (self-published, 1991). Two recent books that explore issues relating to public lands, the public domain, and property in the West are Dorothee Kocks, *Dream a Little: Land and Social Justice in America* (Berkeley and Los Angeles: University of California Press, 1999), and *Land in the American West: Private Claims and the Common Good*, ed. William G. Robbins and James C. Foster (Seattle: University of Washington Press, 2000).

As Terry Jordan has written, the amount of work on the cattle industry is positively "mind-numbing," but one can do no better than to start with his *North American Cattle-Ranching Frontiers* (Albuquerque: University of New Mexico Press, 1993). I also relied on several classics in the field: Robert G. Athearn's *High Country Empire: The High Plains and Rockies* (Lincoln: University of Nebraska Press, 1960); Lewis Atherton, *The Cattle Kings* (Bloomington: Indiana University Press, 1961); Edward Everett Dale, *The Range Cattle Industry: Ranching on the Great Plains from 1865 to 1925* (1930; Norman: University of Oklahoma Press, 1960); Ernest Staples Osgood, *The Day of the Cattleman* (1929; Chicago: University of Chicago Press, 1968); John T. Schlebecker, *Cattle Raising on the Plains, 1900–61* (Lincoln: University of Nebraska Press, 1963); and Walter Prescott Webb, *The Great Plains* (1931; reprint, Boston: Ginn, 1959). Other works that I drew from included Gene Gressley, *Bankers and Cattlemen* (New York: Knopf, 1966); William MacLeod and Will C. Barnes, *Cattle* (Garden City, N.Y.: Doubleday, Doran, 1930); Theodore Roosevelt, *Ranch Life and the Hunting-Trail* (1888; New York: Century Co., 1899); Laurence M. Woods, *British Gentlemen in the Wild West: The Era of the Intensely English Cowboy* (New York: Free Press, 1989). For perhaps some obvious reasons, sheep raising in the West has not inspired nearly as much work, and I depended mostly on the *National Wool Grower* for necessary information. But see also Alexander Campbell McGregor's *Counting Sheep: From Open Range to Agribusiness on the Columbia Plateau* (Seattle: University of Washington Press, 1982) and Edward

Norris Wentworth, *America's Sheep Trails* (Ames: Iowa State College Press, 1948).

Of course, shaping the argument of this book required learning something about property law. For a casebook, I used Roger A. Cunningham, William B. Stoebuck, and Dale A. Whitman, *The Law of Property* (St. Paul, Minn: West Publishing Co., 1984), which helped me to understand some of the essential categories in property law. For inspiration I found a number of legal scholars whose work spoke eloquently to my interests. I returned often to Carol Rose's *Property and Persuasion: Essays on the History, Theory, and Rhetoric of Ownership* (Boulder, Colo.: Westview Press, 1994), as well as to C. B. Macpherson's edited volume, *Property: Mainstream and Critical Positions* (Toronto: University of Toronto Press, 1978), which includes Morris Cohen's essay on "Property and Sovereignty" and an excerpt from Charles Reich's "The New Economy." Joseph Singer's "Sovereignty and Property," *Northwestern University Law Review* 86 (1991): 1–56, and "The Reliance Interest in Property," *Stanford Law Review* 40 (February 1988) have been especially critical pieces in opening my eyes to the relational aspects of property law. Margaret Jane Radin's essay "Property and Personhood," which shaped my argument in chapter 5, can be found in her collection of essays *Reinterpreting Property* (Chicago: University of Chicago Press, 1993). Hendrik Hartog's *Public Property and Private Power: The Corporation of the City of New York in American Law* (Chapel Hill: University of North Carolina Press, 1983) was the first book to get me thinking about the connection between the government's property ownership and its political authority. *Land Law and Real Property in American History: Major Historical Interpretations,* ed. Kermit Hall (New York: Garland, 1987) gave me a deeper sense for issues of landed property over the nation's history, particularly in the nineteenth century, while Lawrence Friedman's *A History of American Law,* 2d ed. (New York: Simon & Schuster, 1985), was a helpful reference. On specific issues, Charles E. Clark's *Real Covenants and Other Interests Which "Run with the Land,"* 2d ed. (Chicago: Callaghan, 1947), gave clarity on this important issue in Farrington Carpenter's understanding of the Taylor Grazing Act; Jack H. Archer et al., *The Public Trust Doctrine and the Management of America's Coasts* (Amherst: University of Massachusetts Press, 1994) provided a lucid account of this doctrine, which stands in fascinating contrast to the legal framework for the public domain.

On public grazing law specifically, an excellent place to start is Charles Wilkinson's *Crossing the Next Meridian: Land, Water, and the Future of the West* (Washington, D.C.: Island Press, 1992). The work of George Cameron Coggins is also central. See his five-part series of articles published in 1982 and 1983 in *Environmental Law,* all beginning with the title, "The Law of Public Rangeland Management." The most relevant of these to this work are "The Extent and Distribution of Federal Power," *Environmental Law* 12 (1982): 535–621 (co-authored with Parthenia Blessing Evans and Margaret Lindberg-Johnson), and "The Commons and the Taylor Act," *Environmental Law* 13 (1982): 1–101 (co-authored with Margaret Lindberg-Johnson). And on the current controversies over property rights and the wise use movement, I found most helpful *A*

Wolf in the Garden: The Land Rights Movement and the New Environmental Debate, ed. Philip D. Brick and R. McGreggor Cawley (Lanham, Md.: Rowman & Littlefield, 1999); John Echeverria and Raymond Booth Eby, *Let the People Judge: Wise Use and the Private Property Rights Movement* (Washington, D.C.: Island Press, 1995), *Who Owns America? Social Conflict over Property Rights,* ed. Harvey M. Jacobs (Madison: University of Wisconsin Press, 1998); and the Heritage Foundation's *Private Rights and Public Lands* (Washington D.C.: Heritage Foundation, 1983).

Finally, this book clearly engages with a set of questions in American political history. Since beginning this project in graduate school, I have followed the debates about the formation of the American state. *Bringing the State Back In,* ed. Peter B. Evans, Dietrich Rueschmeyer, and Theda Skocpol (New York: Cambridge University Press, 1985), and Stephen Skowronek, *Building a New American State: The Expansion of National Administrative Capacities, 1877–1920* (New York: Cambridge University Press, 1982) were among the books influential on my early thinking about this project. Like many political historians, however, I began to seek a more nuanced understanding of state power. I explored this issue historiographically as it relates to the American West in "In Search of the 'Federal Presence' in the America West," *Western Historical Quarterly* 30 (Winter 1999): 449–73, where readers can find additional citations to works on the state. Many other works that would fall into the broad category of political history and that contributed to my research can be found in the notes.

Index